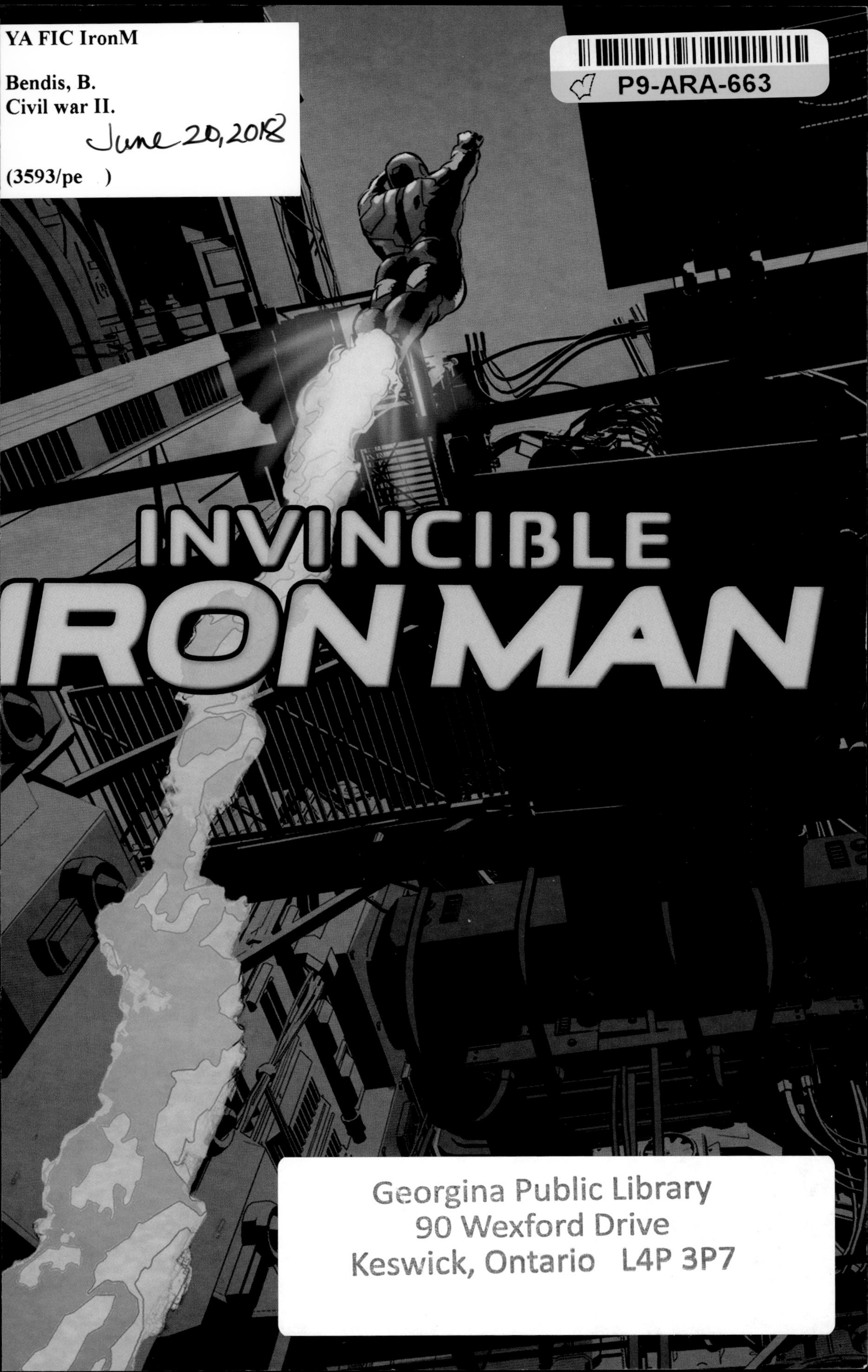
INVINCIBLE
IRON MAN

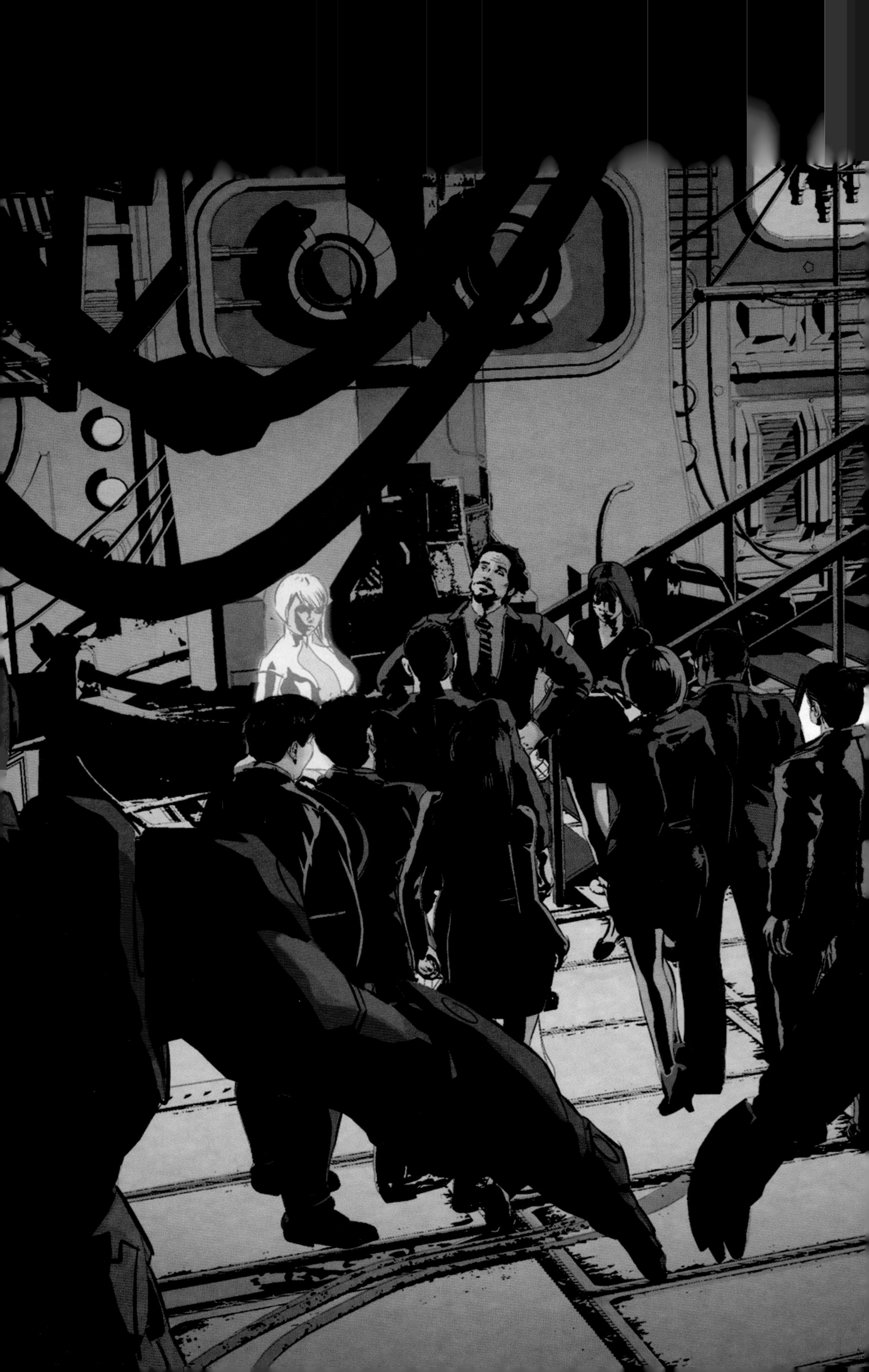

LIONAIRE PLAYBOY AND GENIUS INDUSTRIALIST TONY STARK WAS KIDNAPPED DURING A ROUTINE WEAPONS TEST. HIS TORS ATTEMPTED TO FORCE HIM TO BUILD A WEAPON OF MASS DESTRUCTION. INSTEAD HE CREATED A POWERED SUIT OF ARMOR THAT SAVED HIS LIFE. FROM THAT DAY ON, HE USED THE SUIT TO PROTECT THE WORLD AS THE...

INVINCIBLE IRON MAN

CIVIL WAR II

BRIAN MICHAEL BENDIS
WRITER

MIKE DEODATO JR.
ARTIST

FRANK MARTIN
COLOR ARTIST

VC's CLAYTON COWLES
LETTERER

**MIKE DEODATO JR. &
FRANK MARTIN** [#12-13]
AND **DALE KEOWN &
JASON KEITH** [#14]
COVER ART

ALANNA SMITH
ASSISTANT EDITOR

TOM BREVOORT
EDITOR

IRON MAN CREATED BY STAN LEE, LARRY LIEBER, DON HECK & JACK KIRBY

COLLECTION EDITOR: **JENNIFER GRÜNWALD**
ASSISTANT EDITOR: **CAITLIN O'CONNELL**
ASSOCIATE MANAGING EDITOR: **KATERI WOODY**
EDITOR, SPECIAL PROJECTS: **MARK D. BEAZLEY**
VP PRODUCTION & SPECIAL PROJECTS: **JEFF YOUNGQUIST**
SVP PRINT, SALES & MARKETING: **DAVID GABRIEL**
BOOK DESIGNER: **JAY BOWEN**

EDITOR IN CHIEF: **AXEL ALONSO**
CHIEF CREATIVE OFFICER: **JOE QUESADA**
PRESIDENT: **DAN BUCKLEY**
EXECUTIVE PRODUCER: **ALAN FINE**

BLE IRON MAN VOL. 3: CIVIL WAR II. Contains material originally published in magazine form as INVINCIBLE IRON MAN #12-14 and MIGHTY AVENGERS #9-11. First printing 2017. ISBN# 978-1-302-90321-3. Published by MARVEL WIDE, INC., a subsidiary of MARVEL ENTERTAINMENT, LLC. OFFICE OF PUBLICATION: 135 West 50th Street, New York, NY 10020. Copyright © 2017 MARVEL No similarity between any of the names, characters, persons, and/or ns in this magazine with those of any living or dead person or institution is intended, and any such similarity which may exist is purely coincidental. **Printed in the U.S.A.** DAN BUCKLEY, President, Marvel Entertainment; JOE QUESADA, eative Officer; TOM BREVOORT, SVP of Publishing; DAVID BOGART, SVP of Business Affairs & Operations, Publishing & Partnership; C.B. CEBULSKI, VP of Brand Management & Development, Asia; DAVID GABRIEL, SVP of Sales & g. Publishing; JEFF YOUNGQUIST, VP of Production & Special Projects; DAN CARR, Executive Director of Publishing Technology; ALEX MORALES, Director of Publishing Operations; SUSAN CRESPI, Production Manager; STAN LEE, n Emeritus. For information regarding advertising in Marvel Comics or on Marvel.com, please contact Vit DeBellis, Integrated Sales Manager, at vdebellis@marvel.com. For Marvel subscription inquiries, please call 888-511-5480. ctured between 9/1/2017 and 10/3/2017 by LSC COMMUNICATIONS INC., KENDALLVILLE, IN, USA.

FRIDAY'S LOG:

RECENTLY COMPLETED AGENDA ITEMS:

- FAKE YOUR OWN DEATH TO INFILTRATE A JAPANESE TERRORIST CELL.

- KIDNAP THE NEW INHUMAN KNOWN AS ULYSSES WHO CLAIMS HE CAN SEE THE FUTURE AND FIND OUT HOW HE DOES IT.

IN-PROGRESS AGENDA ITEMS:

- APOLOGIZE TO YOUR INVESTORS AND AMARA FOR FAKING YOUR OWN DEATH.

- RESPOND TO PRESS CONCERNS THAT YOU'RE PLANNING TO START A WAR WITH CAPTAIN MARVEL OVER ULYSSES.

- TALK TO SOMEONE ABOUT RHODEY'S DEATH BEFORE YOU DO SOMETHING STUPID (I MEAN IT, TONY).

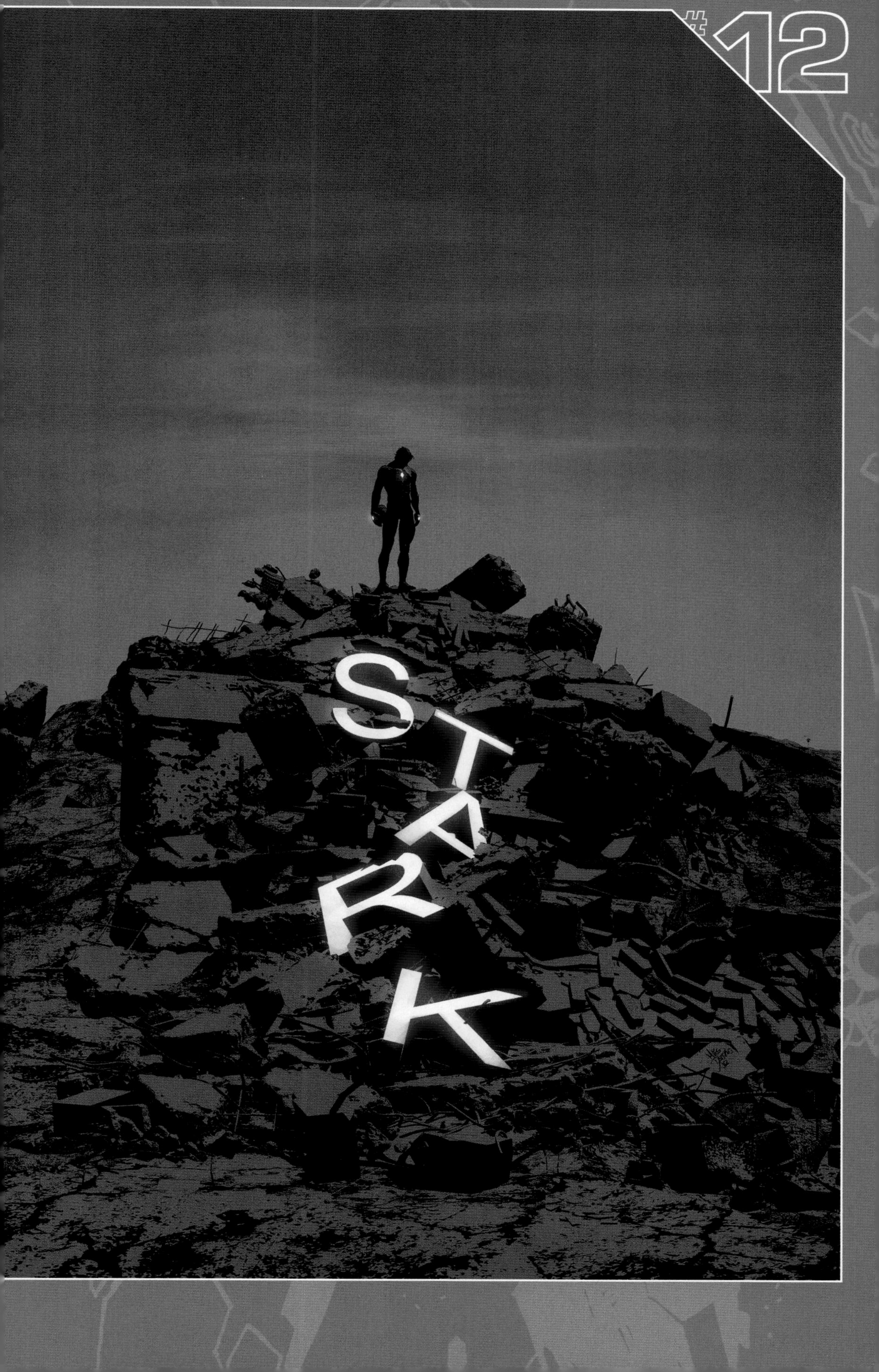
#12
STARK

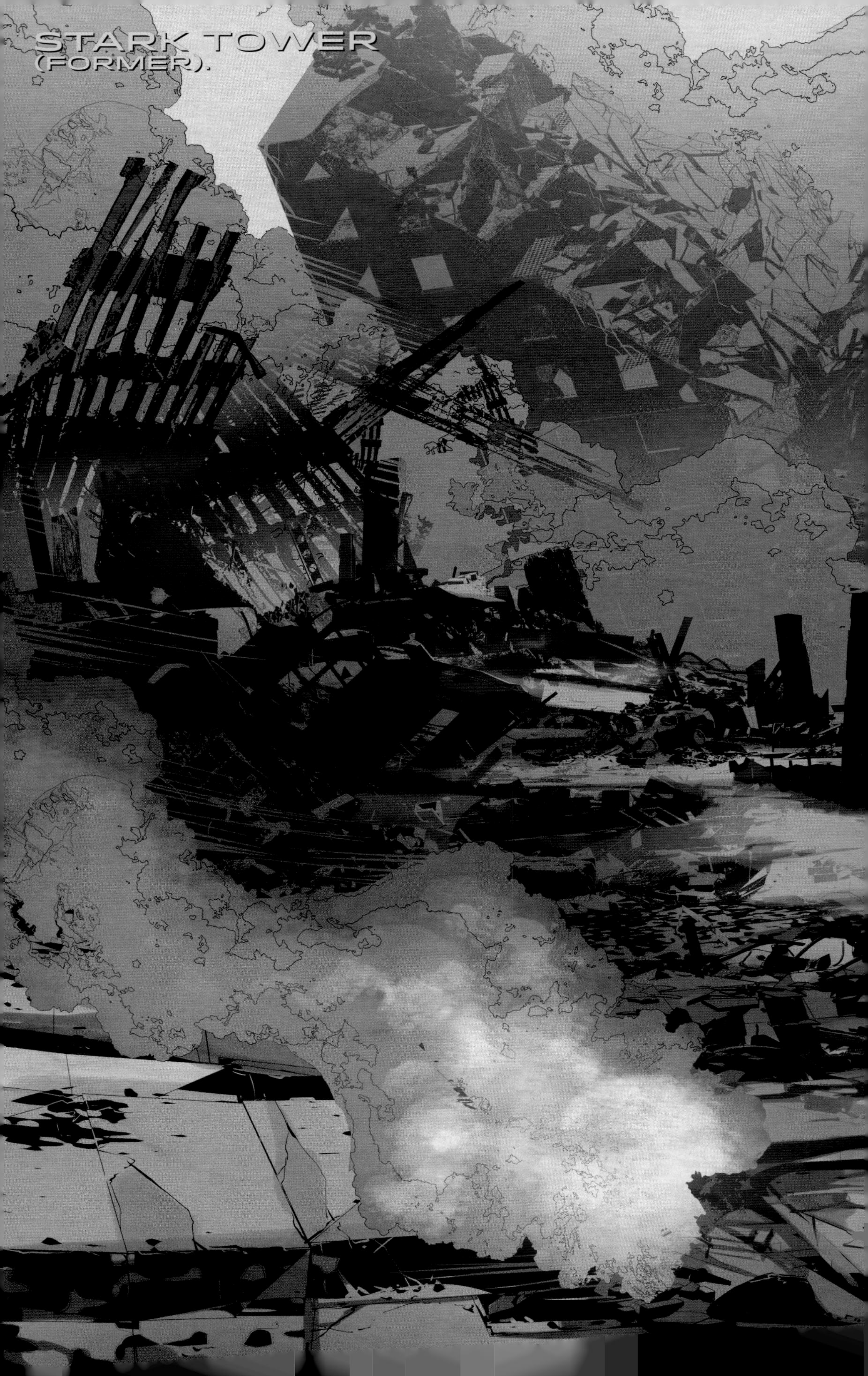
STARK TOWER
(FORMER).

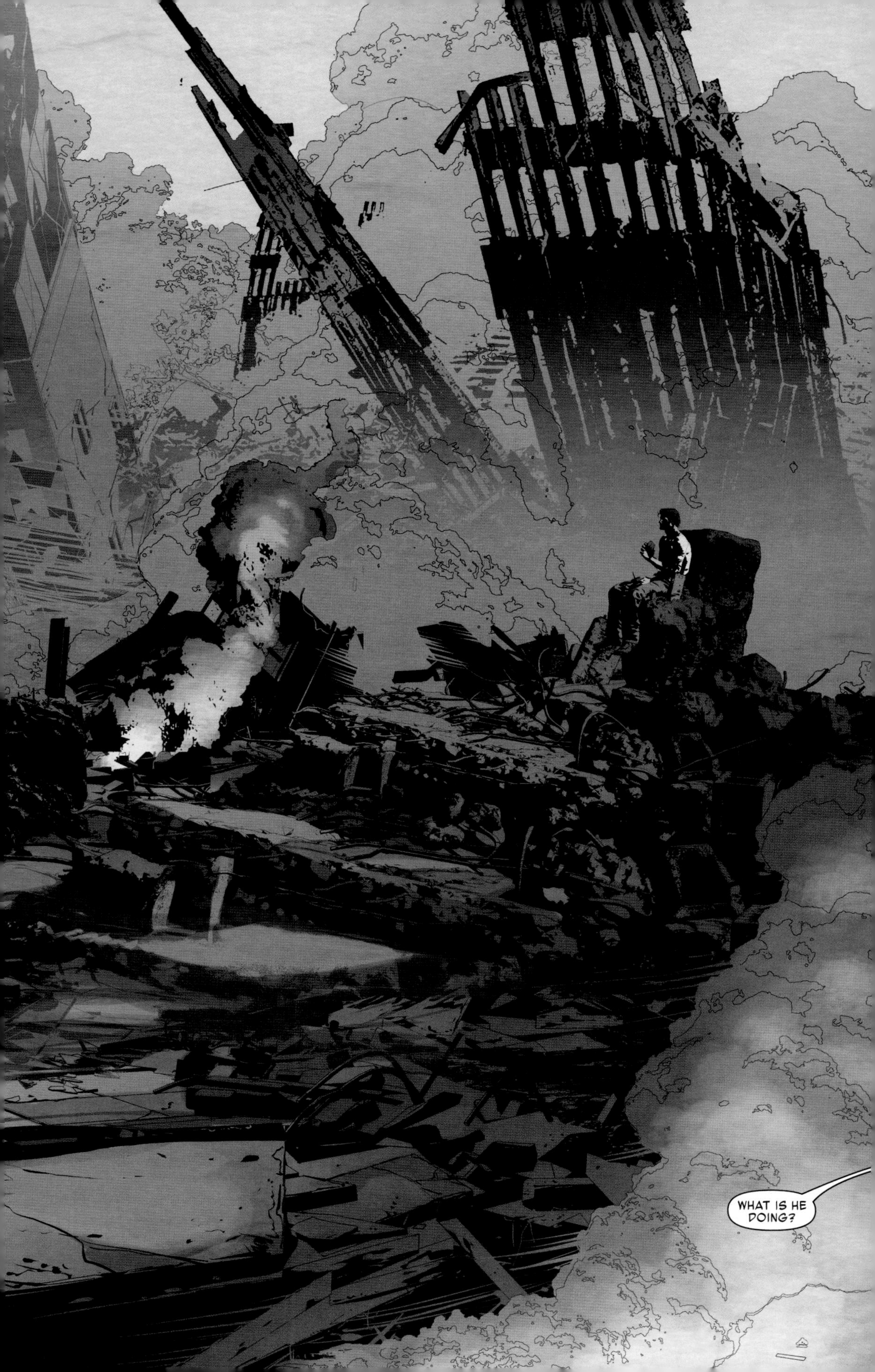
WHAT IS HE DOING?

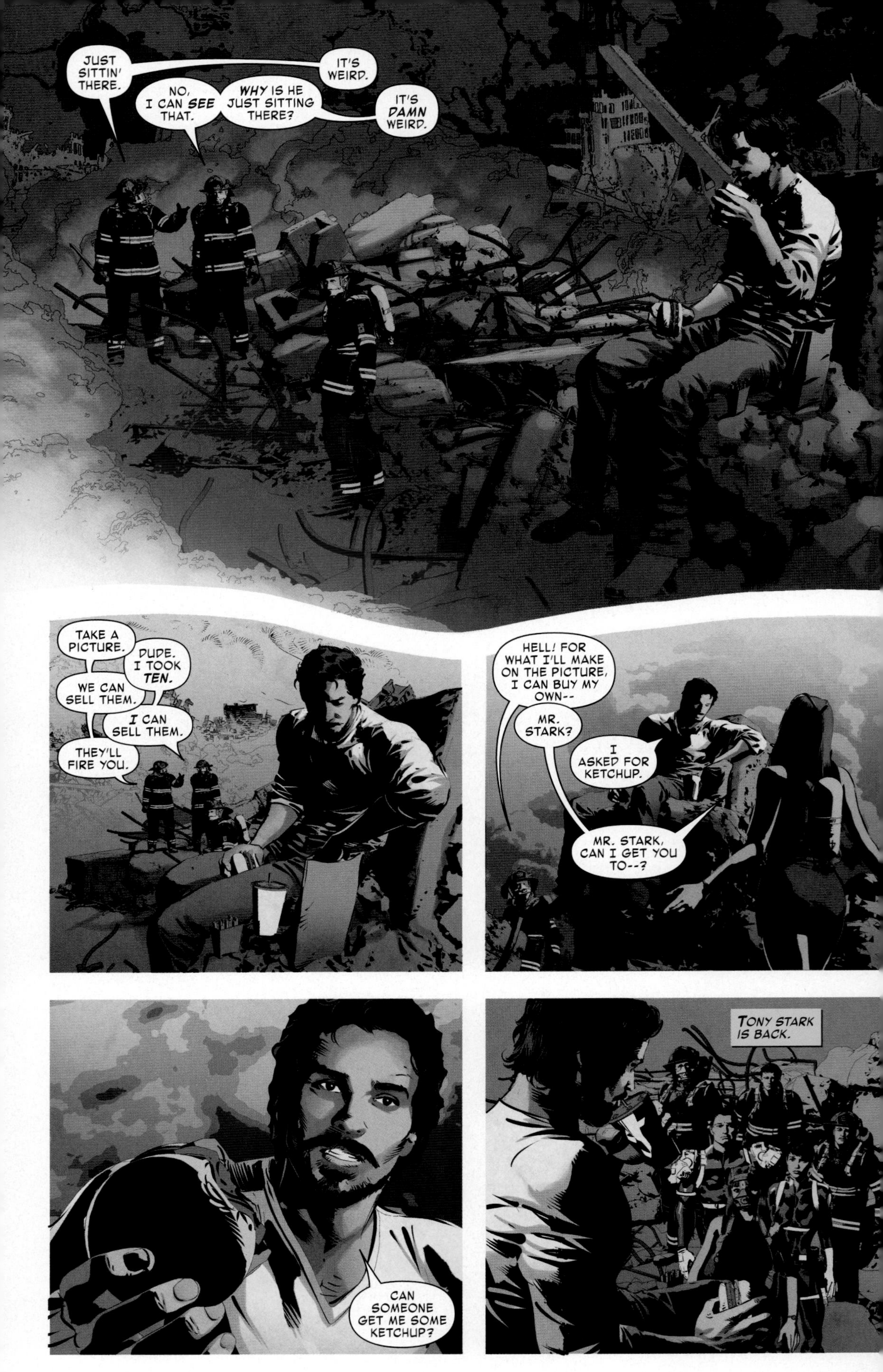
JUST SITTIN' THERE.
IT'S WEIRD.
NO, I CAN SEE THAT.
WHY IS HE JUST SITTING THERE?
IT'S DAMN WEIRD.
TAKE A PICTURE.
DUDE. I TOOK TEN.
WE CAN SELL THEM.
I CAN SELL THEM.
THEY'LL FIRE YOU.
HELL! FOR WHAT I'LL MAKE ON THE PICTURE, I CAN BUY MY OWN--
MR. STARK?
I ASKED FOR KETCHUP.
MR. STARK, CAN I GET YOU TO--?
CAN SOMEONE GET ME SOME KETCHUP?
TONY STARK IS BACK.

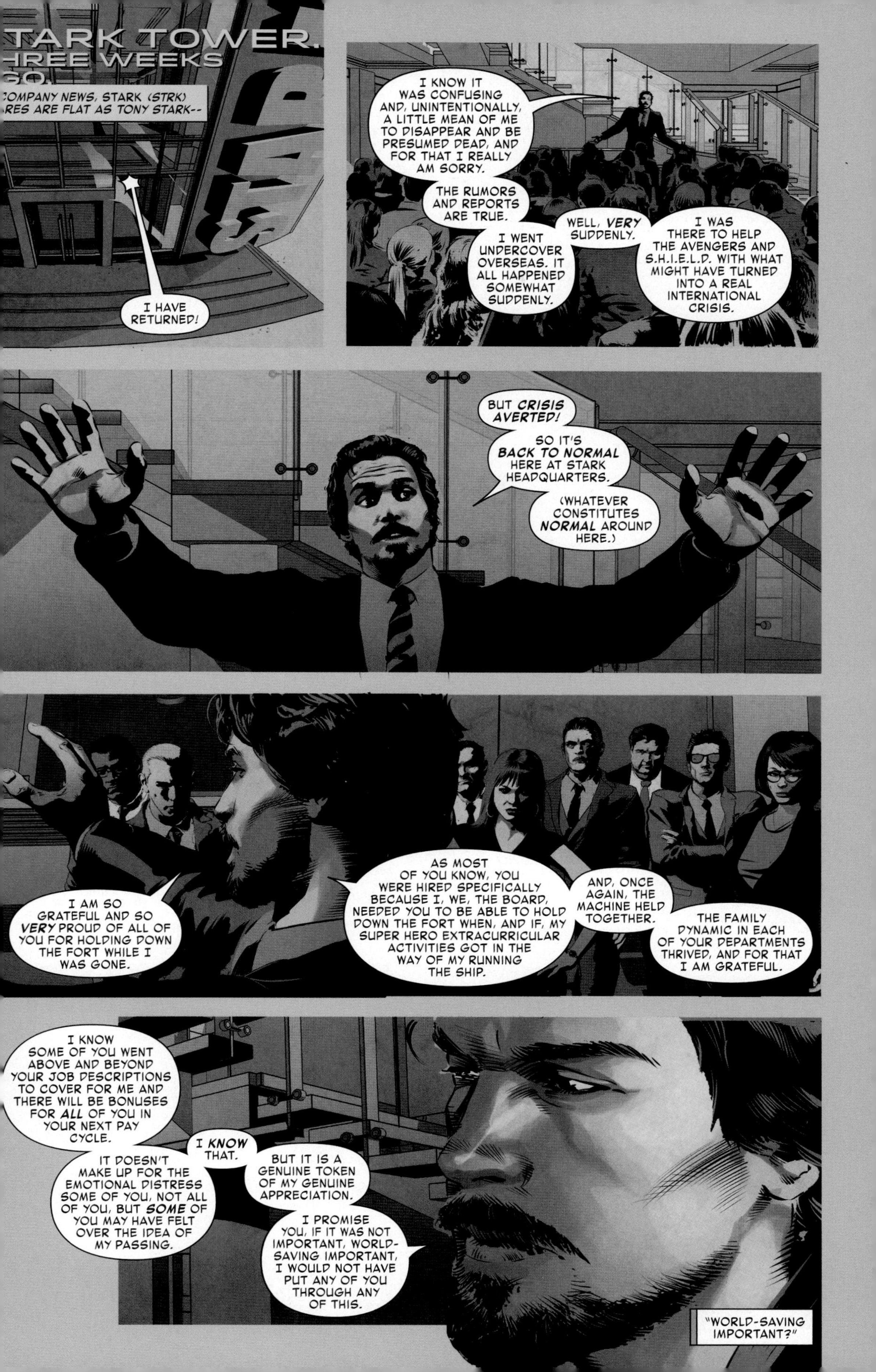
TARK TOWER. HREE WEEKS GO.
COMPANY NEWS, STARK (STRK) RES ARE FLAT AS TONY STARK--
I HAVE RETURNED!
I KNOW IT WAS CONFUSING AND, UNINTENTIONALLY, A LITTLE MEAN OF ME TO DISAPPEAR AND BE PRESUMED DEAD, AND FOR THAT I REALLY AM SORRY.
THE RUMORS AND REPORTS ARE TRUE.
I WENT UNDERCOVER OVERSEAS. IT ALL HAPPENED SOMEWHAT SUDDENLY.
WELL, VERY SUDDENLY.
I WAS THERE TO HELP THE AVENGERS AND S.H.I.E.L.D. WITH WHAT MIGHT HAVE TURNED INTO A REAL INTERNATIONAL CRISIS.
BUT CRISIS AVERTED!
SO IT'S BACK TO NORMAL HERE AT STARK HEADQUARTERS.
(WHATEVER CONSTITUTES NORMAL AROUND HERE.)
I AM SO GRATEFUL AND SO VERY PROUD OF ALL OF YOU FOR HOLDING DOWN THE FORT WHILE I WAS GONE.
AS MOST OF YOU KNOW, YOU WERE HIRED SPECIFICALLY BECAUSE I, WE, THE BOARD, NEEDED YOU TO BE ABLE TO HOLD DOWN THE FORT WHEN, AND IF, MY SUPER HERO EXTRACURRICULAR ACTIVITIES GOT IN THE WAY OF MY RUNNING THE SHIP.
AND, ONCE AGAIN, THE MACHINE HELD TOGETHER.
THE FAMILY DYNAMIC IN EACH OF YOUR DEPARTMENTS THRIVED, AND FOR THAT I AM GRATEFUL.
I KNOW SOME OF YOU WENT ABOVE AND BEYOND YOUR JOB DESCRIPTIONS TO COVER FOR ME AND THERE WILL BE BONUSES FOR ALL OF YOU IN YOUR NEXT PAY CYCLE.
IT DOESN'T MAKE UP FOR THE EMOTIONAL DISTRESS SOME OF YOU, NOT ALL OF YOU, BUT SOME OF YOU MAY HAVE FELT OVER THE IDEA OF MY PASSING.
I KNOW THAT.
BUT IT IS A GENUINE TOKEN OF MY GENUINE APPRECIATION.
I PROMISE YOU, IF IT WAS NOT IMPORTANT, WORLD-SAVING IMPORTANT, I WOULD NOT HAVE PUT ANY OF YOU THROUGH ANY OF THIS.
"WORLD-SAVING IMPORTANT?"

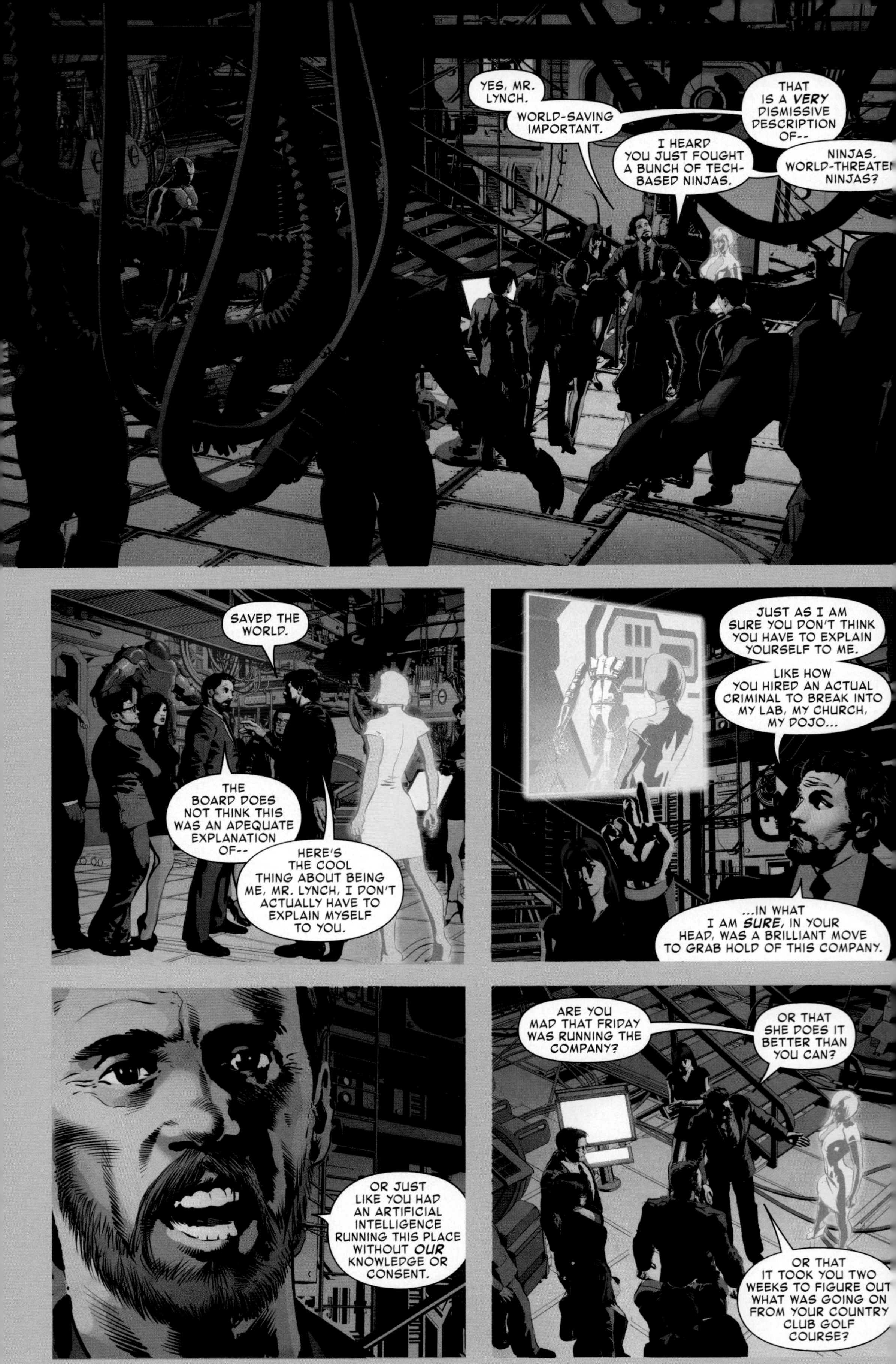
YES, MR. LYNCH.
WORLD-SAVING IMPORTANT.
THAT IS A VERY DISMISSIVE DESCRIPTION OF--
I HEARD YOU JUST FOUGHT A BUNCH OF TECH-BASED NINJAS.
NINJAS. WORLD-THREATEN NINJAS?
SAVED THE WORLD.
THE BOARD DOES NOT THINK THIS WAS AN ADEQUATE EXPLANATION OF--
HERE'S THE COOL THING ABOUT BEING ME, MR. LYNCH, I DON'T ACTUALLY HAVE TO EXPLAIN MYSELF TO YOU.
JUST AS I AM SURE YOU DON'T THINK YOU HAVE TO EXPLAIN YOURSELF TO ME.
LIKE HOW YOU HIRED AN ACTUAL CRIMINAL TO BREAK INTO MY LAB, MY CHURCH, MY DOJO...
...IN WHAT I AM SURE, IN YOUR HEAD, WAS A BRILLIANT MOVE TO GRAB HOLD OF THIS COMPANY.
OR JUST LIKE YOU HAD AN ARTIFICIAL INTELLIGENCE RUNNING THIS PLACE WITHOUT OUR KNOWLEDGE OR CONSENT.
ARE YOU MAD THAT FRIDAY WAS RUNNING THE COMPANY?
OR THAT SHE DOES IT BETTER THAN YOU CAN?
OR THAT IT TOOK YOU TWO WEEKS TO FIGURE OUT WHAT WAS GOING ON FROM YOUR COUNTRY CLUB GOLF COURSE?

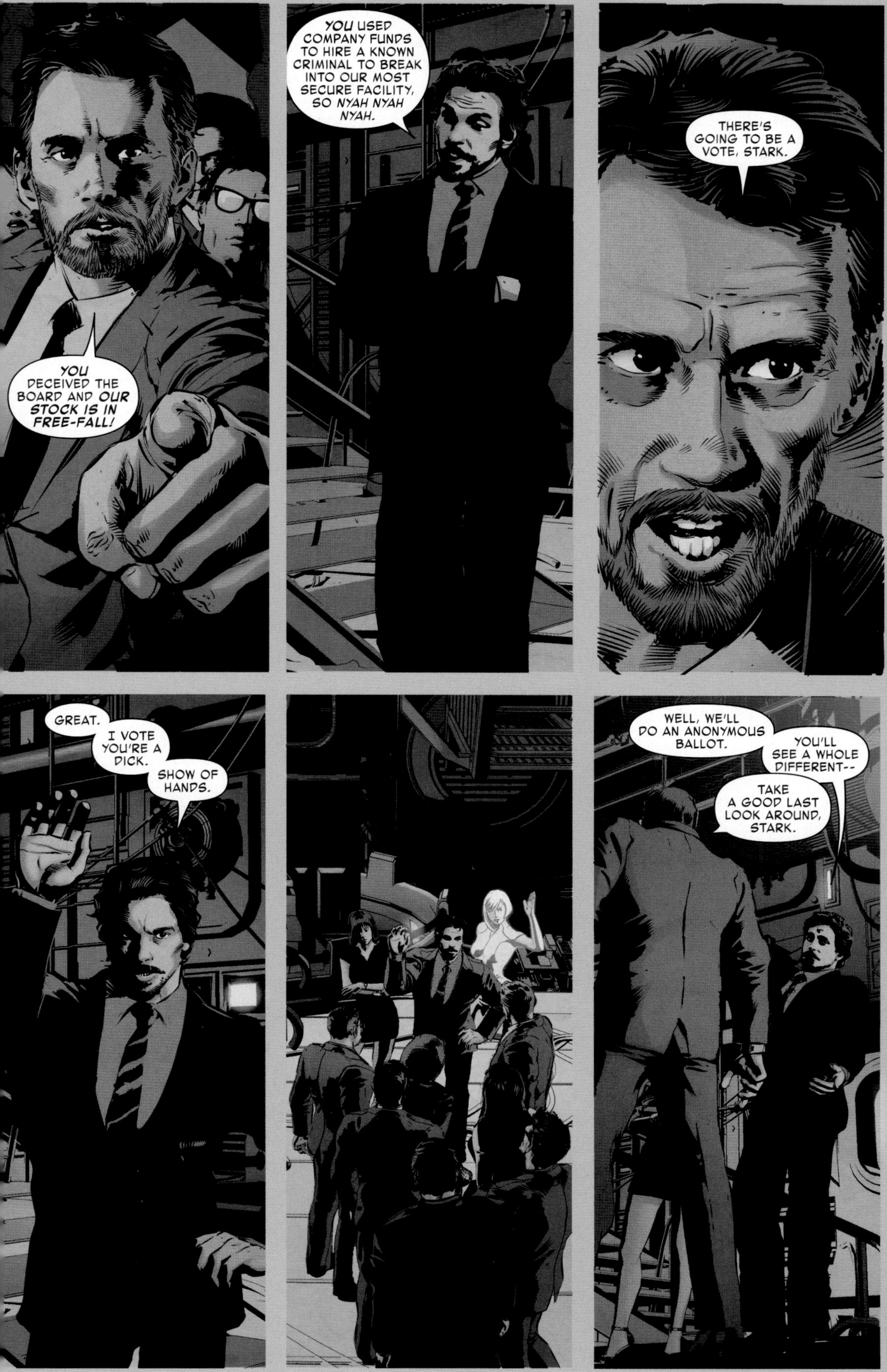
YOU DECEIVED THE BOARD AND OUR STOCK IS IN FREE-FALL!
YOU USED COMPANY FUNDS TO HIRE A KNOWN CRIMINAL TO BREAK INTO OUR MOST SECURE FACILITY, SO NYAH NYAH NYAH.
THERE'S GOING TO BE A VOTE, STARK.
GREAT.
I VOTE YOU'RE A DICK.
SHOW OF HANDS.
WELL, WE'LL DO AN ANONYMOUS BALLOT.
YOU'LL SEE A WHOLE DIFFERENT--
TAKE A GOOD LAST LOOK AROUND, STARK.

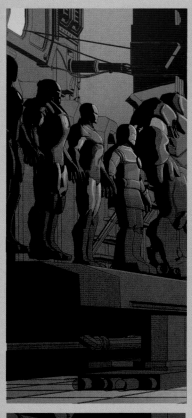

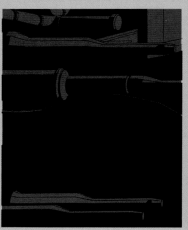

AND I'M SORRY, MJ.

OKAY? THAT'S IT?

OKAY.

HEY, WORK F YOU

YOU DO HAVE TO EX YOURSEL ME.

WELL, THE JOB IS A CHALLENGE.

AND I FEEL LIKE IT MIGHT BE A *TEMP JOB* ANYWAY.

I'M HARDLY AN EXPERT IN HIGH FINANCE BUT...YOU'RE IN TROUBLE.

I KNOW.

YEAH.

DO YOU?

HE DOES.

ANYTHING YOU CAN INVENT OR SELL REAL FAST TO TURN IT AROUND?

I CAME UP WITH THIS HYBRID DONUT PIZZA THING.

YEAH.

BA

EW.

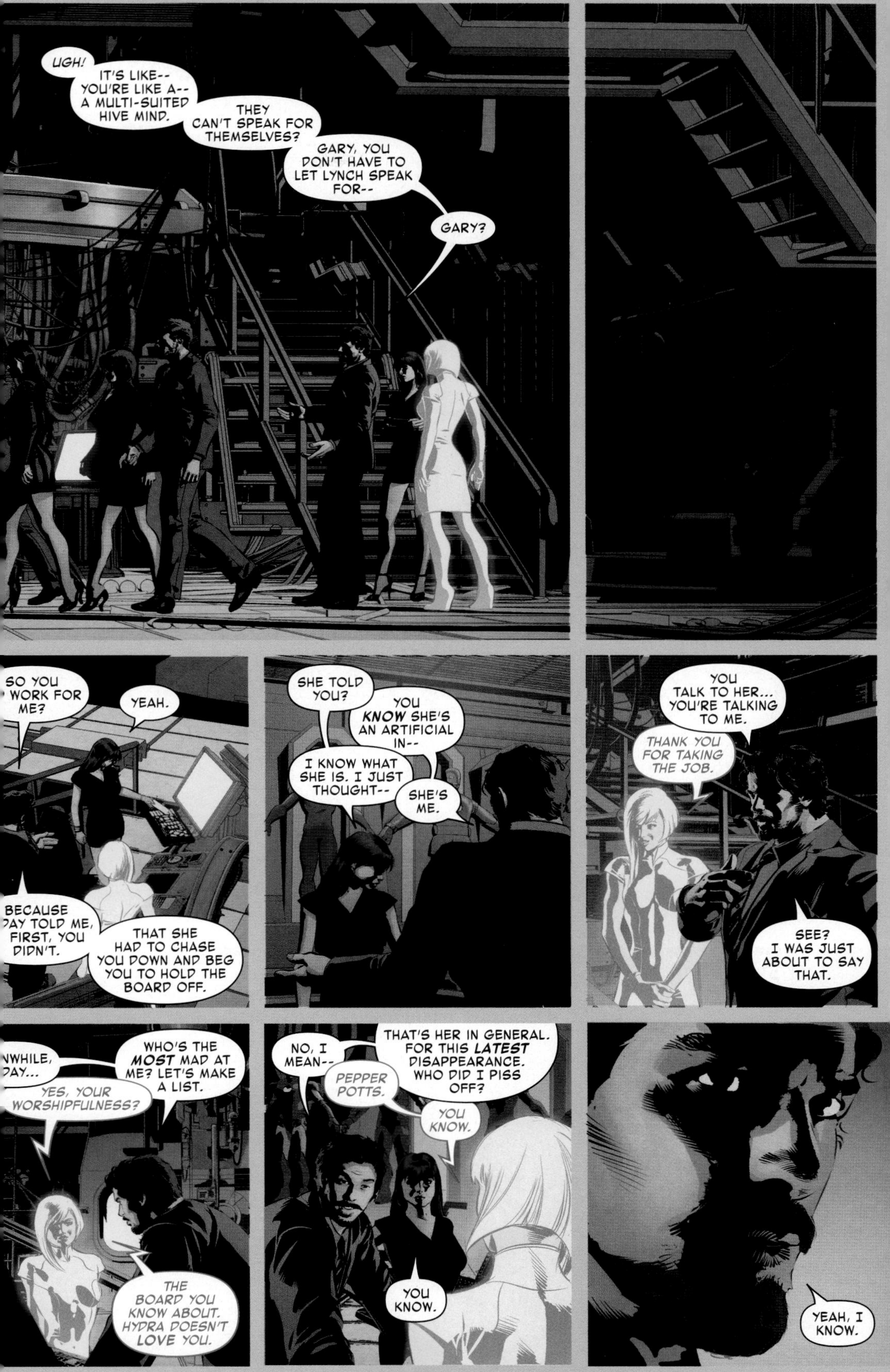
UGH!
IT'S LIKE-- YOU'RE LIKE A-- A MULTI-SUITED HIVE MIND.
THEY CAN'T SPEAK FOR THEMSELVES?
GARY, YOU DON'T HAVE TO LET LYNCH SPEAK FOR--
GARY?
SO YOU WORK FOR ME?
YEAH.
BECAUSE TOLD ME, FIRST, YOU DIDN'T.
THAT SHE HAD TO CHASE YOU DOWN AND BEG YOU TO HOLD THE BOARD OFF.
SHE TOLD YOU?
YOU KNOW SHE'S AN ARTIFICIAL IN--
I KNOW WHAT SHE IS. I JUST THOUGHT--
SHE'S ME.
YOU TALK TO HER... YOU'RE TALKING TO ME.
THANK YOU FOR TAKING THE JOB.
SEE? I WAS JUST ABOUT TO SAY THAT.
WHO'S THE MOST MAD AT ME? LET'S MAKE A LIST.
YES, YOUR WORSHIPFULNESS?
THE BOARD YOU KNOW ABOUT. HYDRA DOESN'T LOVE YOU.
NO, I MEAN--
THAT'S HER IN GENERAL. FOR THIS LATEST DISAPPEARANCE. WHO DID I PISS OFF?
PEPPER POTTS.
YOU KNOW.
YOU KNOW.
YEAH, I KNOW.

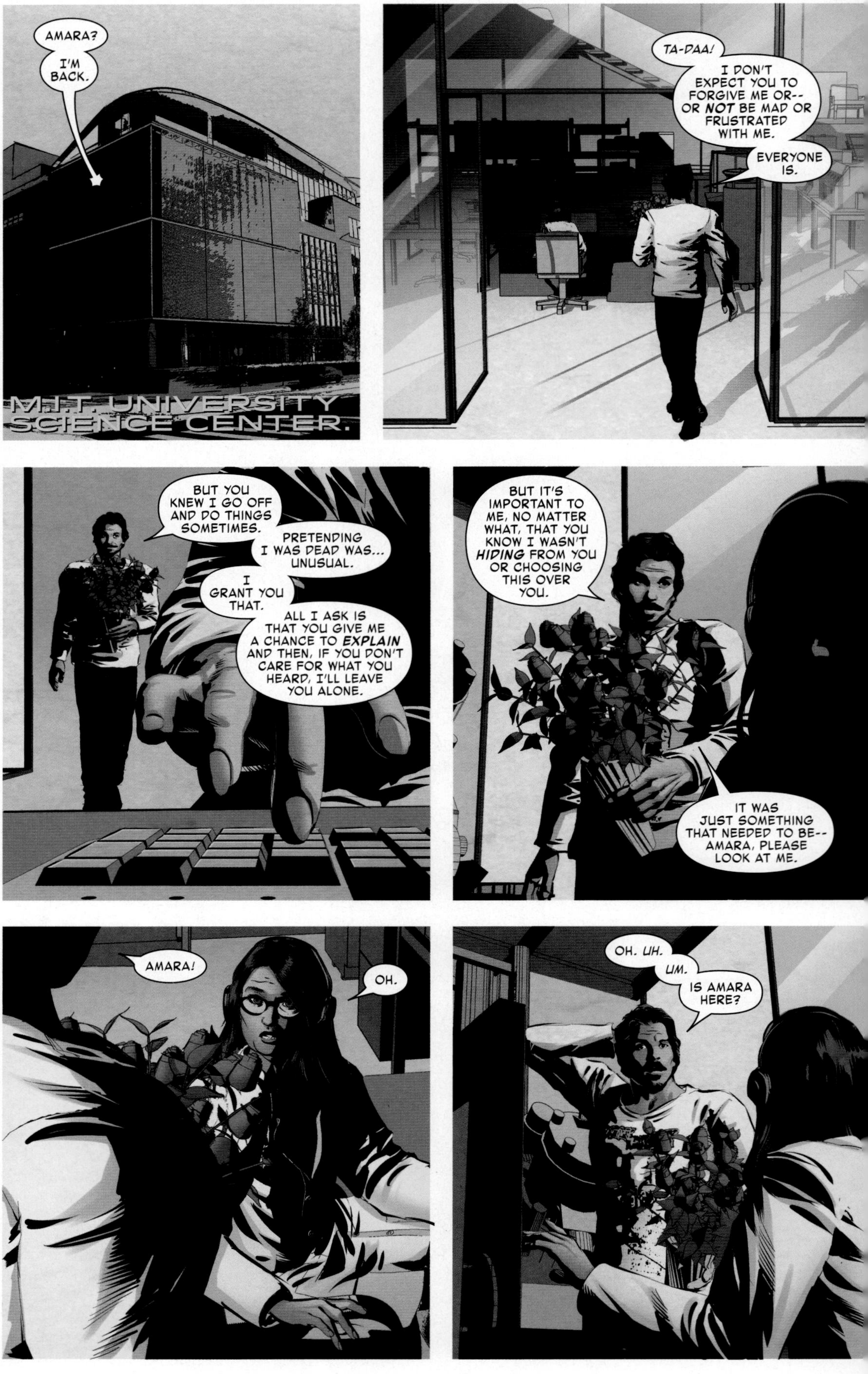
AMARA?
I'M BACK.
M.I.T. UNIVERSITY SCIENCE CENTER.
TA-DAA!
I DON'T EXPECT YOU TO FORGIVE ME OR-- OR NOT BE MAD OR FRUSTRATED WITH ME.
EVERYONE IS.
BUT YOU KNEW I GO OFF AND DO THINGS SOMETIMES.
PRETENDING I WAS DEAD WAS... UNUSUAL.
I GRANT YOU THAT.
ALL I ASK IS THAT YOU GIVE ME A CHANCE TO EXPLAIN AND THEN, IF YOU DON'T CARE FOR WHAT YOU HEARD, I'LL LEAVE YOU ALONE.
BUT IT'S IMPORTANT TO ME, NO MATTER WHAT, THAT YOU KNOW I WASN'T HIDING FROM YOU OR CHOOSING THIS OVER YOU.
IT WAS JUST SOMETHING THAT NEEDED TO BE-- AMARA, PLEASE LOOK AT ME.
AMARA!
OH.
OH. UH.
UM.
IS AMARA HERE?

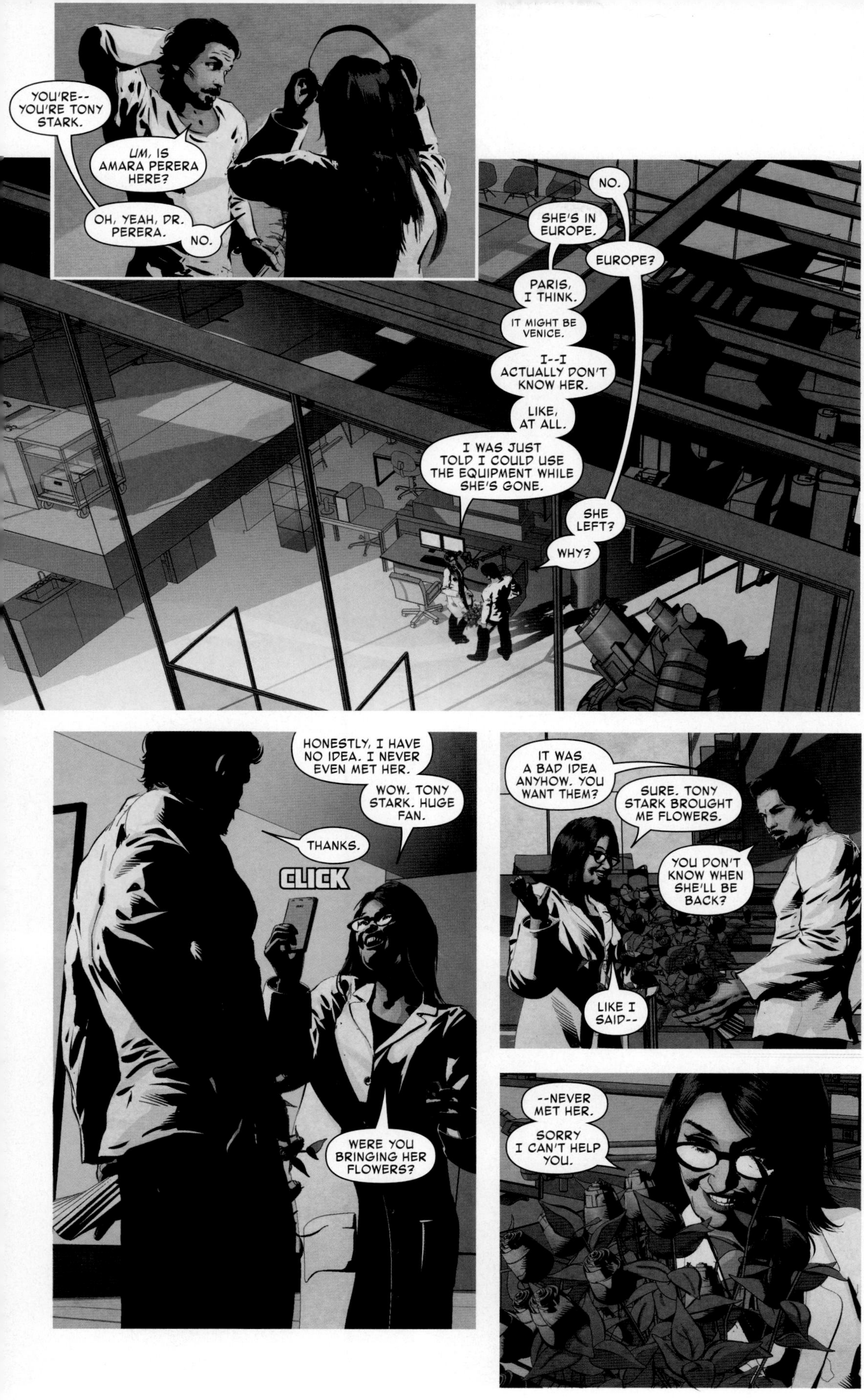
YOU'RE--
YOU'RE TONY STARK.
UM, IS AMARA PERERA HERE?
OH, YEAH, DR. PERERA.
NO.
NO.
SHE'S IN EUROPE.
EUROPE?
PARIS, I THINK.
IT MIGHT BE VENICE.
I--I ACTUALLY DON'T KNOW HER.
LIKE, AT ALL.
I WAS JUST TOLD I COULD USE THE EQUIPMENT WHILE SHE'S GONE.
SHE LEFT?
WHY?
HONESTLY, I HAVE NO IDEA. I NEVER EVEN MET HER.
WOW. TONY STARK. HUGE FAN.
THANKS.
CLICK
WERE YOU BRINGING HER FLOWERS?
IT WAS A BAD IDEA ANYHOW. YOU WANT THEM?
SURE. TONY STARK BROUGHT ME FLOWERS.
YOU DON'T KNOW WHEN SHE'LL BE BACK?
LIKE I SAID--
--NEVER MET HER.
SORRY I CAN'T HELP YOU.

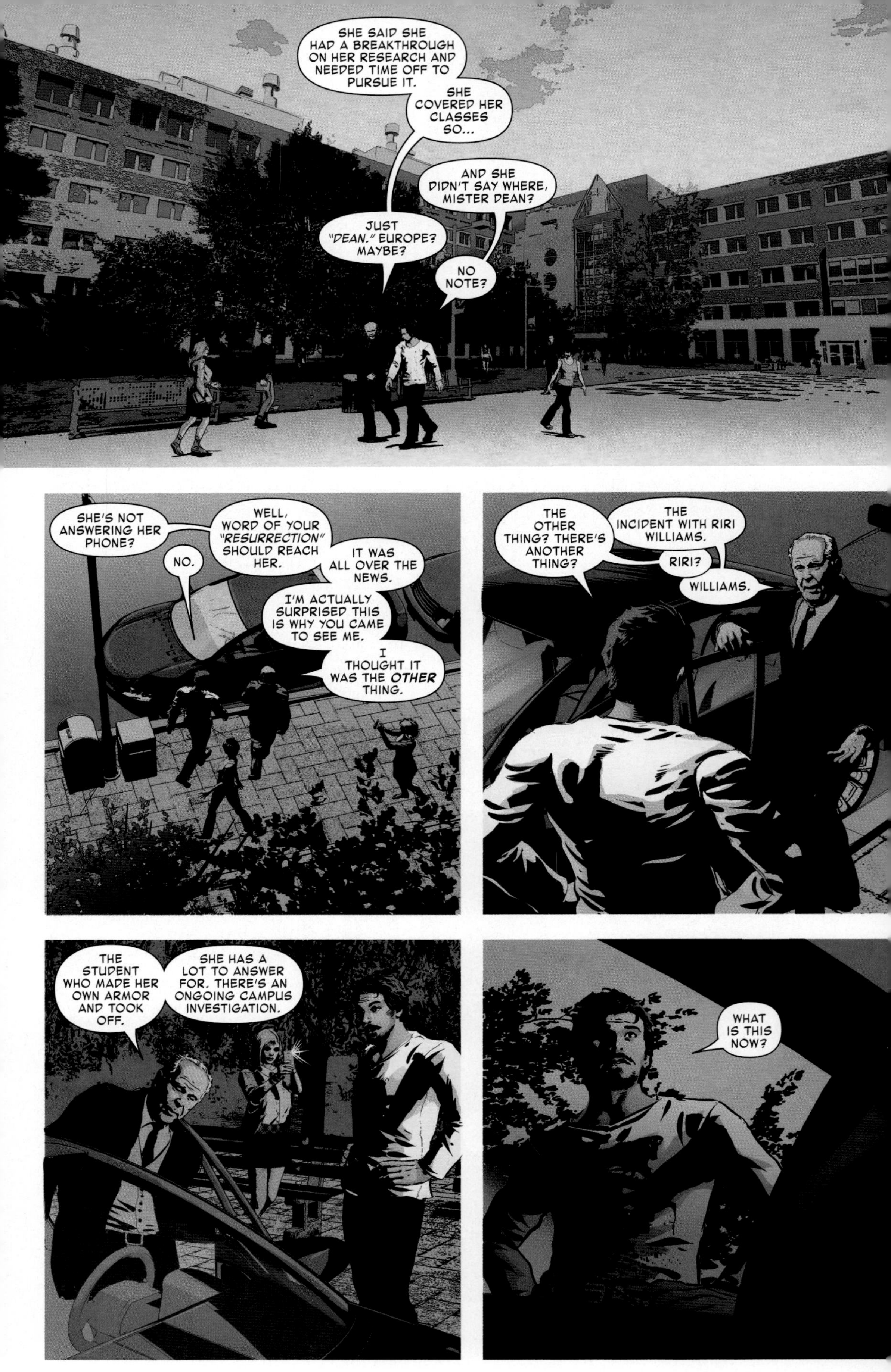
SHE SAID SHE HAD A BREAKTHROUGH ON HER RESEARCH AND NEEDED TIME OFF TO PURSUE IT.
SHE COVERED HER CLASSES SO...
AND SHE DIDN'T SAY WHERE, MISTER DEAN?
JUST "DEAN." EUROPE? MAYBE?
NO NOTE?
SHE'S NOT ANSWERING HER PHONE?
NO.
WELL, WORD OF YOUR "RESURRECTION" SHOULD REACH HER.
IT WAS ALL OVER THE NEWS.
I'M ACTUALLY SURPRISED THIS IS WHY YOU CAME TO SEE ME.
I THOUGHT IT WAS THE OTHER THING.
THE OTHER THING? THERE'S ANOTHER THING?
THE INCIDENT WITH RIRI WILLIAMS.
RIRI?
WILLIAMS.
THE STUDENT WHO MADE HER OWN ARMOR AND TOOK OFF.
SHE HAS A LOT TO ANSWER FOR. THERE'S AN ONGOING CAMPUS INVESTIGATION.
WHAT IS THIS NOW?

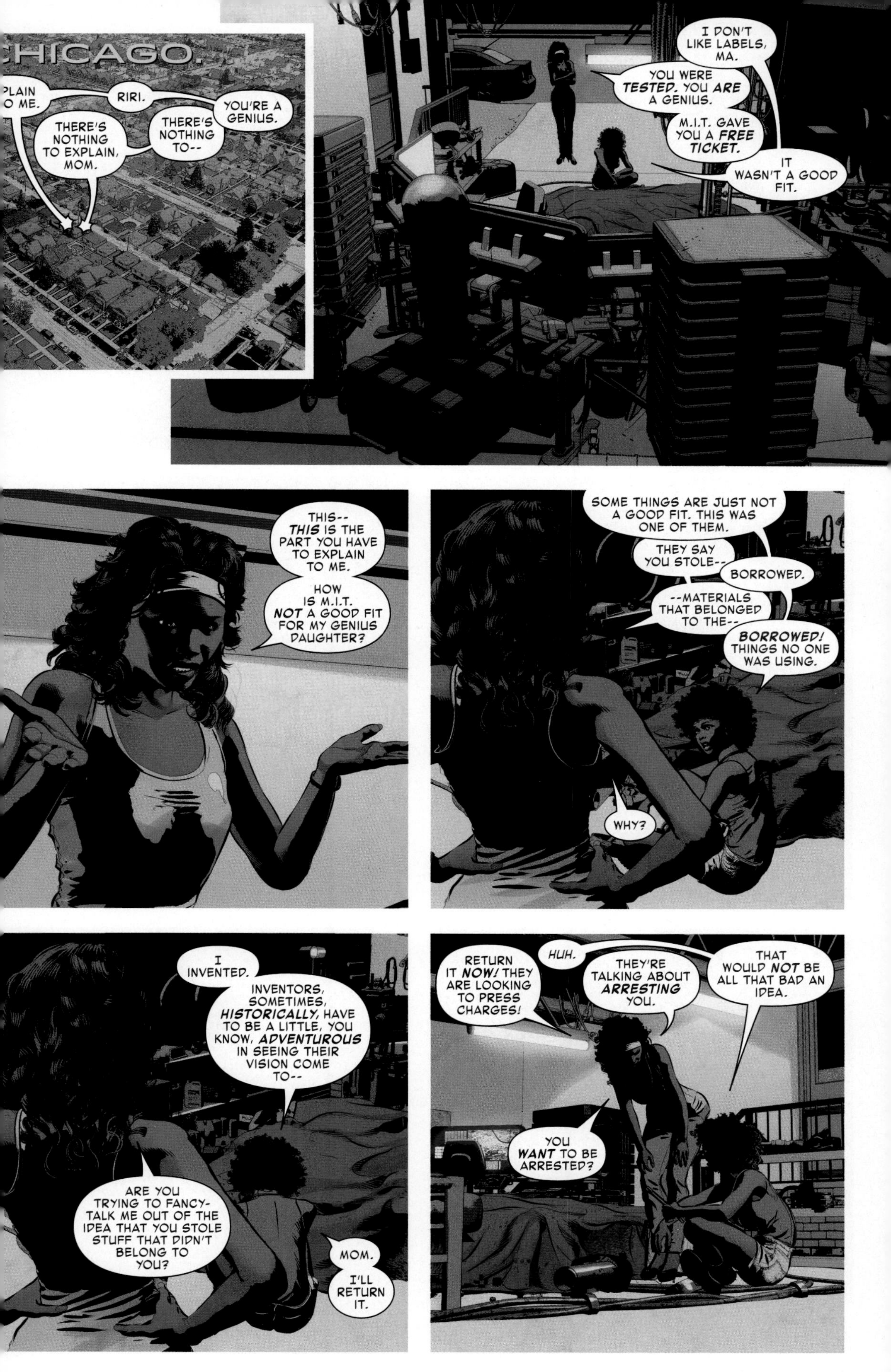
CHICAGO.
PLAIN
O ME.
RIRI.
YOU'RE A GENIUS.
THERE'S NOTHING TO EXPLAIN, MOM.
THERE'S NOTHING TO--
I DON'T LIKE LABELS, MA.
YOU WERE TESTED. YOU ARE A GENIUS.
M.I.T. GAVE YOU A FREE TICKET.
IT WASN'T A GOOD FIT.
THIS-- THIS IS THE PART YOU HAVE TO EXPLAIN TO ME.
HOW IS M.I.T. NOT A GOOD FIT FOR MY GENIUS DAUGHTER?
SOME THINGS ARE JUST NOT A GOOD FIT. THIS WAS ONE OF THEM.
THEY SAY YOU STOLE--
BORROWED.
--MATERIALS THAT BELONGED TO THE--
BORROWED! THINGS NO ONE WAS USING.
WHY?
I INVENTED.
INVENTORS, SOMETIMES, HISTORICALLY, HAVE TO BE A LITTLE, YOU KNOW, ADVENTUROUS IN SEEING THEIR VISION COME TO--
ARE YOU TRYING TO FANCY-TALK ME OUT OF THE IDEA THAT YOU STOLE STUFF THAT DIDN'T BELONG TO YOU?
MOM.
I'LL RETURN IT.
RETURN IT NOW! THEY ARE LOOKING TO PRESS CHARGES!
HUH.
THEY'RE TALKING ABOUT ARRESTING YOU.
THAT WOULD NOT BE ALL THAT BAD AN IDEA.
YOU WANT TO BE ARRESTED?

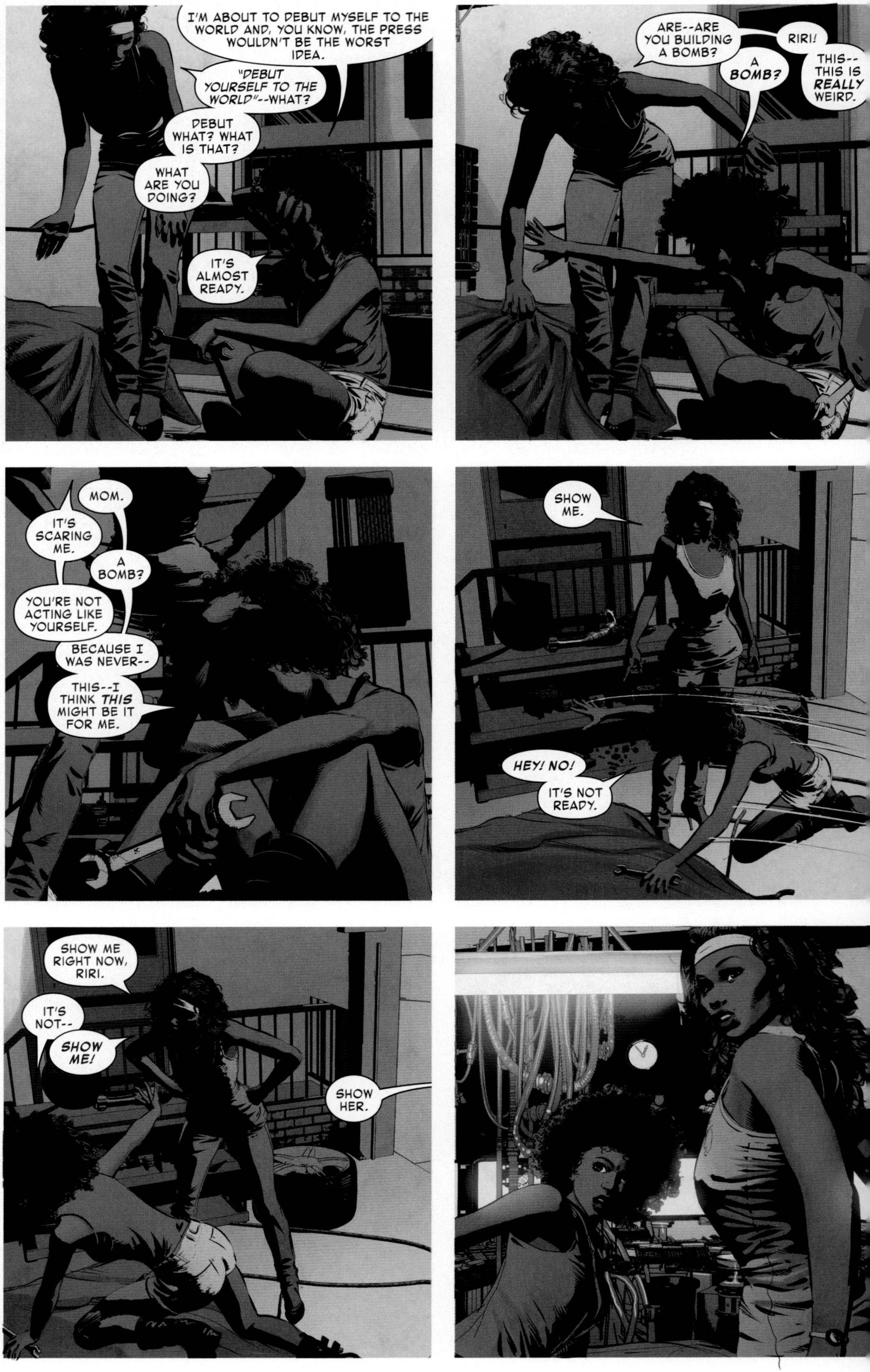

I'M ABOUT TO DEBUT MYSELF TO THE WORLD AND, YOU KNOW, THE PRESS WOULDN'T BE THE WORST IDEA.
"DEBUT YOURSELF TO THE WORLD"--WHAT?
DEBUT WHAT? WHAT IS THAT?
WHAT ARE YOU DOING?
IT'S ALMOST READY.
ARE--ARE YOU BUILDING A BOMB?
RIRI!
A BOMB?
THIS--THIS IS REALLY WEIRD.
MOM.
IT'S SCARING ME.
A BOMB?
YOU'RE NOT ACTING LIKE YOURSELF.
BECAUSE I WAS NEVER--
THIS--I THINK THIS MIGHT BE IT FOR ME.
SHOW ME.
HEY! NO!
IT'S NOT READY.
SHOW ME RIGHT NOW, RIRI.
IT'S NOT--
SHOW ME!
SHOW HER.

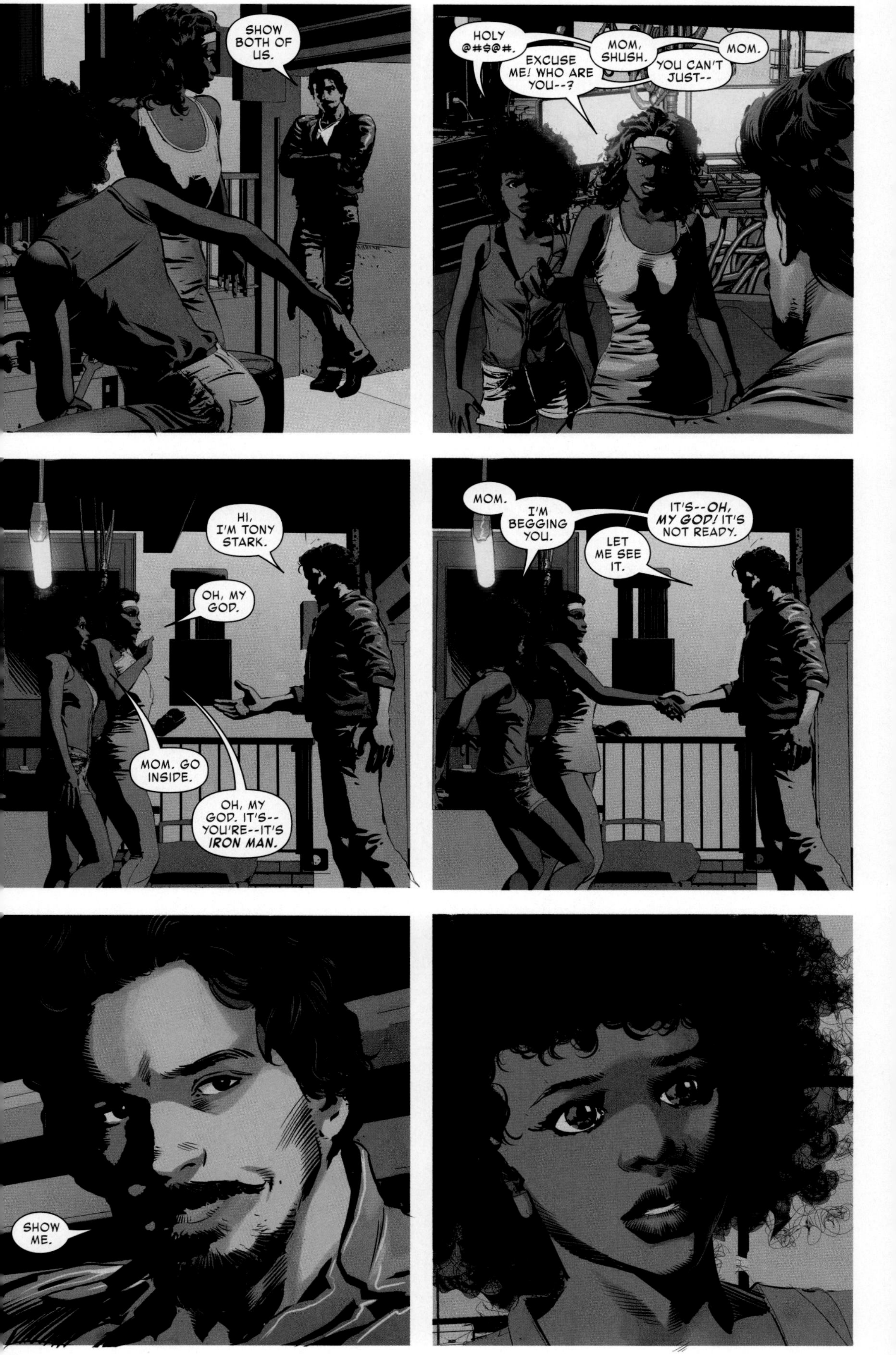
SHOW BOTH OF US.
HOLY @#$@#.
EXCUSE ME! WHO ARE YOU--?
MOM, SHUSH.
MOM.
YOU CAN'T JUST--
HI, I'M TONY STARK.
OH, MY GOD.
MOM. GO INSIDE.
OH, MY GOD. IT'S-- YOU'RE--IT'S IRON MAN.
MOM.
I'M BEGGING YOU.
IT'S--OH, MY GOD! IT'S NOT READY.
LET ME SEE IT.
SHOW ME.

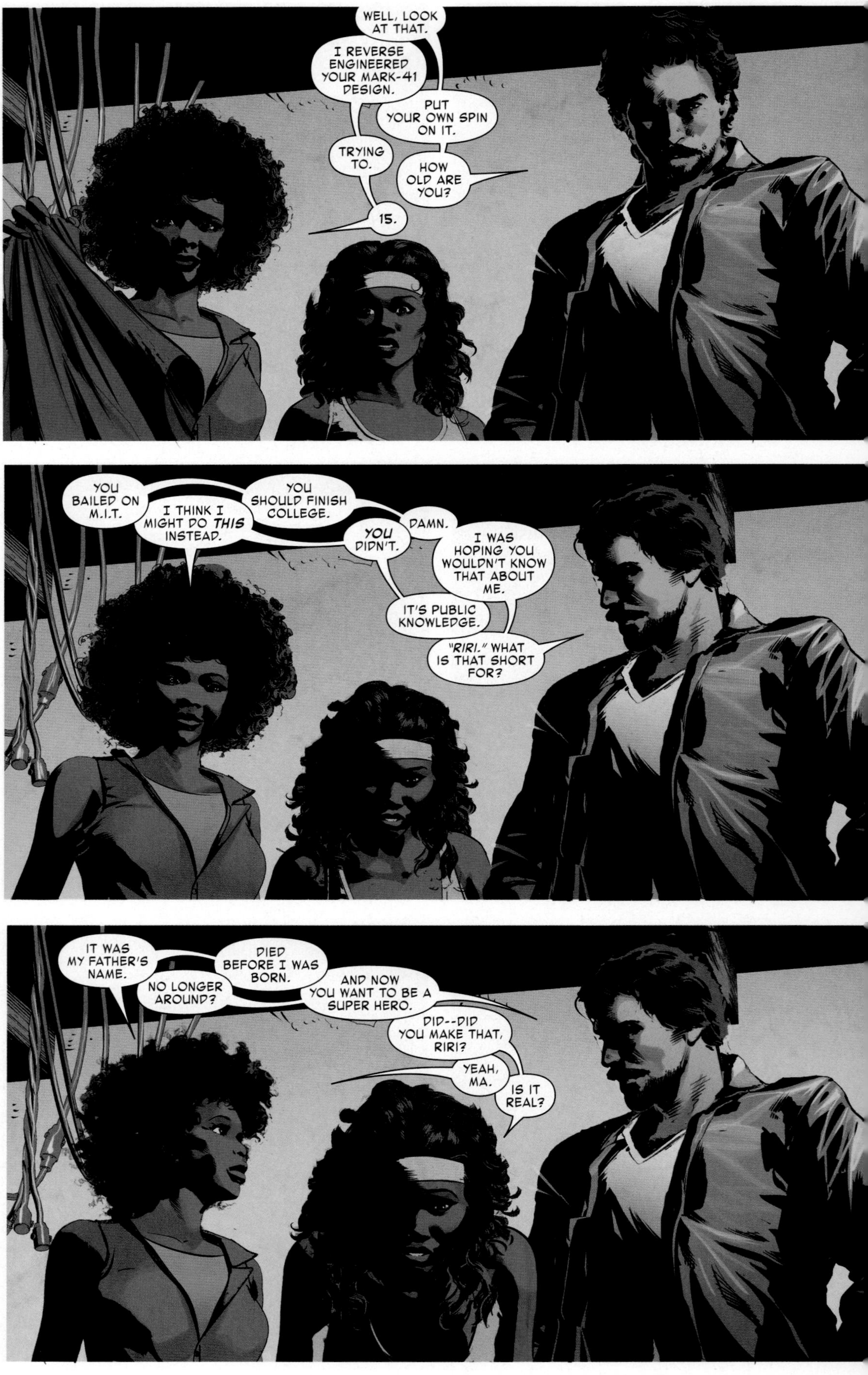
WELL, LOOK AT THAT.
I REVERSE ENGINEERED YOUR MARK-41 DESIGN.
PUT YOUR OWN SPIN ON IT.
TRYING TO.
HOW OLD ARE YOU?
15.
YOU BAILED ON M.I.T.
YOU SHOULD FINISH COLLEGE.
I THINK I MIGHT DO *THIS* INSTEAD.
DAMN.
YOU DIDN'T.
I WAS HOPING YOU WOULDN'T KNOW THAT ABOUT ME.
IT'S PUBLIC KNOWLEDGE.
"*RIRI.*" WHAT IS THAT SHORT FOR?
IT WAS MY FATHER'S NAME.
DIED BEFORE I WAS BORN.
NO LONGER AROUND?
AND NOW YOU WANT TO BE A SUPER HERO.
DID--DID YOU MAKE THAT, RIRI?
YEAH, MA.
IS IT REAL?

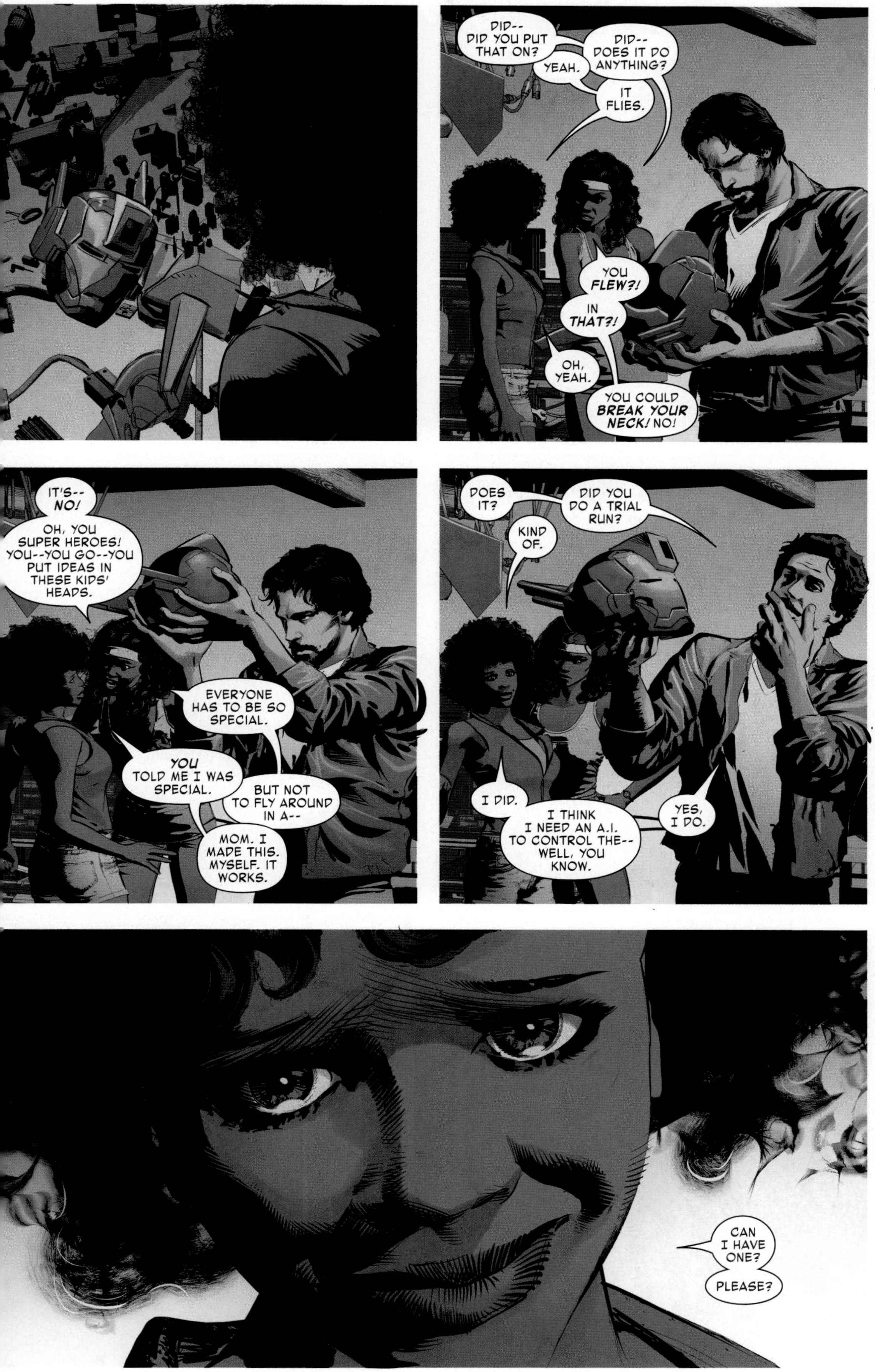
DID--
DID YOU PUT THAT ON?
YEAH.
DID--
DOES IT DO ANYTHING?
IT FLIES.
YOU FLEW?!
IN THAT?!
OH, YEAH.
YOU COULD BREAK YOUR NECK! NO!
IT'S--
NO!
OH, YOU SUPER HEROES! YOU--YOU GO--YOU PUT IDEAS IN THESE KIDS' HEADS.
EVERYONE HAS TO BE SO SPECIAL.
YOU TOLD ME I WAS SPECIAL.
BUT NOT TO FLY AROUND IN A--
MOM. I MADE THIS. MYSELF. IT WORKS.
DOES IT?
DID YOU DO A TRIAL RUN?
KIND OF.
I DID.
I THINK I NEED AN A.I. TO CONTROL THE--WELL, YOU KNOW.
YES, I DO.
CAN I HAVE ONE?
PLEASE?

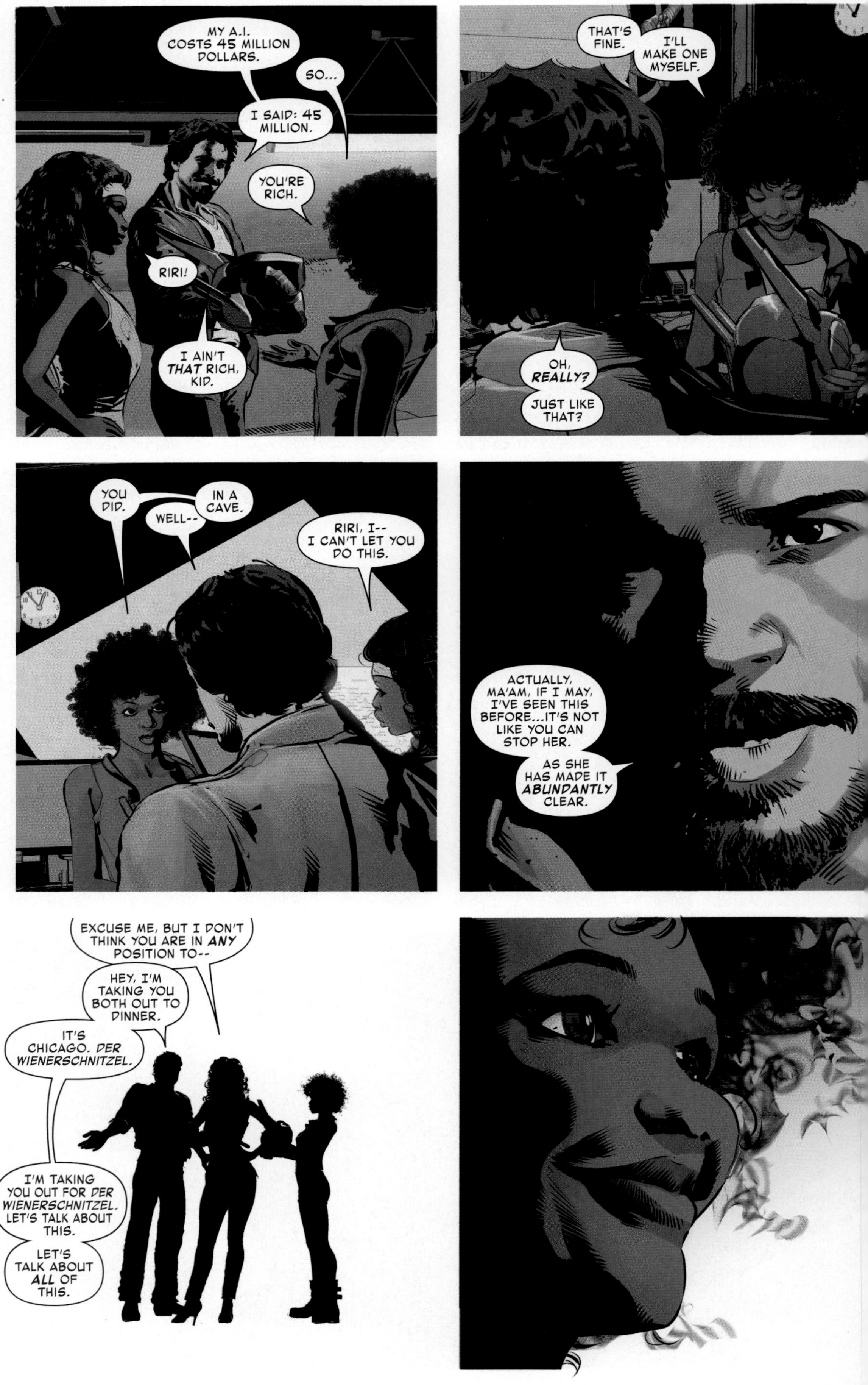
MY A.I. COSTS 45 MILLION DOLLARS.
SO...
I SAID: 45 MILLION.
YOU'RE RICH.
RIRI!
I AIN'T *THAT* RICH, KID.
THAT'S FINE.
I'LL MAKE ONE MYSELF.
OH, *REALLY?*
JUST LIKE THAT?
YOU DID.
WELL--
IN A CAVE.
RIRI, I-- I CAN'T LET YOU DO THIS.
ACTUALLY, MA'AM, IF I MAY, I'VE SEEN THIS BEFORE...IT'S NOT LIKE YOU CAN STOP HER.
AS SHE HAS MADE IT *ABUNDANTLY* CLEAR.
EXCUSE ME, BUT I DON'T THINK YOU ARE IN *ANY* POSITION TO--
HEY, I'M TAKING YOU BOTH OUT TO DINNER.
IT'S CHICAGO. *DER WIENERSCHNITZEL.*
I'M TAKING YOU OUT FOR *DER WIENERSCHNITZEL.* LET'S TALK ABOUT THIS.
LET'S TALK ABOUT *ALL* OF THIS.

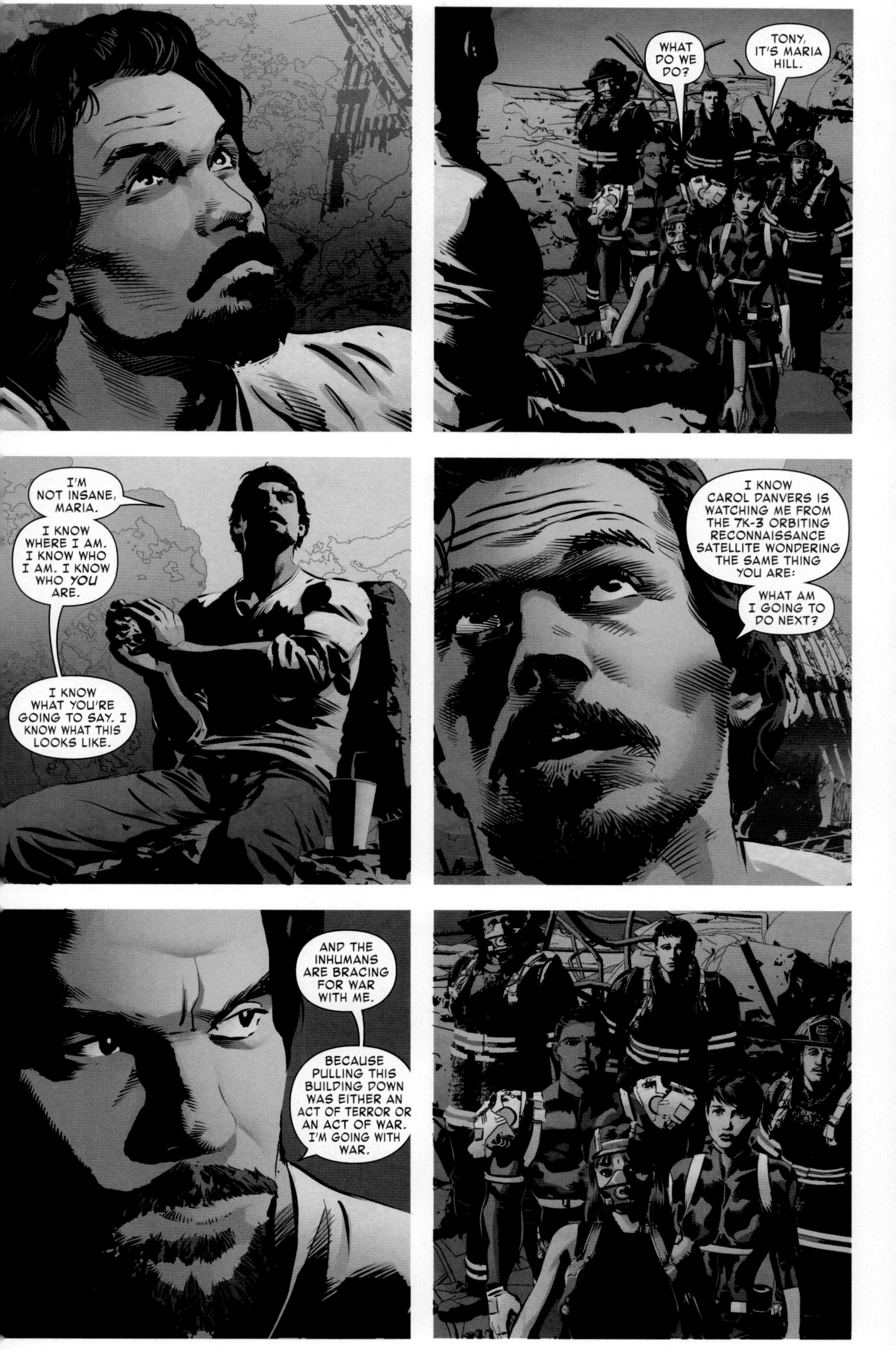
TONY, IT'S MARIA HILL.
WHAT DO WE DO?
I'M NOT INSANE, MARIA.
I KNOW WHERE I AM. I KNOW WHO I AM. I KNOW WHO *YOU* ARE.
I KNOW WHAT YOU'RE GOING TO SAY. I KNOW WHAT THIS LOOKS LIKE.
I KNOW CAROL DANVERS IS WATCHING ME FROM THE 7K-3 ORBITING RECONNAISSANCE SATELLITE WONDERING THE SAME THING YOU ARE:
WHAT AM I GOING TO DO NEXT?
AND THE INHUMANS ARE BRACING FOR WAR WITH ME.
BECAUSE PULLING THIS BUILDING DOWN WAS EITHER AN ACT OF TERROR OR AN ACT OF WAR. I'M GOING WITH WAR.

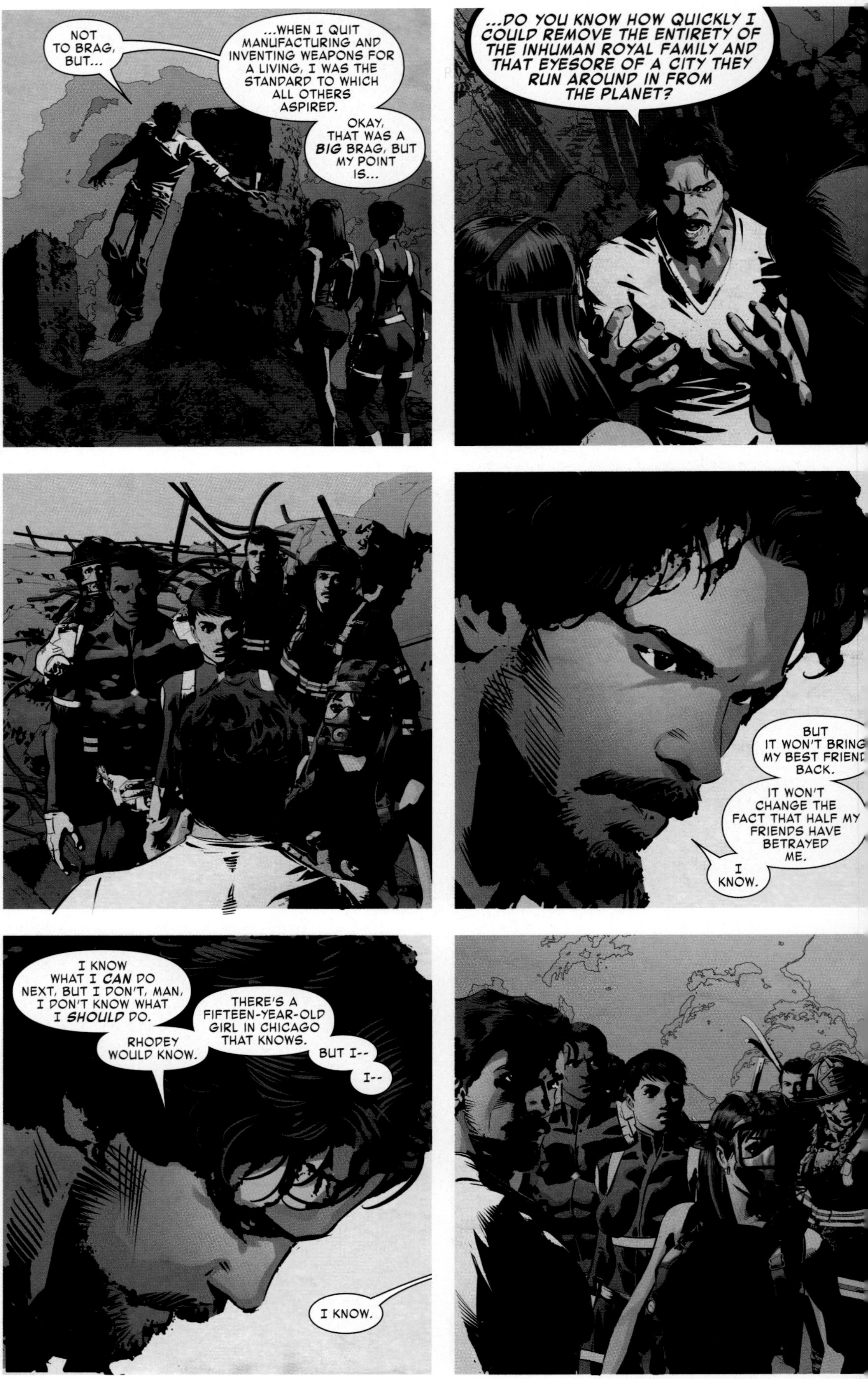
NOT TO BRAG, BUT...
...WHEN I QUIT MANUFACTURING AND INVENTING WEAPONS FOR A LIVING, I WAS THE STANDARD TO WHICH ALL OTHERS ASPIRED.
OKAY, THAT WAS A BIG BRAG, BUT MY POINT IS...
...DO YOU KNOW HOW QUICKLY I COULD REMOVE THE ENTIRETY OF THE INHUMAN ROYAL FAMILY AND THAT EYESORE OF A CITY THEY RUN AROUND IN FROM THE PLANET?
BUT IT WON'T BRING MY BEST FRIEND BACK.
IT WON'T CHANGE THE FACT THAT HALF MY FRIENDS HAVE BETRAYED ME.
I KNOW.
I KNOW WHAT I CAN DO NEXT, BUT I DON'T, MAN, I DON'T KNOW WHAT I SHOULD DO.
RHODEY WOULD KNOW.
THERE'S A FIFTEEN-YEAR-OLD GIRL IN CHICAGO THAT KNOWS.
BUT I--
I--
I KNOW.

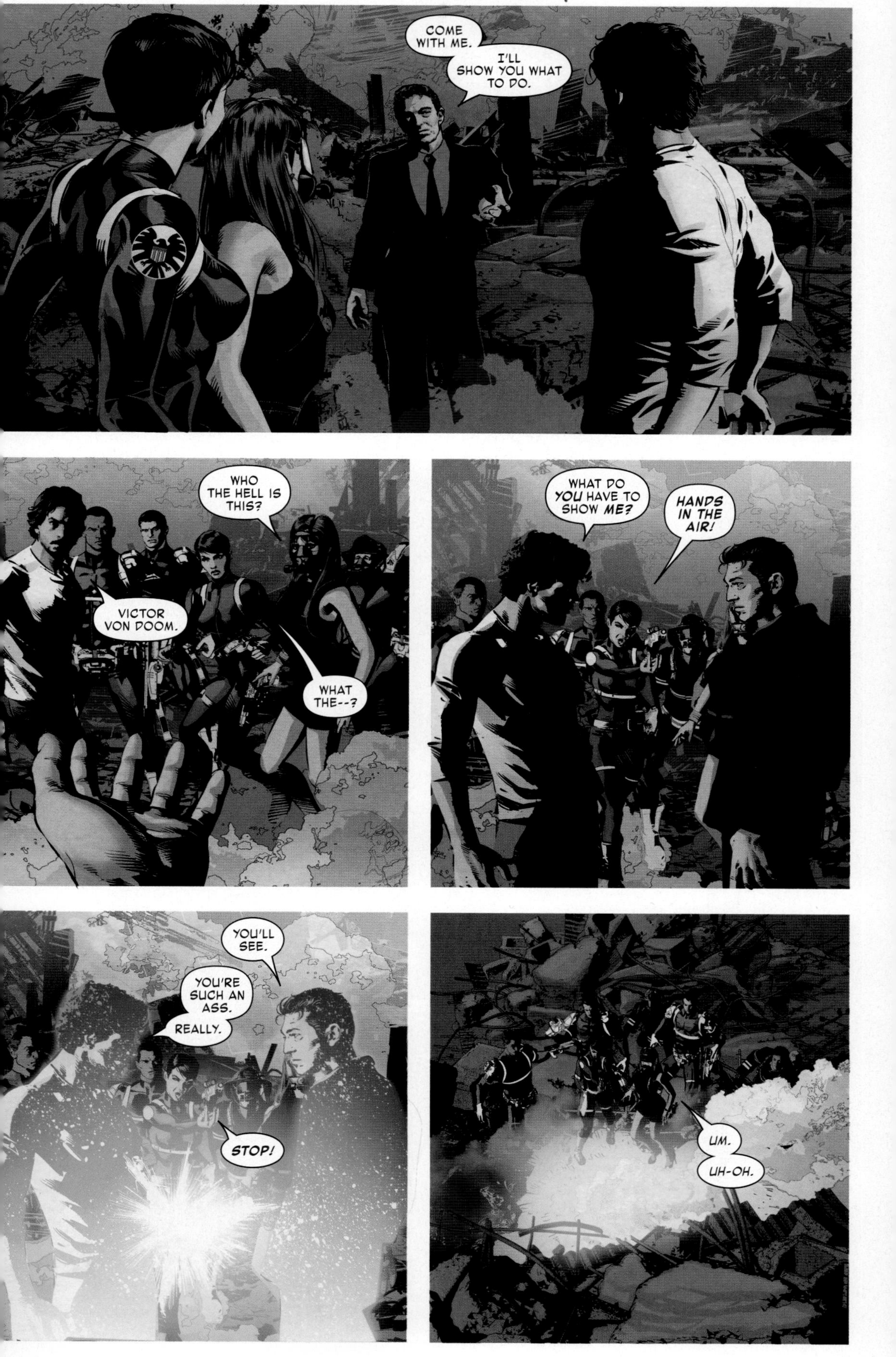
COME WITH ME.
I'LL SHOW YOU WHAT TO DO.
WHO THE HELL IS THIS?
VICTOR VON DOOM.
WHAT THE--?
WHAT DO YOU HAVE TO SHOW ME?
HANDS IN THE AIR!
YOU'LL SEE.
YOU'RE SUCH AN ASS.
REALLY.
STOP!
UM.
UH-OH.

#13

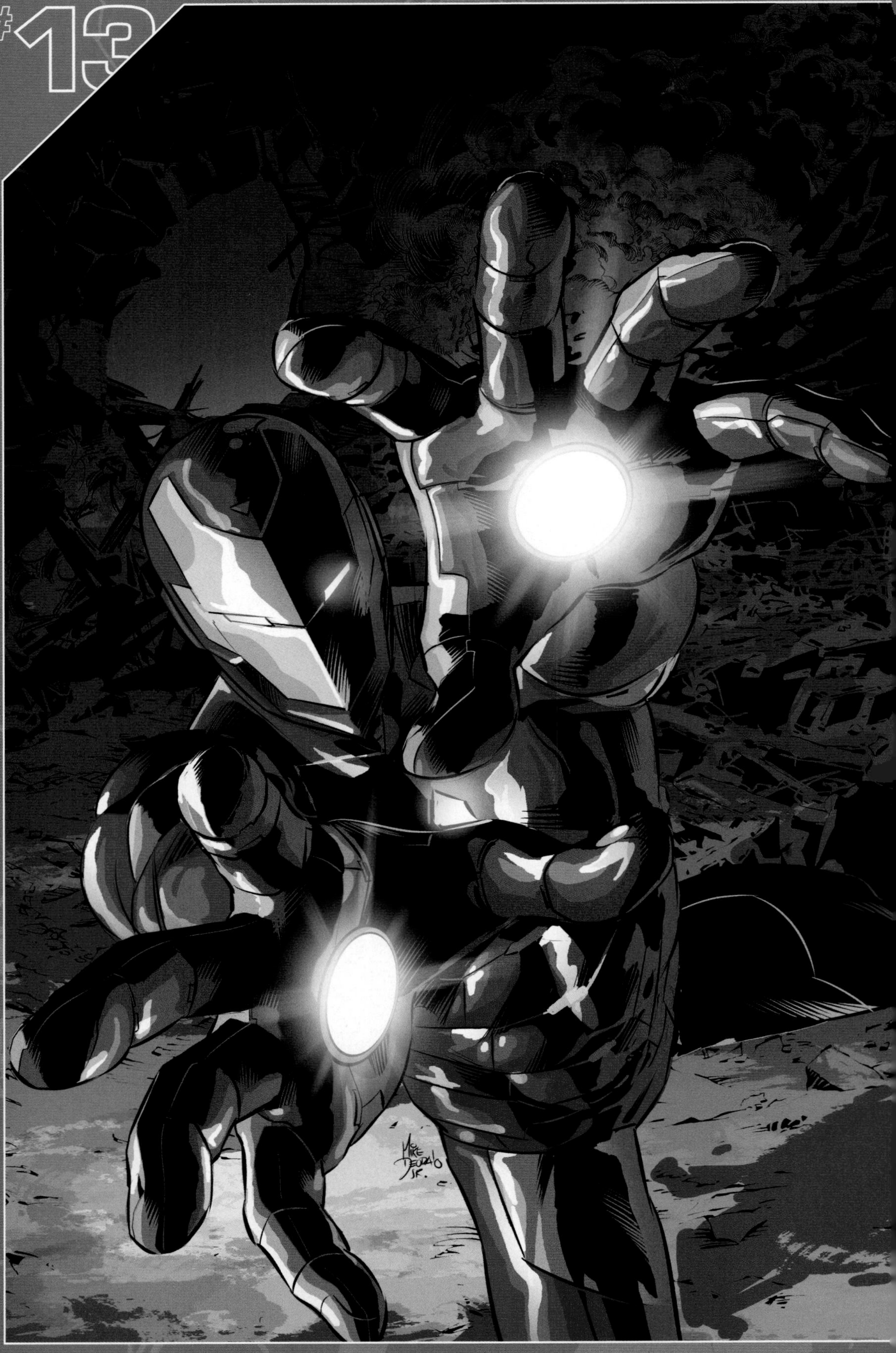

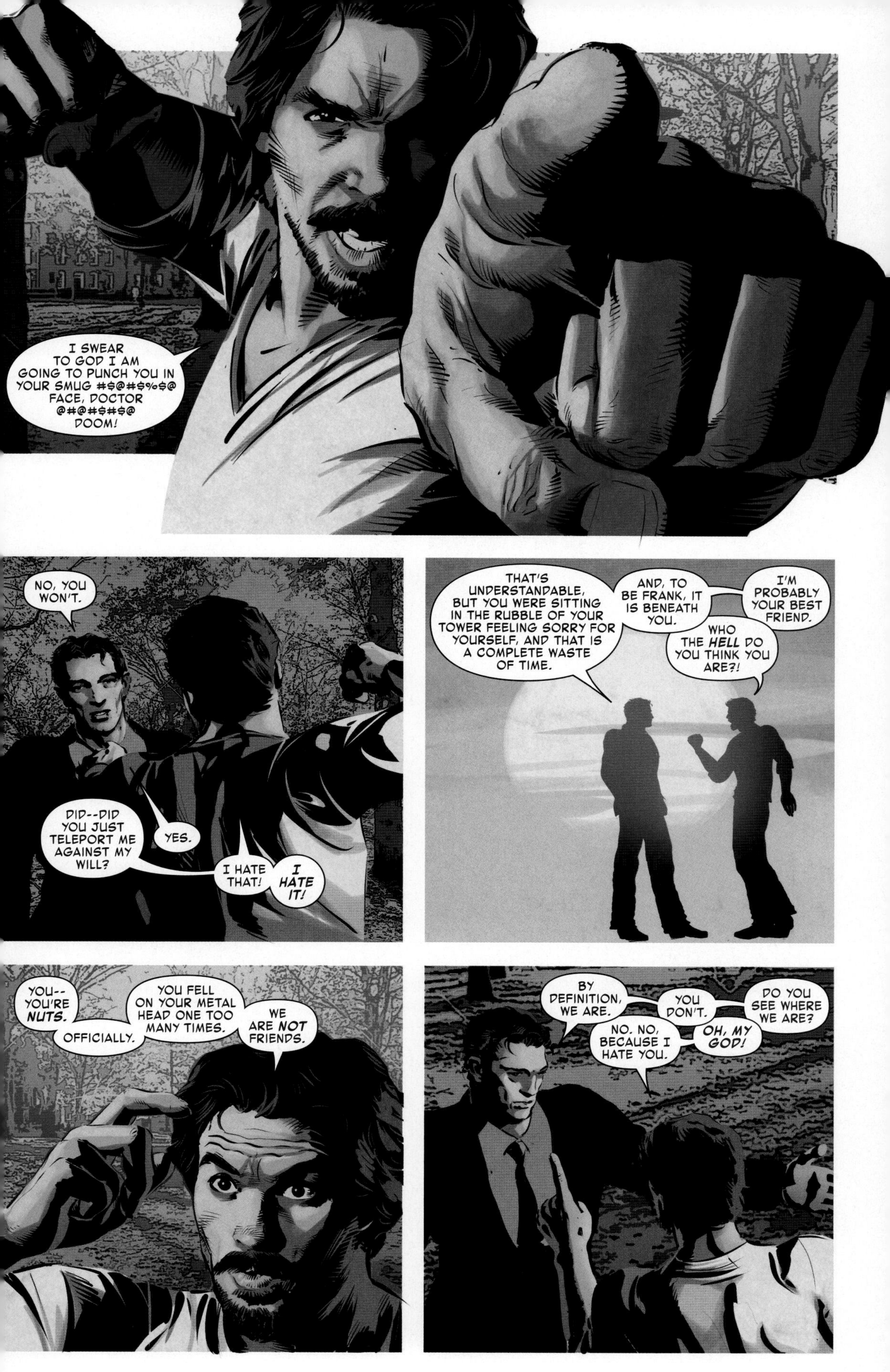
I SWEAR TO GOD I AM GOING TO PUNCH YOU IN YOUR SMUG #$@#$%$@ FACE, DOCTOR @#@#$#$@ DOOM!
NO, YOU WON'T.
DID--DID YOU JUST TELEPORT ME AGAINST MY WILL?
YES.
I HATE THAT!
I HATE IT!
THAT'S UNDERSTANDABLE, BUT YOU WERE SITTING IN THE RUBBLE OF YOUR TOWER FEELING SORRY FOR YOURSELF, AND THAT IS A COMPLETE WASTE OF TIME.
AND, TO BE FRANK, IT IS BENEATH YOU.
I'M PROBABLY YOUR BEST FRIEND.
WHO THE HELL DO YOU THINK YOU ARE?!
YOU--YOU'RE NUTS.
OFFICIALLY.
YOU FELL ON YOUR METAL HEAD ONE TOO MANY TIMES.
WE ARE NOT FRIENDS.
BY DEFINITION, WE ARE.
YOU DON'T.
DO YOU SEE WHERE WE ARE?
NO. NO, BECAUSE I HATE YOU.
OH, MY GOD!

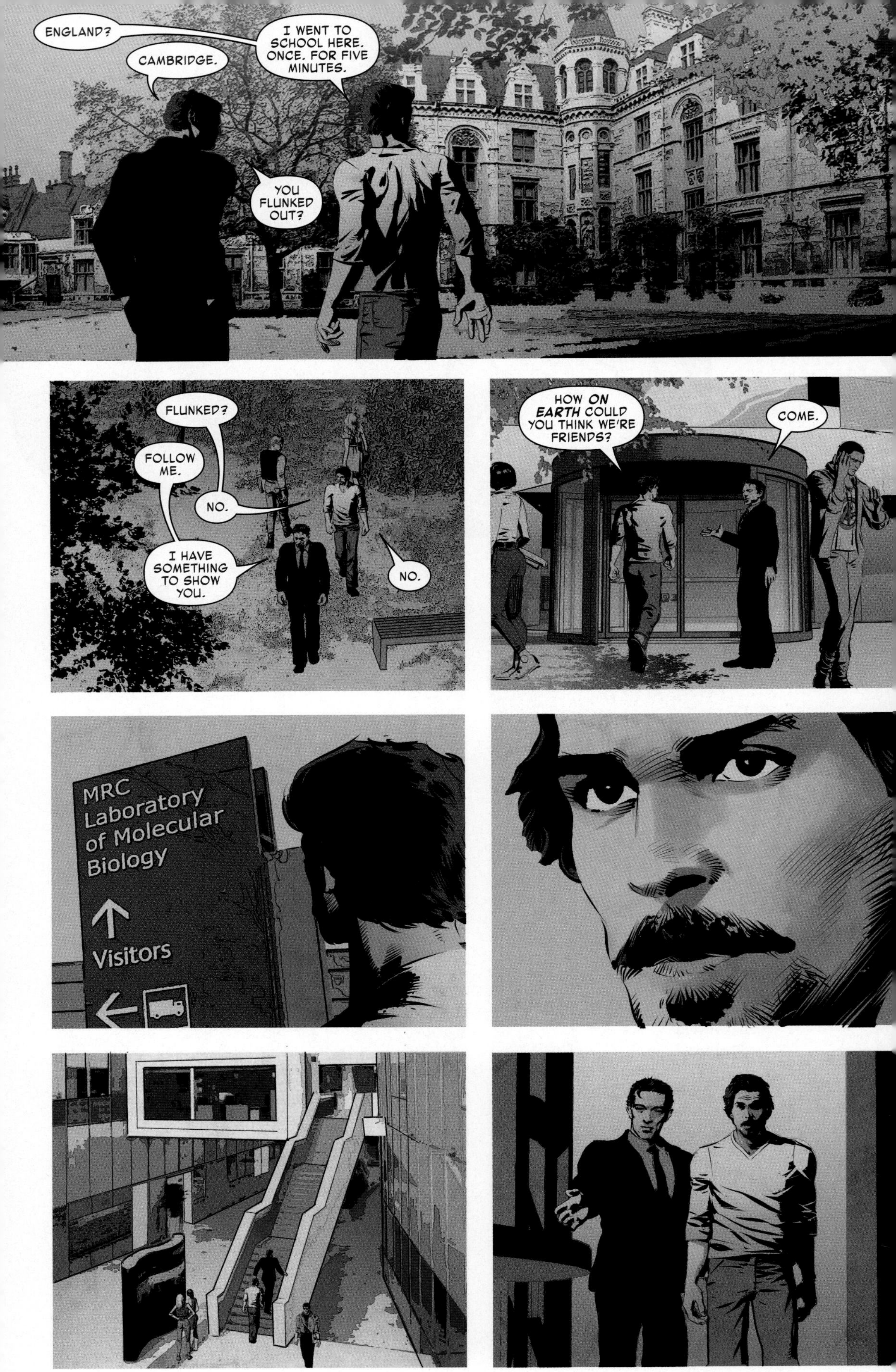
ENGLAND?
I WENT TO SCHOOL HERE. ONCE. FOR FIVE MINUTES.
CAMBRIDGE.
YOU FLUNKED OUT?
FLUNKED?
NO.
FOLLOW ME.
I HAVE SOMETHING TO SHOW YOU.
NO.
HOW ON EARTH COULD YOU THINK WE'RE FRIENDS?
COME.
MRC Laboratory of Molecular Biology
Visitors

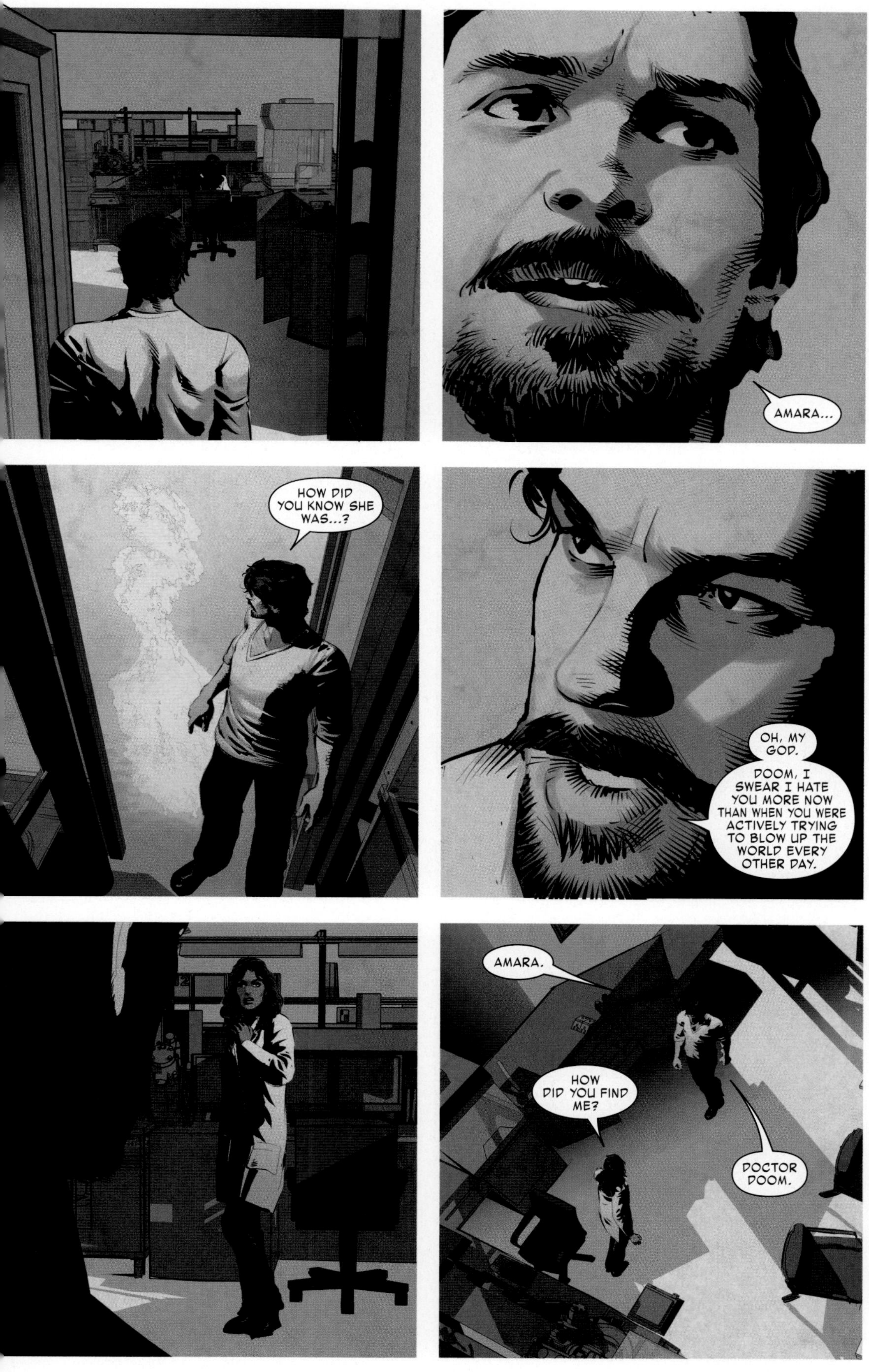
AMARA...
HOW DID YOU KNOW SHE WAS...?
OH, MY GOD.
DOOM, I SWEAR I HATE YOU MORE NOW THAN WHEN YOU WERE ACTIVELY TRYING TO BLOW UP THE WORLD EVERY OTHER DAY.
AMARA.
HOW DID YOU FIND ME?
DOCTOR DOOM.

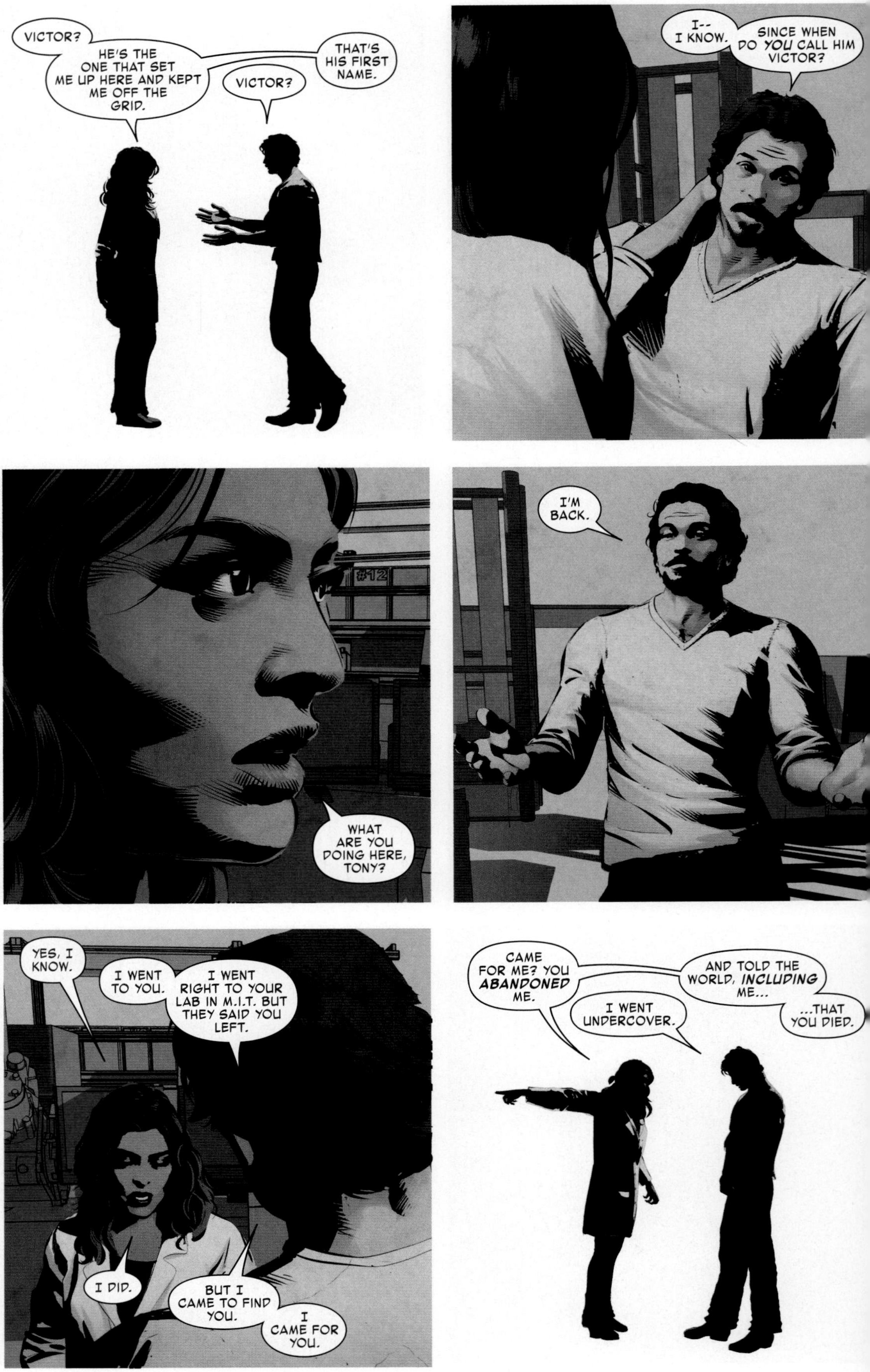
VICTOR?
HE'S THE ONE THAT SET ME UP HERE AND KEPT ME OFF THE GRID.
THAT'S HIS FIRST NAME.
VICTOR?
I-- I KNOW.
SINCE WHEN DO *YOU* CALL HIM VICTOR?
WHAT ARE YOU DOING HERE, TONY?
I'M BACK.
YES, I KNOW.
I WENT TO YOU.
I WENT RIGHT TO YOUR LAB IN M.I.T. BUT THEY SAID YOU LEFT.
I DID.
BUT I CAME TO FIND YOU.
I CAME FOR YOU.
CAME FOR ME? YOU ***ABANDONED*** ME.
I WENT UNDERCOVER.
AND TOLD THE WORLD, ***INCLUDING*** ME...
...THAT YOU DIED.

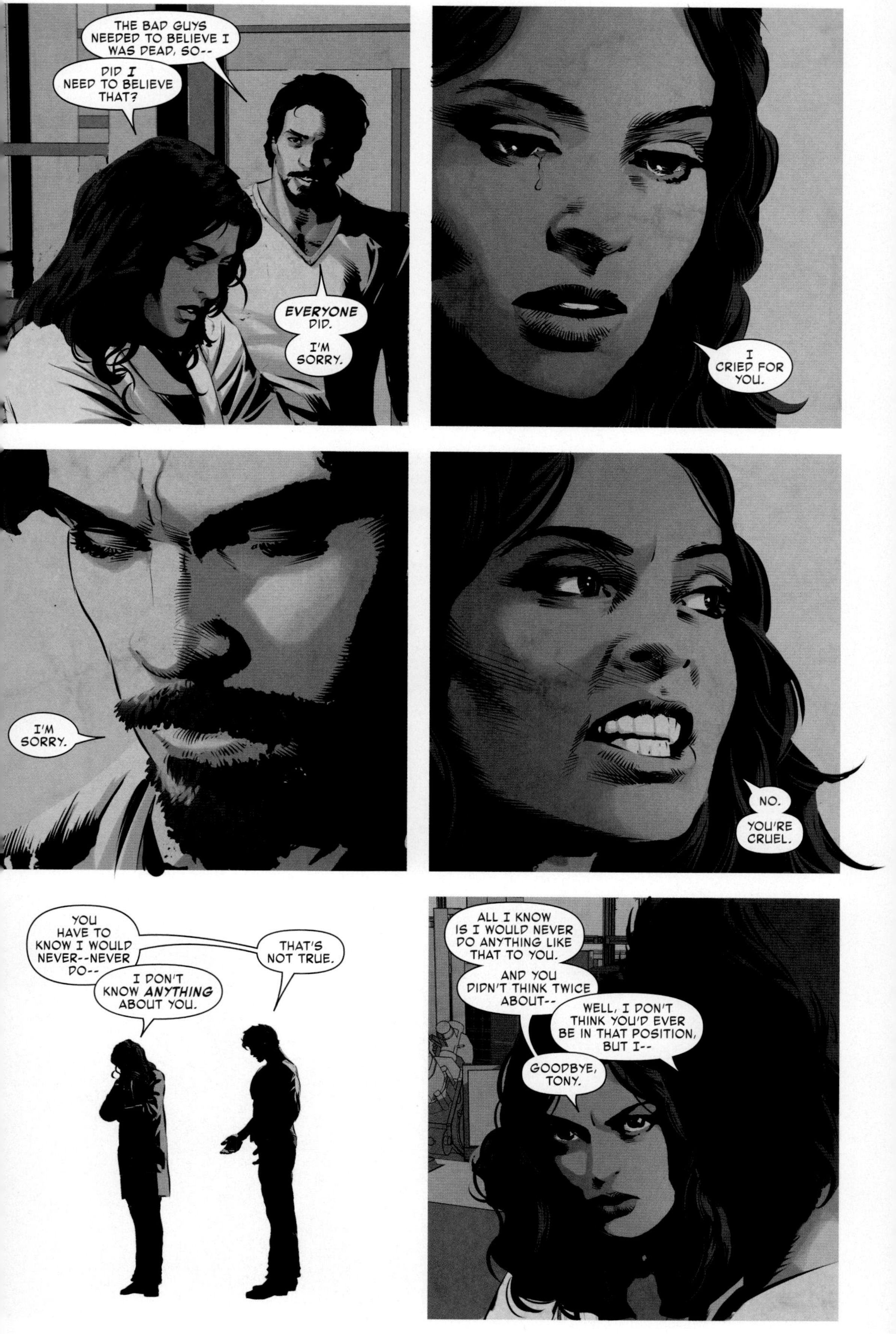
THE BAD GUYS NEEDED TO BELIEVE I WAS DEAD, SO--
DID *I* NEED TO BELIEVE THAT?
EVERYONE DID.
I'M SORRY.
I CRIED FOR YOU.
I'M SORRY.
NO.
YOU'RE CRUEL.
YOU HAVE TO KNOW I WOULD NEVER--NEVER DO--
I DON'T KNOW *ANYTHING* ABOUT YOU.
THAT'S NOT TRUE.
ALL I KNOW IS I WOULD NEVER DO ANYTHING LIKE THAT TO YOU.
AND YOU DIDN'T THINK TWICE ABOUT--
WELL, I DON'T THINK YOU'D EVER BE IN THAT POSITION, BUT I--
GOODBYE, TONY.

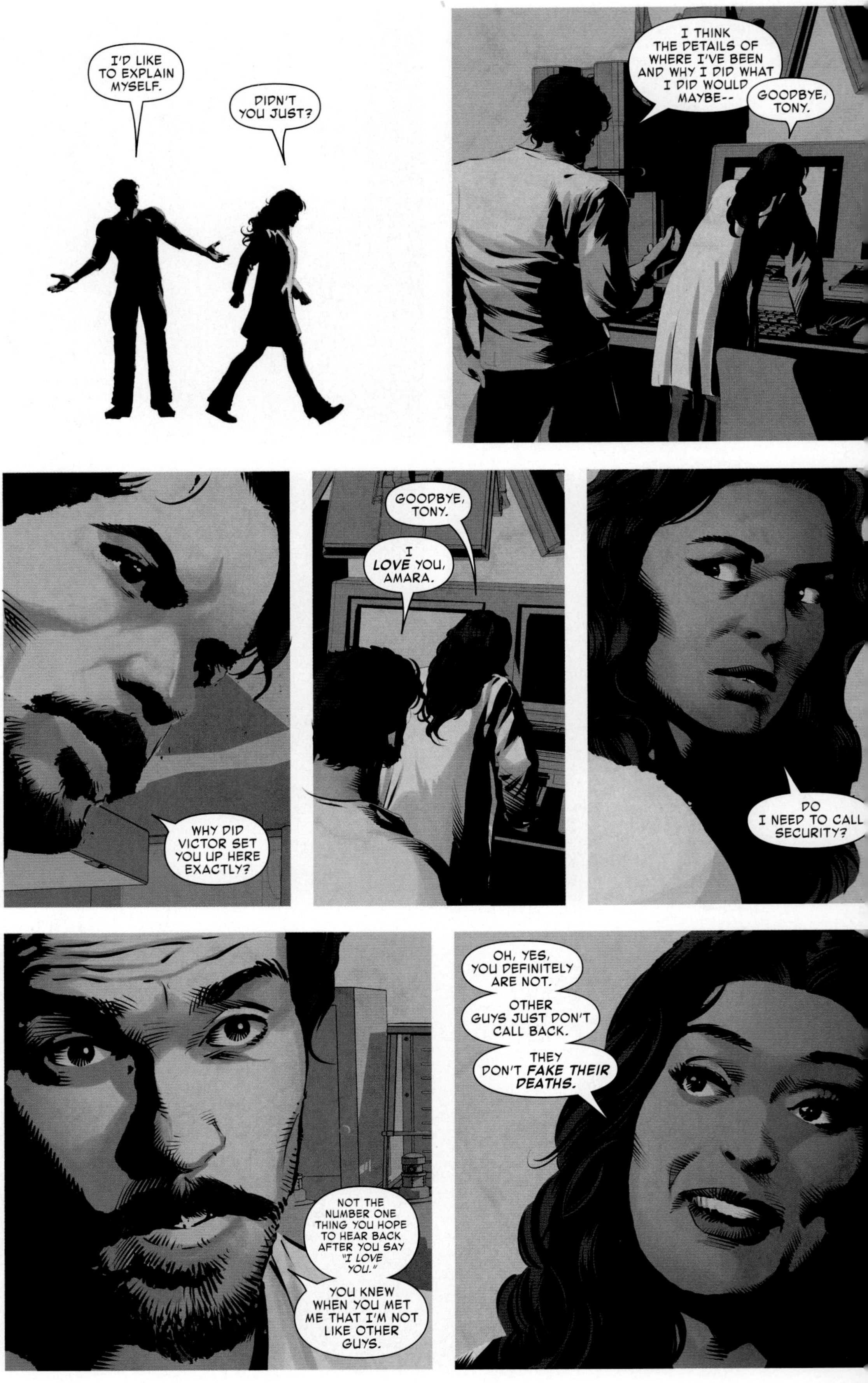
I'D LIKE TO EXPLAIN MYSELF.
DIDN'T YOU JUST?
I THINK THE DETAILS OF WHERE I'VE BEEN AND WHY I DID WHAT I DID WOULD MAYBE--
GOODBYE, TONY.
WHY DID VICTOR SET YOU UP HERE EXACTLY?
GOODBYE, TONY.
I *LOVE* YOU, AMARA.
DO I NEED TO CALL SECURITY?
NOT THE NUMBER ONE THING YOU HOPE TO HEAR BACK AFTER YOU SAY *"I LOVE YOU."*
YOU KNEW WHEN YOU MET ME THAT I'M NOT LIKE OTHER GUYS.
OH, YES, YOU DEFINITELY ARE NOT.
OTHER GUYS JUST DON'T CALL BACK.
THEY DON'T *FAKE THEIR DEATHS.*

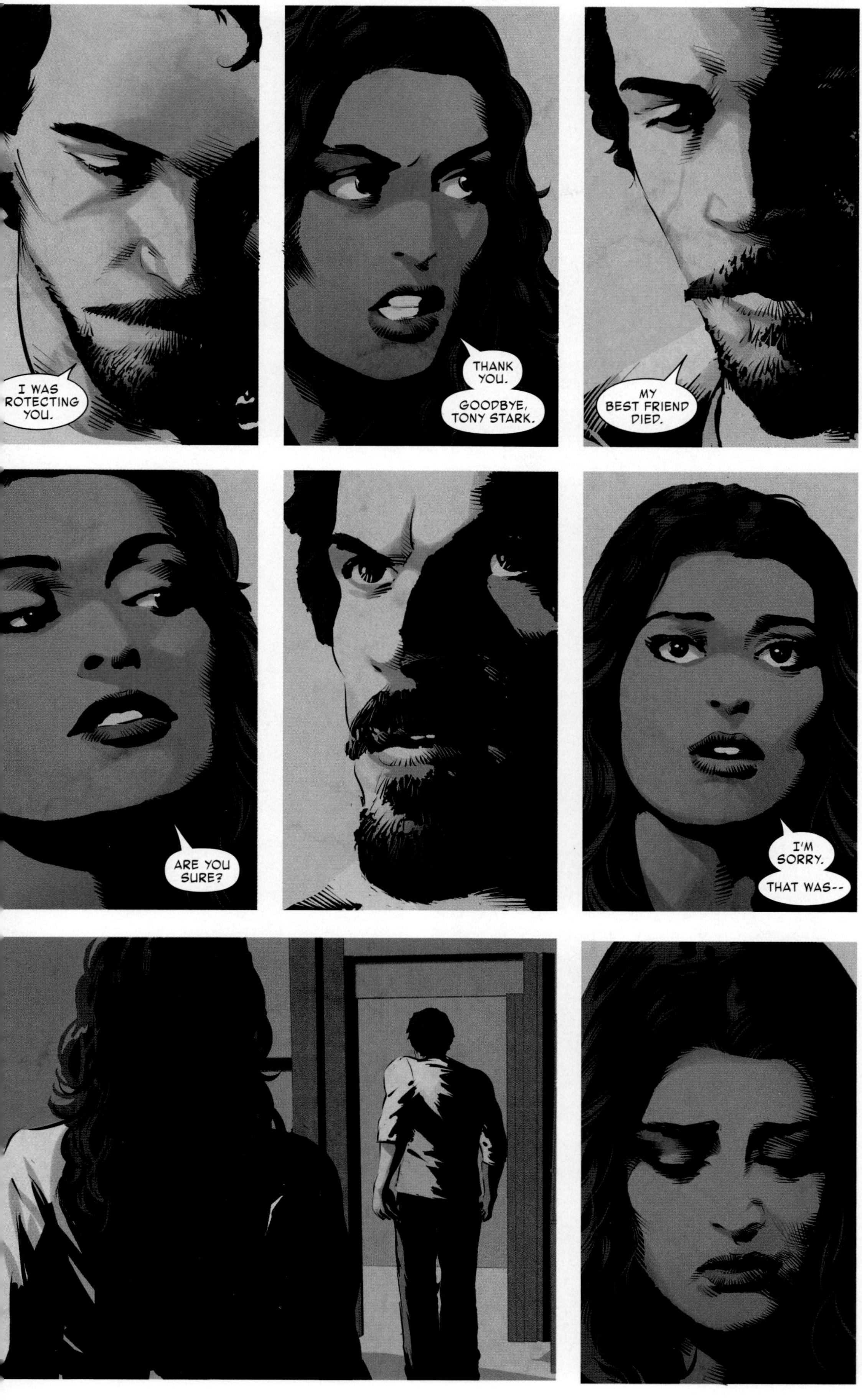
I WAS ROTECTING YOU.
THANK YOU.
GOODBYE, TONY STARK.
MY BEST FRIEND DIED.
ARE YOU SURE?
I'M SORRY.
THAT WAS--

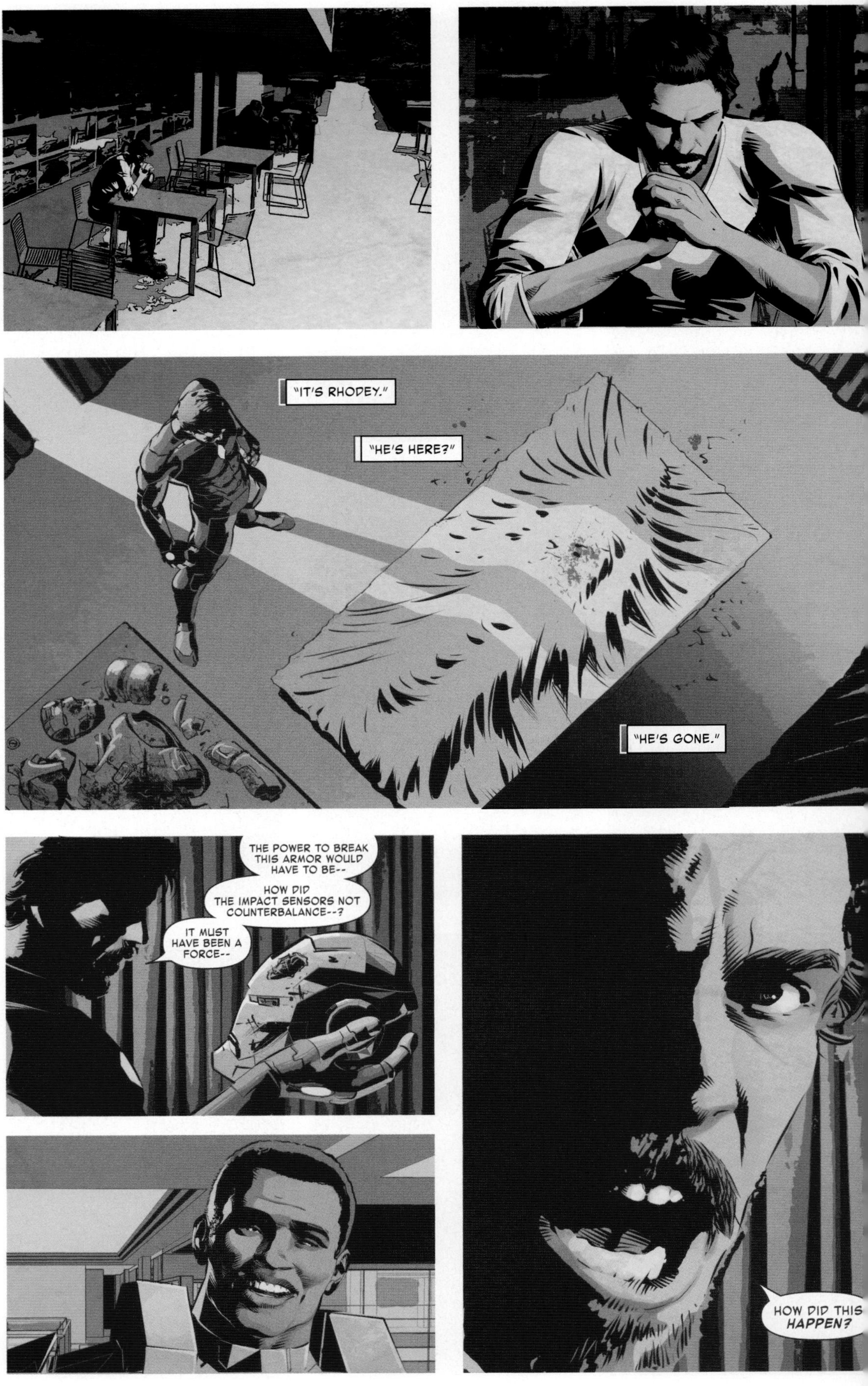
"IT'S RHODEY."
"HE'S HERE?"
"HE'S GONE."
THE POWER TO BREAK THIS ARMOR WOULD HAVE TO BE--
HOW DID THE IMPACT SENSORS NOT COUNTERBALANCE--?
IT MUST HAVE BEEN A FORCE--
HOW DID THIS HAPPEN?

James "Rhodey" Rhodes,
A.K.A. War Machine, is Dead
Stark Stock in Free Fall
War Machine Memorial
Open to the Public
...ns Desperate
...erstood
...Wanted for
... by Defense Council
...rvel
...e World

...to the Public
...nhumans Desperate
to be Understood

Tony Stark Wanted for
Questioning by Defense Coun...
Captain Marvel
Updates the World

THIS IS COLONEL CAROL DANVERS SPEAKING FOR THE ULTIMATES.

IN THE INTEREST OF FULL DISCLOSURE, THIS MESSAGE IS BEING BEAMED WORLDWIDE.

I HAVE JUST RETURNED FROM A DIPLOMATIC MEETING WITH A LONGTIME ALLY AND BENEFCATOR TO THE ENTIRE PLANET...

SOMEONE I AM SO PROUD TO CALL FRIEND...

KING T'CHALLA, THE BLACK PANTHER.

ONE OF THE GREAT JOYS OF MY LIFE IS THAT I GET TO SPEND REAL TIME WITH THESE GREAT HEROES OF SUCH SHEER STRENGTH AND COMPASSION.

T'CHALLA IS, BY ANY DEFINITION, THE REAL DEAL. SO SMART. SUCH A PRESENCE. SUCH A GREAT LEADER TO HIS PEOPLE.

AND HE AND I, WELL, WE TALKED ABOUT THE FUTURE.

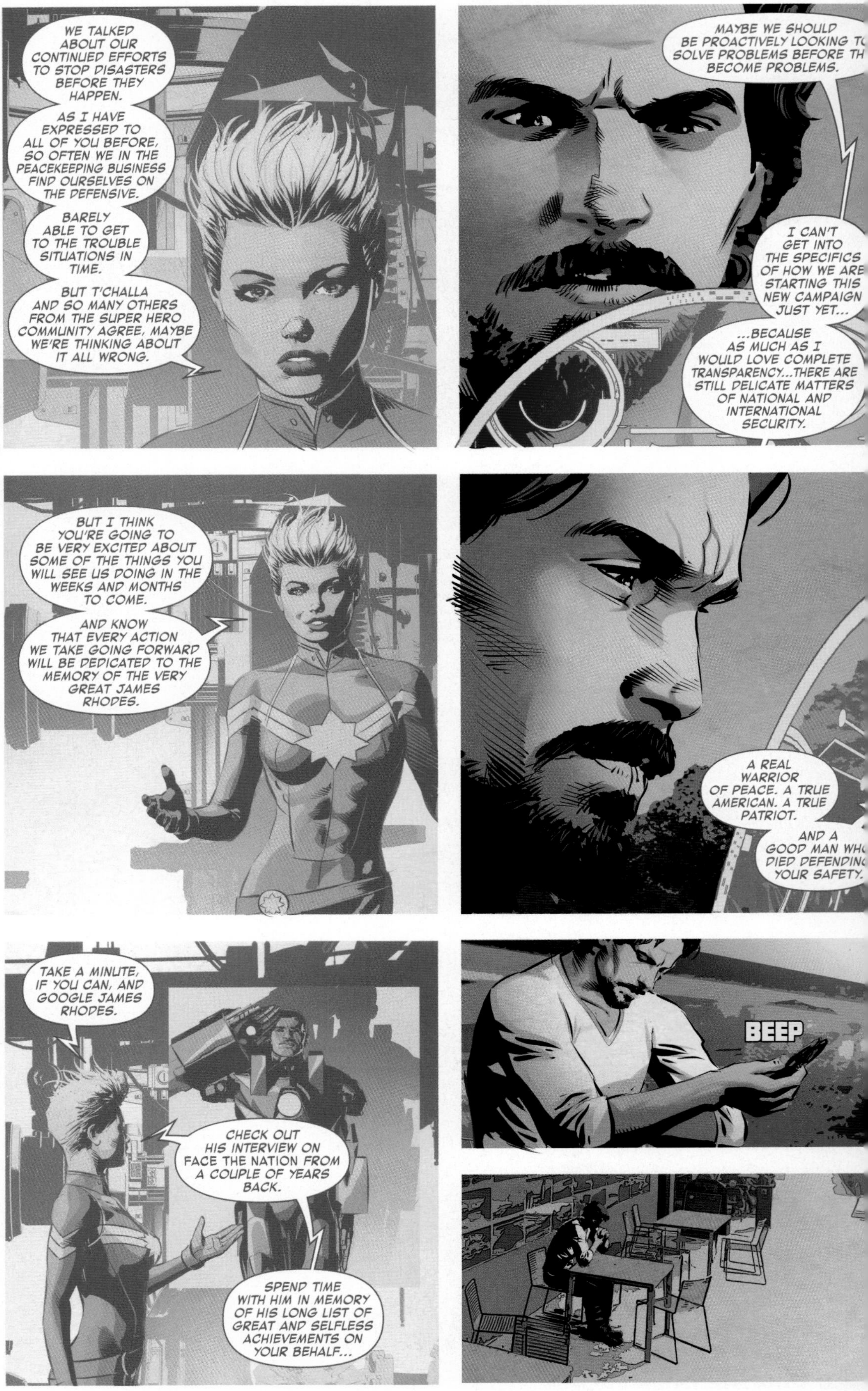
WE TALKED ABOUT OUR CONTINUED EFFORTS TO STOP DISASTERS BEFORE THEY HAPPEN.
AS I HAVE EXPRESSED TO ALL OF YOU BEFORE, SO OFTEN WE IN THE PEACEKEEPING BUSINESS FIND OURSELVES ON THE DEFENSIVE.
BARELY ABLE TO GET TO THE TROUBLE SITUATIONS IN TIME.
BUT T'CHALLA AND SO MANY OTHERS FROM THE SUPER HERO COMMUNITY AGREE, MAYBE WE'RE THINKING ABOUT IT ALL WRONG.
MAYBE WE SHOULD BE PROACTIVELY LOOKING TO SOLVE PROBLEMS BEFORE TH BECOME PROBLEMS.
I CAN'T GET INTO THE SPECIFICS OF HOW WE ARE STARTING THIS NEW CAMPAIGN JUST YET...
...BECAUSE AS MUCH AS I WOULD LOVE COMPLETE TRANSPARENCY...THERE ARE STILL DELICATE MATTERS OF NATIONAL AND INTERNATIONAL SECURITY.
BUT I THINK YOU'RE GOING TO BE VERY EXCITED ABOUT SOME OF THE THINGS YOU WILL SEE US DOING IN THE WEEKS AND MONTHS TO COME.
AND KNOW THAT EVERY ACTION WE TAKE GOING FORWARD WILL BE DEDICATED TO THE MEMORY OF THE VERY GREAT JAMES RHODES.
A REAL WARRIOR OF PEACE. A TRUE AMERICAN. A TRUE PATRIOT.
AND A GOOD MAN WHO DIED DEFENDING YOUR SAFETY.
TAKE A MINUTE, IF YOU CAN, AND GOOGLE JAMES RHODES.
CHECK OUT HIS INTERVIEW ON FACE THE NATION FROM A COUPLE OF YEARS BACK.
SPEND TIME WITH HIM IN MEMORY OF HIS LONG LIST OF GREAT AND SELFLESS ACHIEVEMENTS ON YOUR BEHALF...
BEEP

MOTHER BETHEL
A.M.E. CHURCH.
PHILADELPHIA.

MEMORIAL
SERVICE
FOR JAMES
RHODES.

"THEY'RE
LOOKING
FOR YOU."

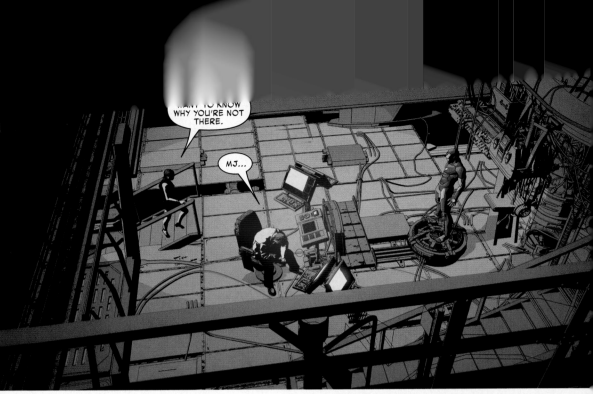

WANT TO KNOW WHY YOU'RE NOT THERE.

MJ...

THEY JUST WANTED TO MAKE SURE YOU'RE OKAY.

LUKE CAGE WAS SURE YOU WERE IN TROUBLE BECAUSE HE COULDN'T THINK OF ANOTHER REASON YOU WEREN'T AT YOUR BEST FRIEND'S SERVICE.

I-- I TOLD THEM--

EVERYONE GRIEVES IN THEIR OWN...

I'M SORRY.

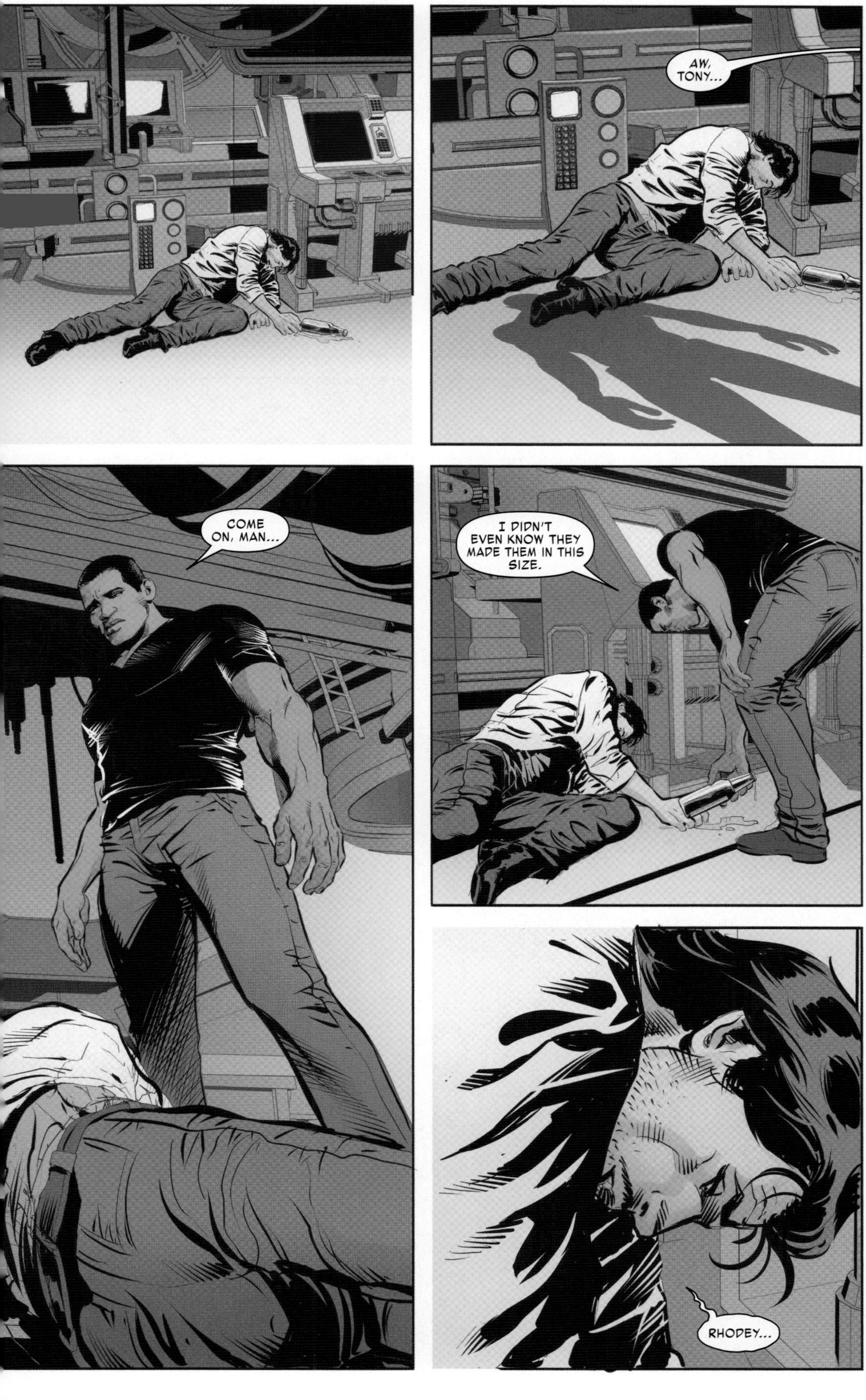
AW, TONY...
COME ON, MAN...
I DIDN'T EVEN KNOW THEY MADE THEM IN THIS SIZE.
RHODEY...

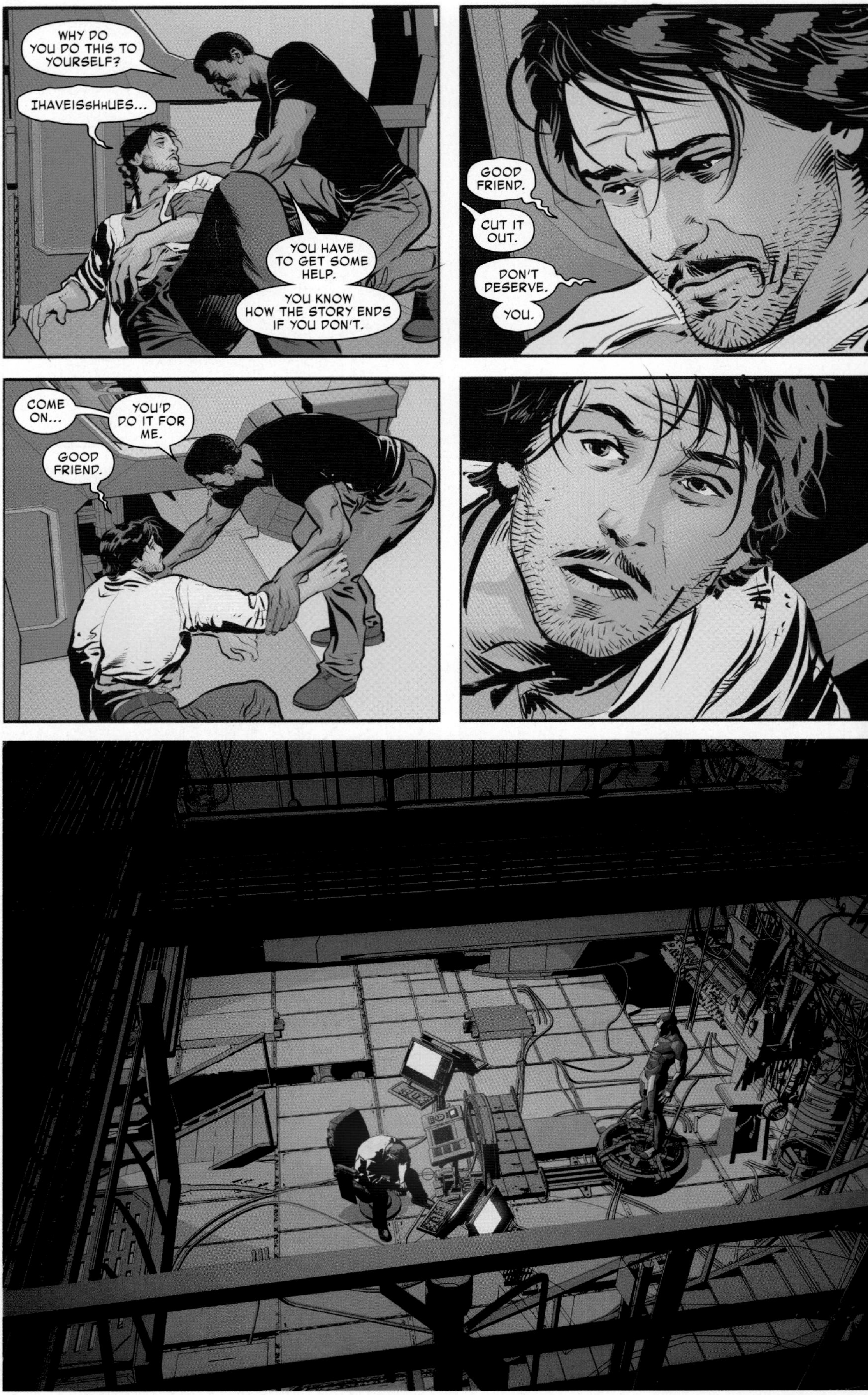
WHY DO YOU DO THIS TO YOURSELF?
IHAVEISSHHUES...
YOU HAVE TO GET SOME HELP.
YOU KNOW HOW THE STORY ENDS IF YOU DON'T.
GOOD FRIEND.
CUT IT OUT.
DON'T DESERVE.
YOU.
COME ON...
YOU'D DO IT FOR ME.
GOOD FRIEND.

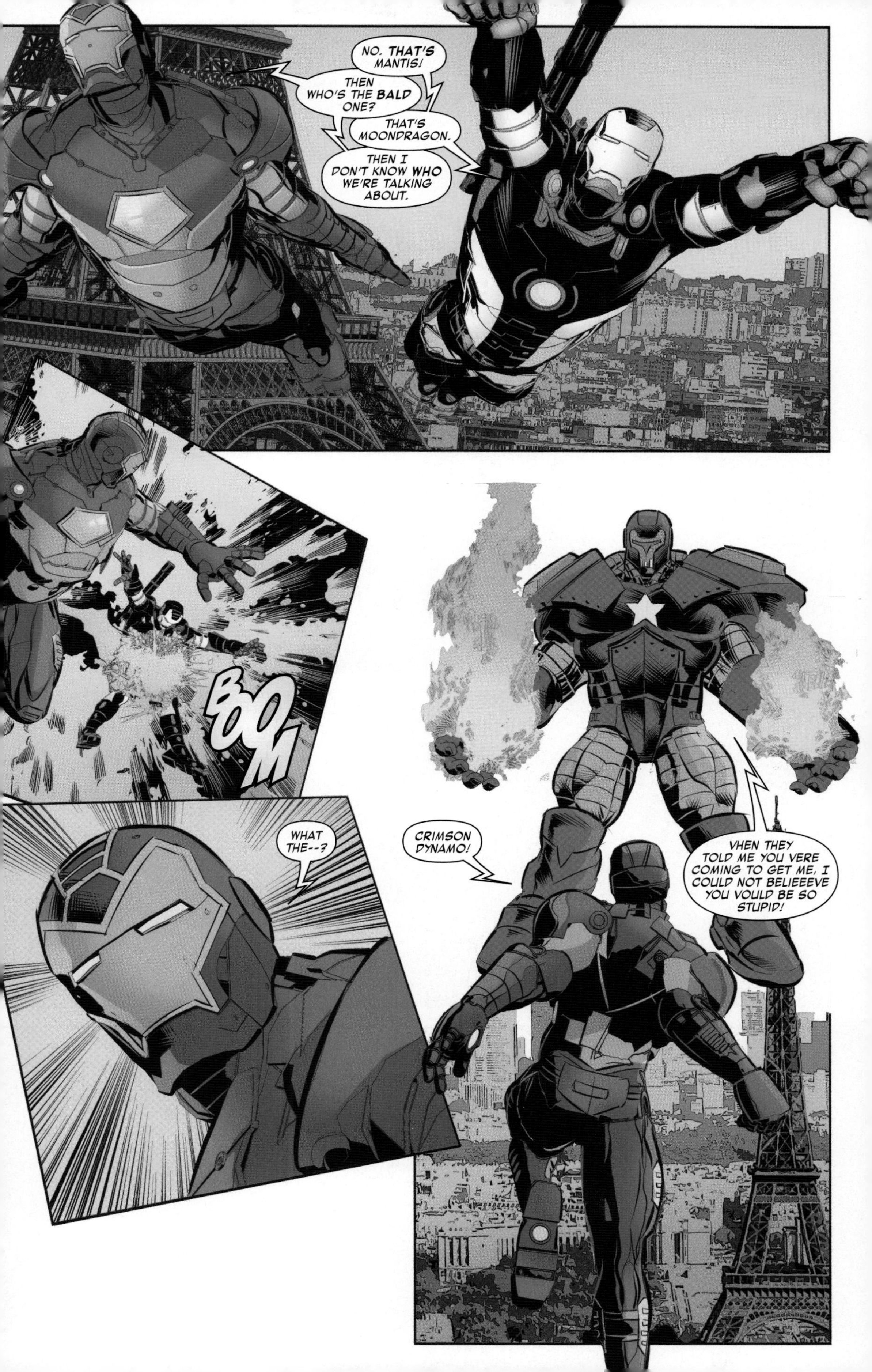
NO. THAT'S MANTIS!
THEN WHO'S THE BALD ONE?
THAT'S MOONDRAGON.
THEN I DON'T KNOW WHO WE'RE TALKING ABOUT.
BOOM
WHAT THE--?
CRIMSON DYNAMO!
VHEN THEY TOLD ME YOU VERE COMING TO GET ME, I COULD NOT BELIEEEVE YOU VOULD BE SO STUPID!

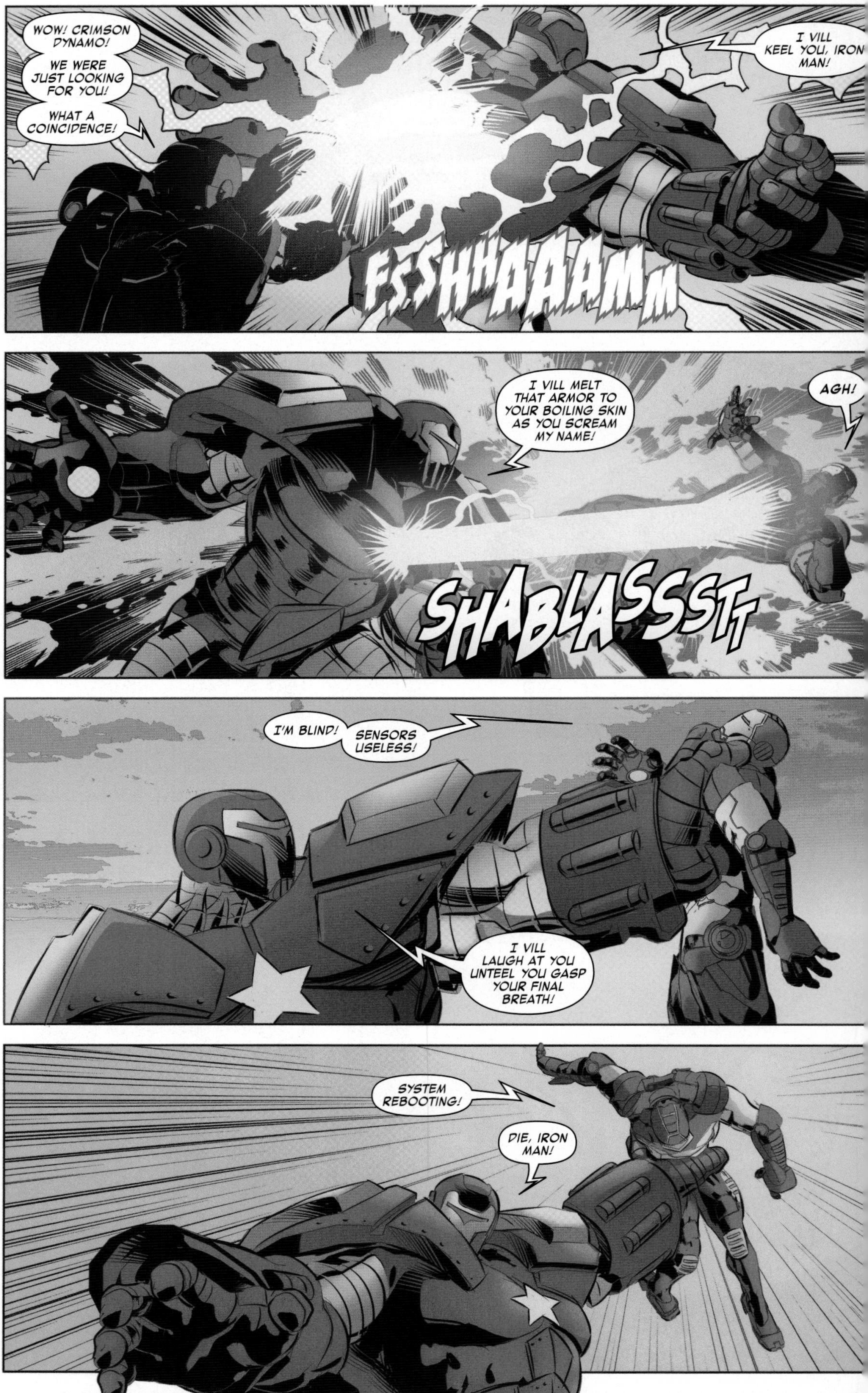
WOW! CRIMSON DYNAMO!
WE WERE JUST LOOKING FOR YOU!
WHAT A COINCIDENCE!
I VILL KEEL YOU, IRON MAN!
FSSHHAAAMM
I VILL MELT THAT ARMOR TO YOUR BOILING SKIN AS YOU SCREAM MY NAME!
AGH!
SHABLASSSTT
I'M BLIND!
SENSORS USELESS!
I VILL LAUGH AT YOU UNTEEL YOU GASP YOUR FINAL BREATH!
SYSTEM REBOOTING!
DIE, IRON MAN!

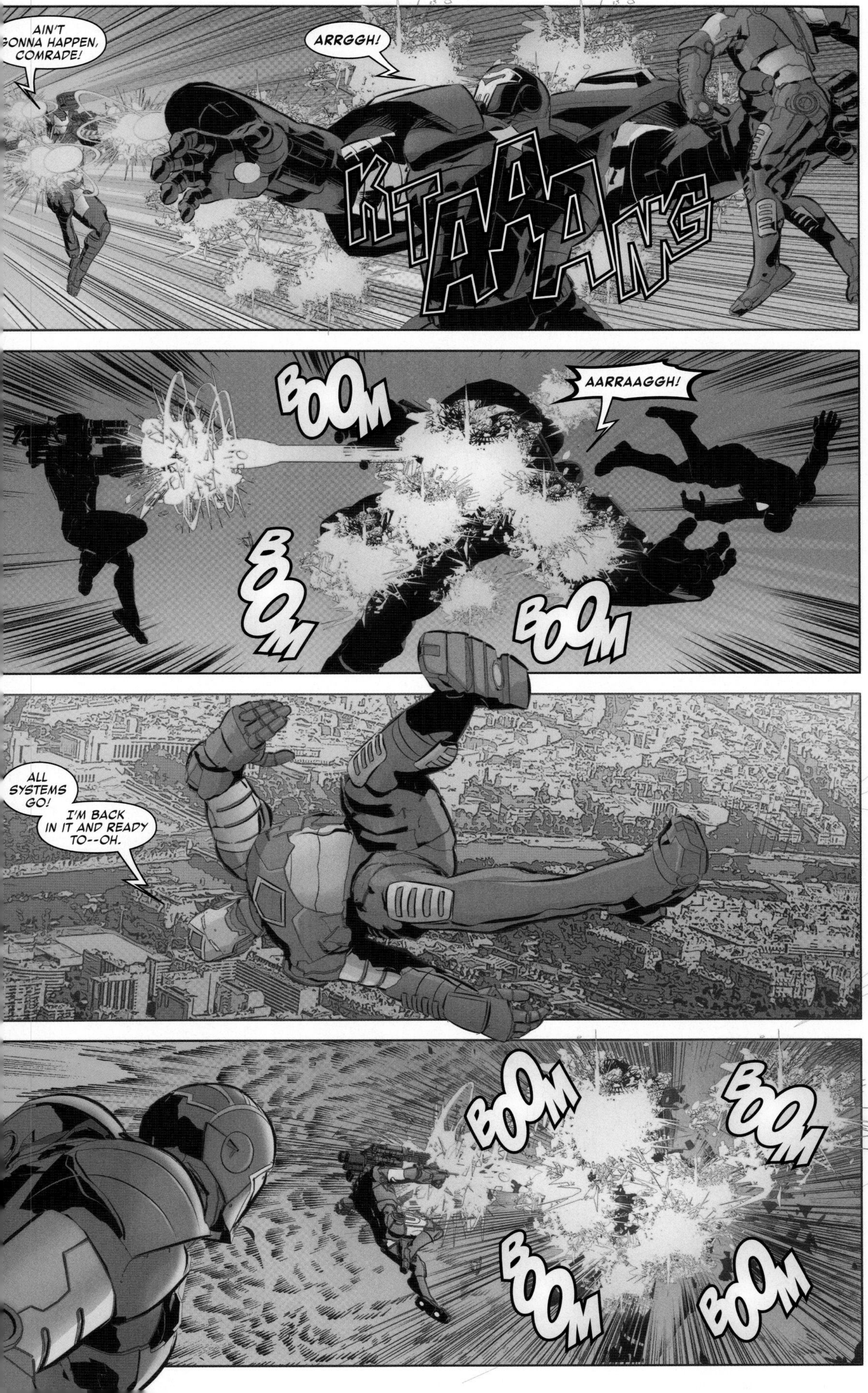
AIN'T GONNA HAPPEN, COMRADE!
ARRGGH!
KTAAAANG
BOOM
AARRAAGGH!
BOOM
BOOM
ALL SYSTEMS GO!
I'M BACK IN IT AND READY TO--OH.
BOOM
BOOM
BOOM
BOOM

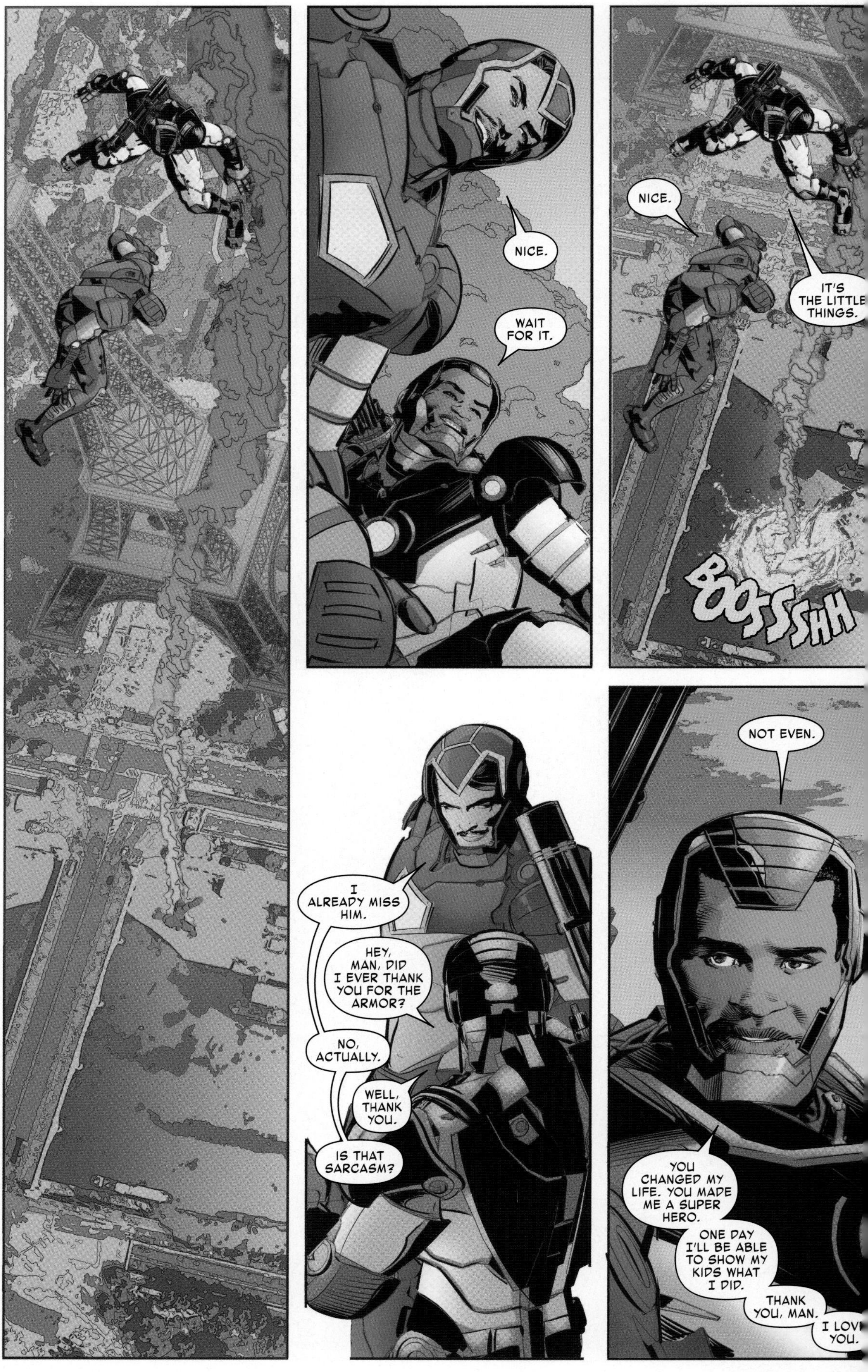
NICE.
WAIT FOR IT.
NICE.
IT'S THE LITTLE THINGS.
BOOSSSHH
I ALREADY MISS HIM.
HEY, MAN, DID I EVER THANK YOU FOR THE ARMOR?
NO, ACTUALLY.
WELL, THANK YOU.
IS THAT SARCASM?
NOT EVEN.
YOU CHANGED MY LIFE. YOU MADE ME A SUPER HERO.
ONE DAY I'LL BE ABLE TO SHOW MY KIDS WHAT I DID.
THANK YOU, MAN.

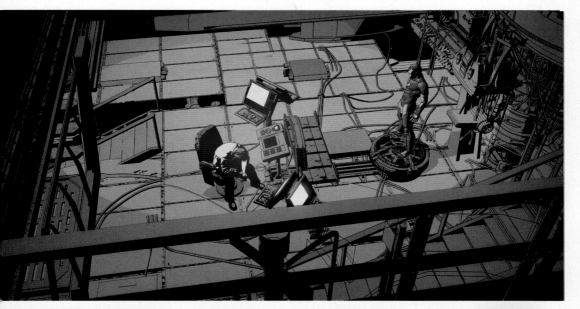

THINK MAYBE I NEED A MEETING.

NO. YOU DON'T.

YOU NEED TO REFOCUS.

GET YOUR COMPANY AFLOAT.

FIND YOUR FOOTING AGAIN AND STOP WALLOWING.

DOOM.

YOU KEEP DISTRACTING YOURSELF.

NOW YOU HAVE *THIS* TO DISTRACT YOURSELF WITH.

DOOM.

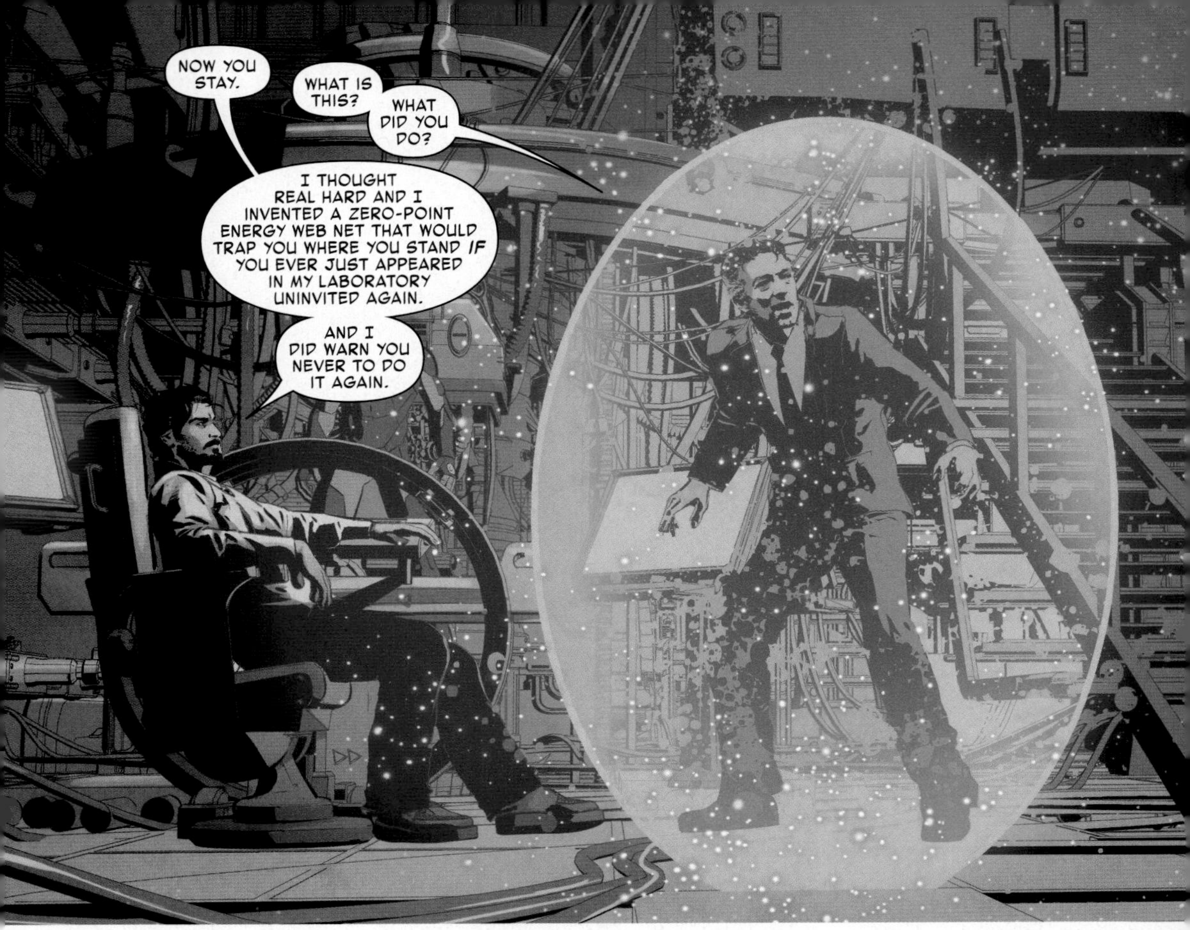
NOW YOU STAY.
WHAT IS THIS?
WHAT DID YOU DO?
I THOUGHT REAL HARD AND I INVENTED A ZERO-POINT ENERGY WEB NET THAT WOULD TRAP YOU WHERE YOU STAND *IF* YOU EVER JUST APPEARED IN MY LABORATORY UNINVITED AGAIN.
AND I DID WARN YOU NEVER TO DO IT AGAIN.

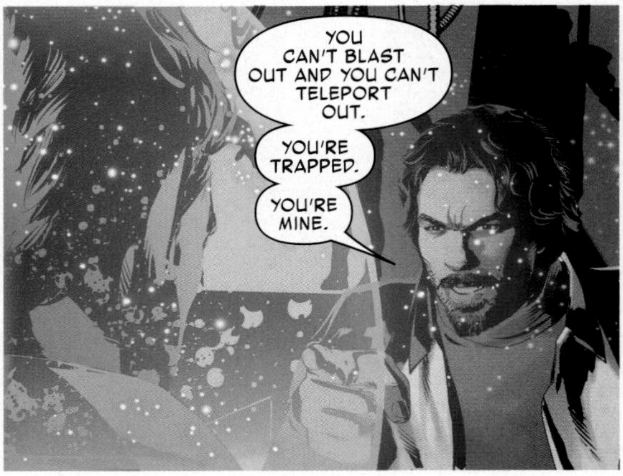
YOU CAN'T BLAST OUT AND YOU CAN'T TELEPORT OUT.
YOU'RE TRAPPED.
YOU'RE MINE.

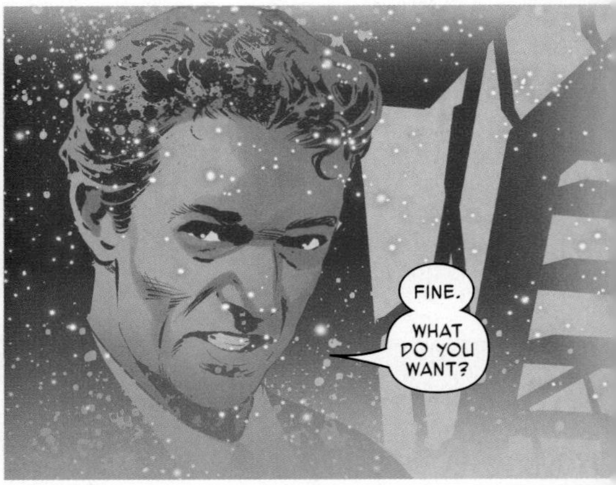
FINE.
WHAT DO YOU WANT?

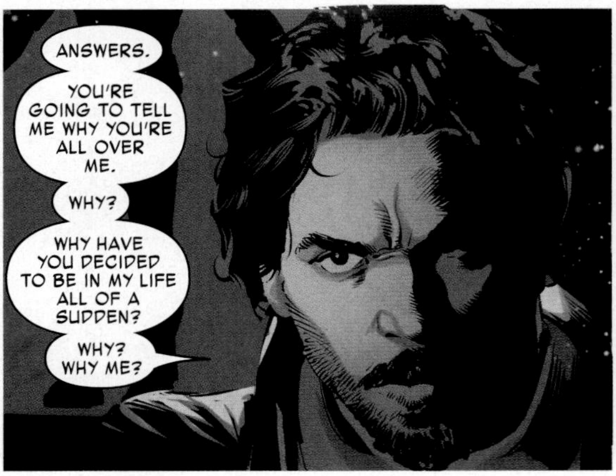
ANSWERS.
YOU'RE GOING TO TELL ME WHY YOU'RE ALL OVER ME.
WHY?
WHY HAVE YOU DECIDED TO BE IN MY LIFE ALL OF A SUDDEN?
WHY? WHY ME?

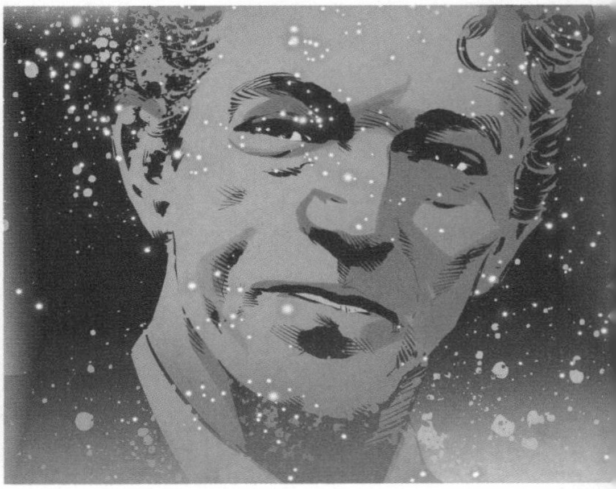

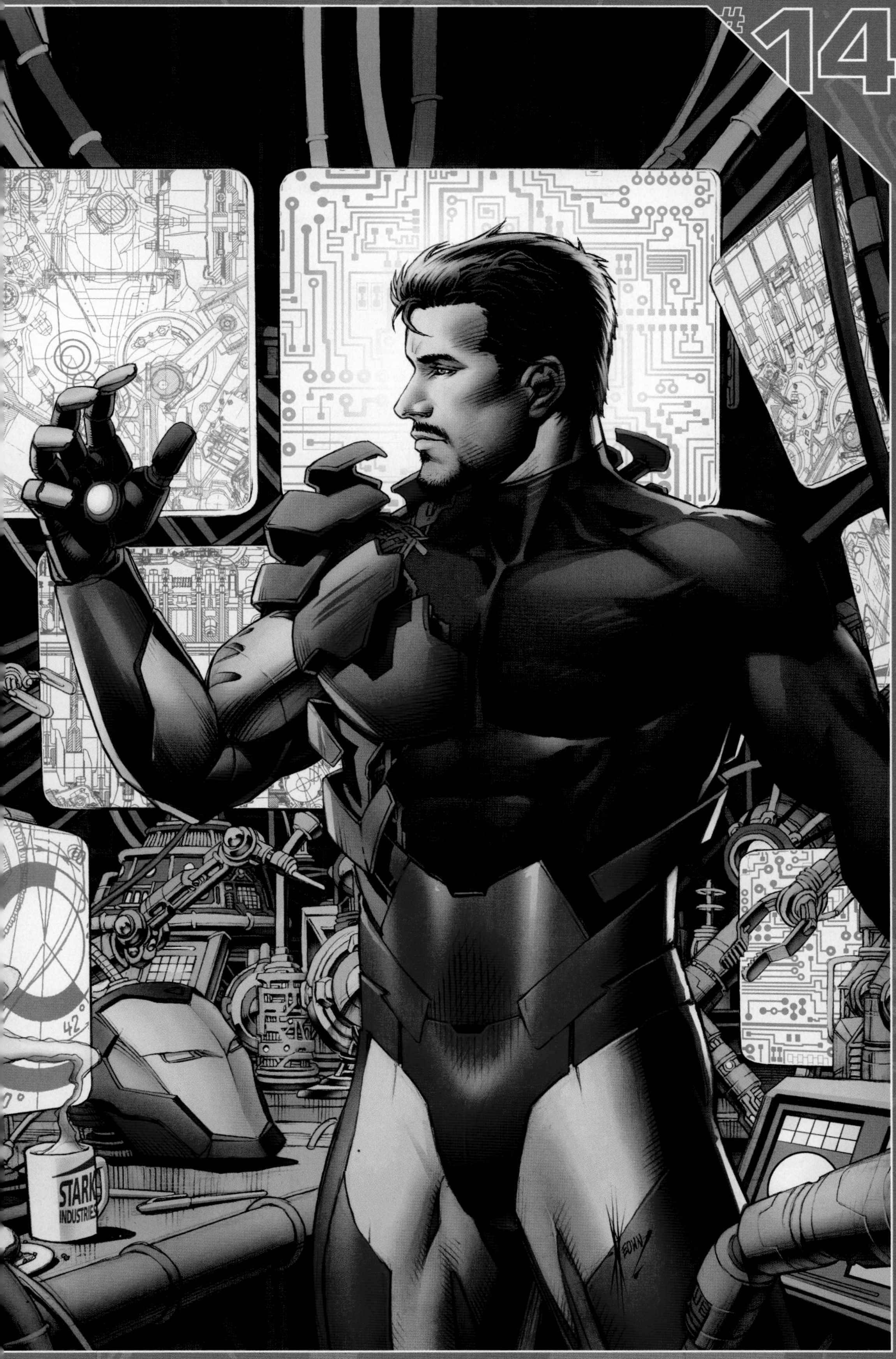
#14
STARK
INDUSTRIES
42

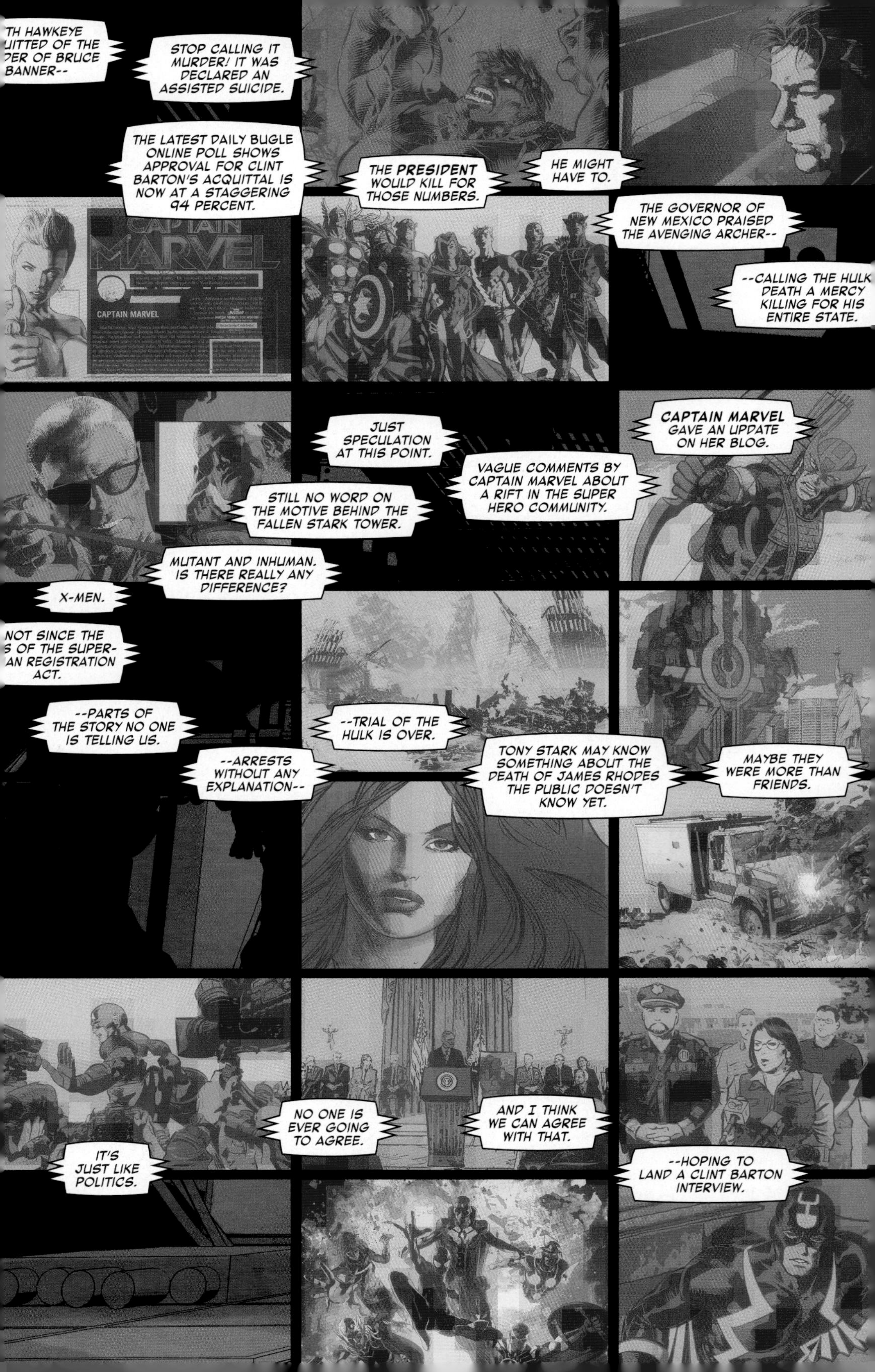

TH HAWKEYE UITTED OF THE RDER OF BRUCE BANNER--
STOP CALLING IT MURDER! IT WAS DECLARED AN ASSISTED SUICIDE.
THE LATEST DAILY BUGLE ONLINE POLL SHOWS APPROVAL FOR CLINT BARTON'S ACQUITTAL IS NOW AT A STAGGERING 94 PERCENT.
THE PRESIDENT WOULD KILL FOR THOSE NUMBERS.
HE MIGHT HAVE TO.
CAPTAIN MARVEL
CAPTAIN MARVEL
THE GOVERNOR OF NEW MEXICO PRAISED THE AVENGING ARCHER--
--CALLING THE HULK DEATH A MERCY KILLING FOR HIS ENTIRE STATE.
JUST SPECULATION AT THIS POINT.
STILL NO WORD ON THE MOTIVE BEHIND THE FALLEN STARK TOWER.
VAGUE COMMENTS BY CAPTAIN MARVEL ABOUT A RIFT IN THE SUPER HERO COMMUNITY.
CAPTAIN MARVEL GAVE AN UPDATE ON HER BLOG.
MUTANT AND INHUMAN. IS THERE REALLY ANY DIFFERENCE?
X-MEN.
NOT SINCE THE S OF THE SUPER- AN REGISTRATION ACT.
--PARTS OF THE STORY NO ONE IS TELLING US.
--ARRESTS WITHOUT ANY EXPLANATION--
--TRIAL OF THE HULK IS OVER.
TONY STARK MAY KNOW SOMETHING ABOUT THE DEATH OF JAMES RHODES THE PUBLIC DOESN'T KNOW YET.
MAYBE THEY WERE MORE THAN FRIENDS.
NO ONE IS EVER GOING TO AGREE.
AND I THINK WE CAN AGREE WITH THAT.
IT'S JUST LIKE POLITICS.
--HOPING TO LAND A CLINT BARTON INTERVIEW.

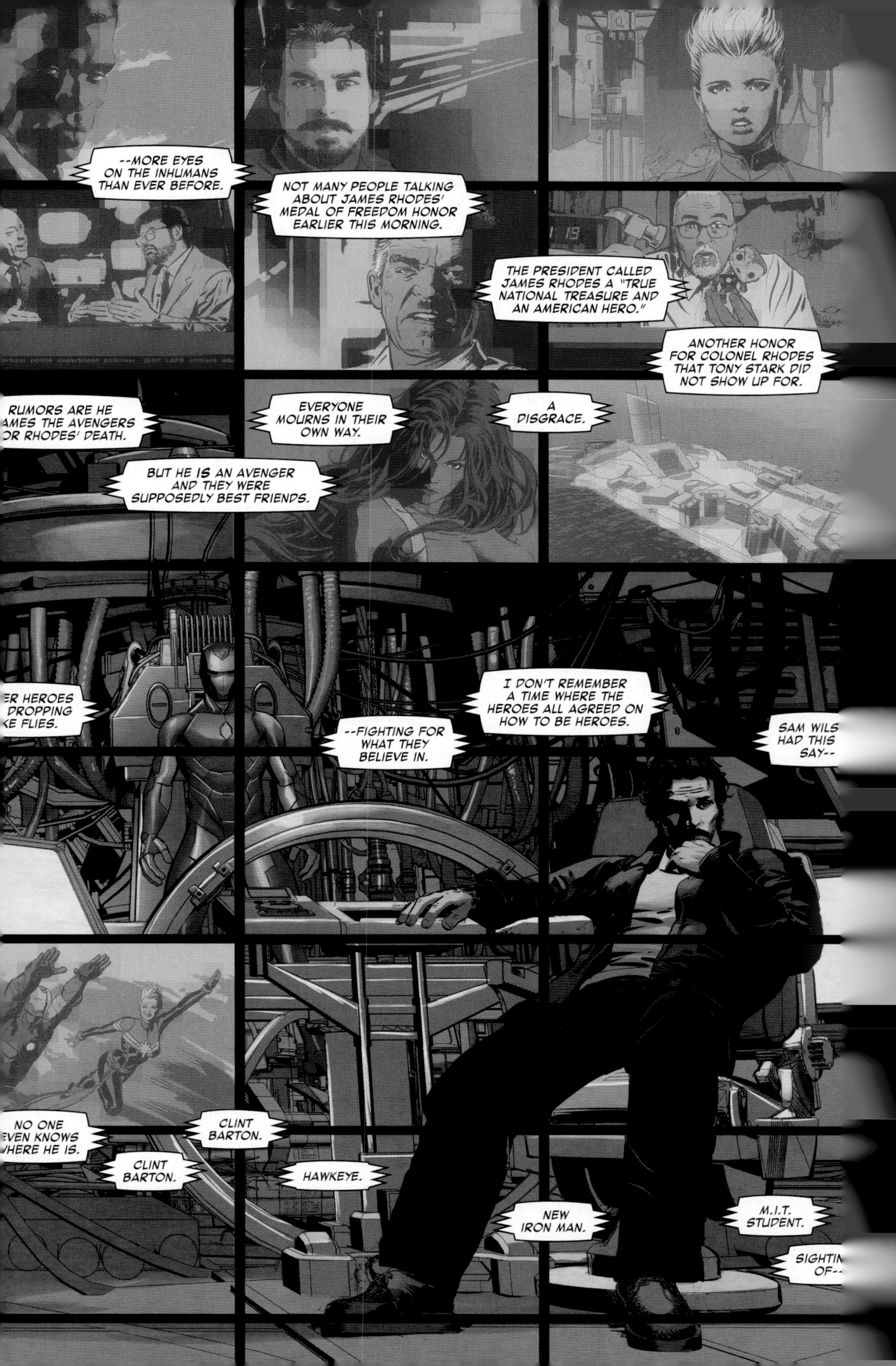
--MORE EYES ON THE INHUMANS THAN EVER BEFORE.
NOT MANY PEOPLE TALKING ABOUT JAMES RHODES' MEDAL OF FREEDOM HONOR EARLIER THIS MORNING.
THE PRESIDENT CALLED JAMES RHODES A "TRUE NATIONAL TREASURE AND AN AMERICAN HERO."
ANOTHER HONOR FOR COLONEL RHODES THAT TONY STARK DID NOT SHOW UP FOR.
RUMORS ARE HE AMES THE AVENGERS OR RHODES' DEATH.
EVERYONE MOURNS IN THEIR OWN WAY.
A DISGRACE.
BUT HE IS AN AVENGER AND THEY WERE SUPPOSEDLY BEST FRIENDS.
ER HEROES DROPPING KE FLIES.
--FIGHTING FOR WHAT THEY BELIEVE IN.
I DON'T REMEMBER A TIME WHERE THE HEROES ALL AGREED ON HOW TO BE HEROES.
SAM WILS HAD THIS SAY--
NO ONE EVEN KNOWS WHERE HE IS.
CLINT BARTON.
CLINT BARTON.
HAWKEYE.
NEW IRON MAN.
M.I.T. STUDENT.
SIGHTIN OF--

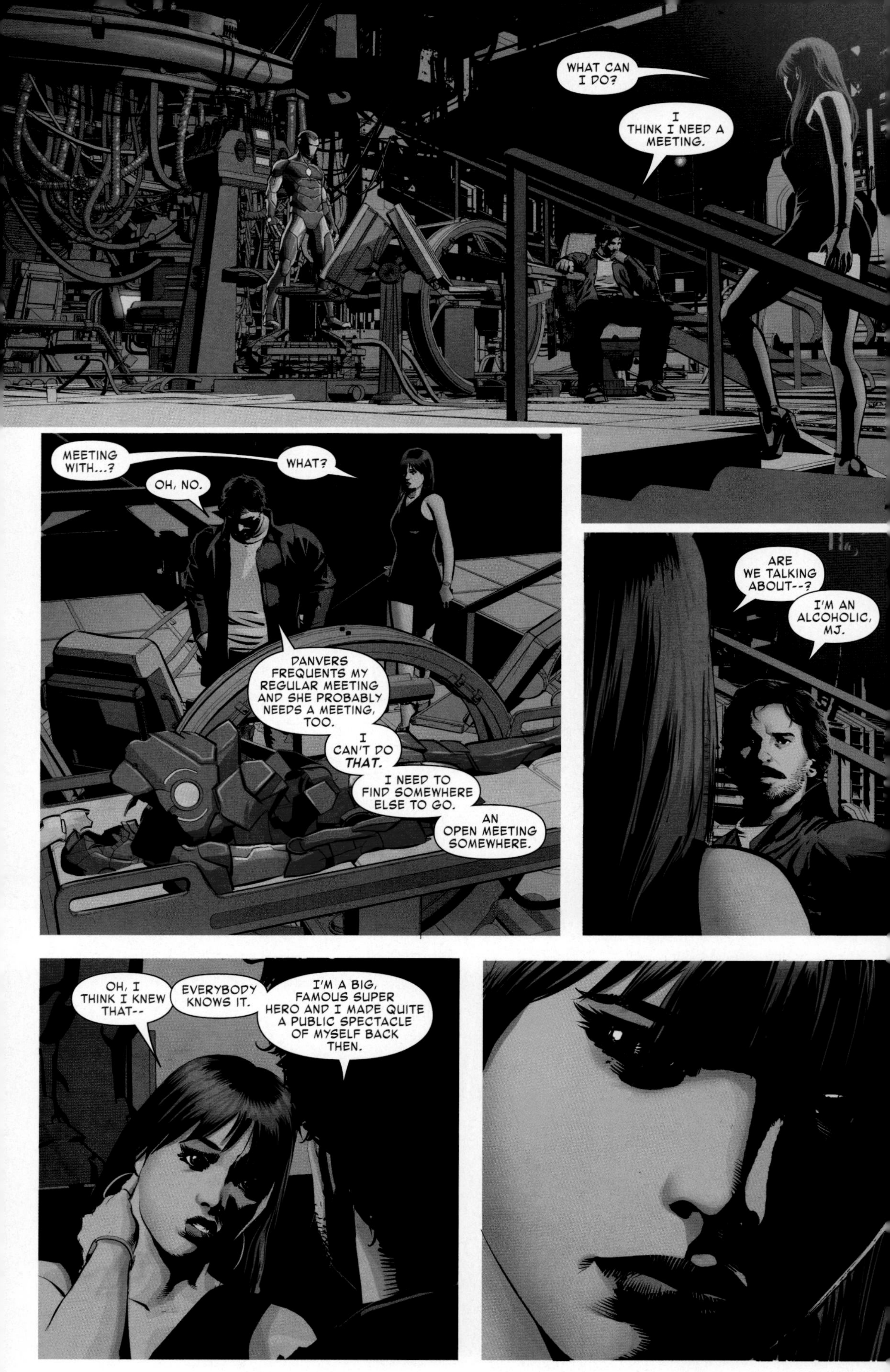
WHAT CAN I DO?
I THINK I NEED A MEETING.
MEETING WITH...?
WHAT?
OH, NO.
DANVERS FREQUENTS MY REGULAR MEETING AND SHE PROBABLY NEEDS A MEETING, TOO.
I CAN'T DO *THAT.*
I NEED TO FIND SOMEWHERE ELSE TO GO.
AN OPEN MEETING SOMEWHERE.
ARE WE TALKING ABOUT--?
I'M AN ALCOHOLIC, MJ.
OH, I THINK I KNEW THAT--
EVERYBODY KNOWS IT.
I'M A BIG, FAMOUS SUPER HERO AND I MADE QUITE A PUBLIC SPECTACLE OF MYSELF BACK THEN.

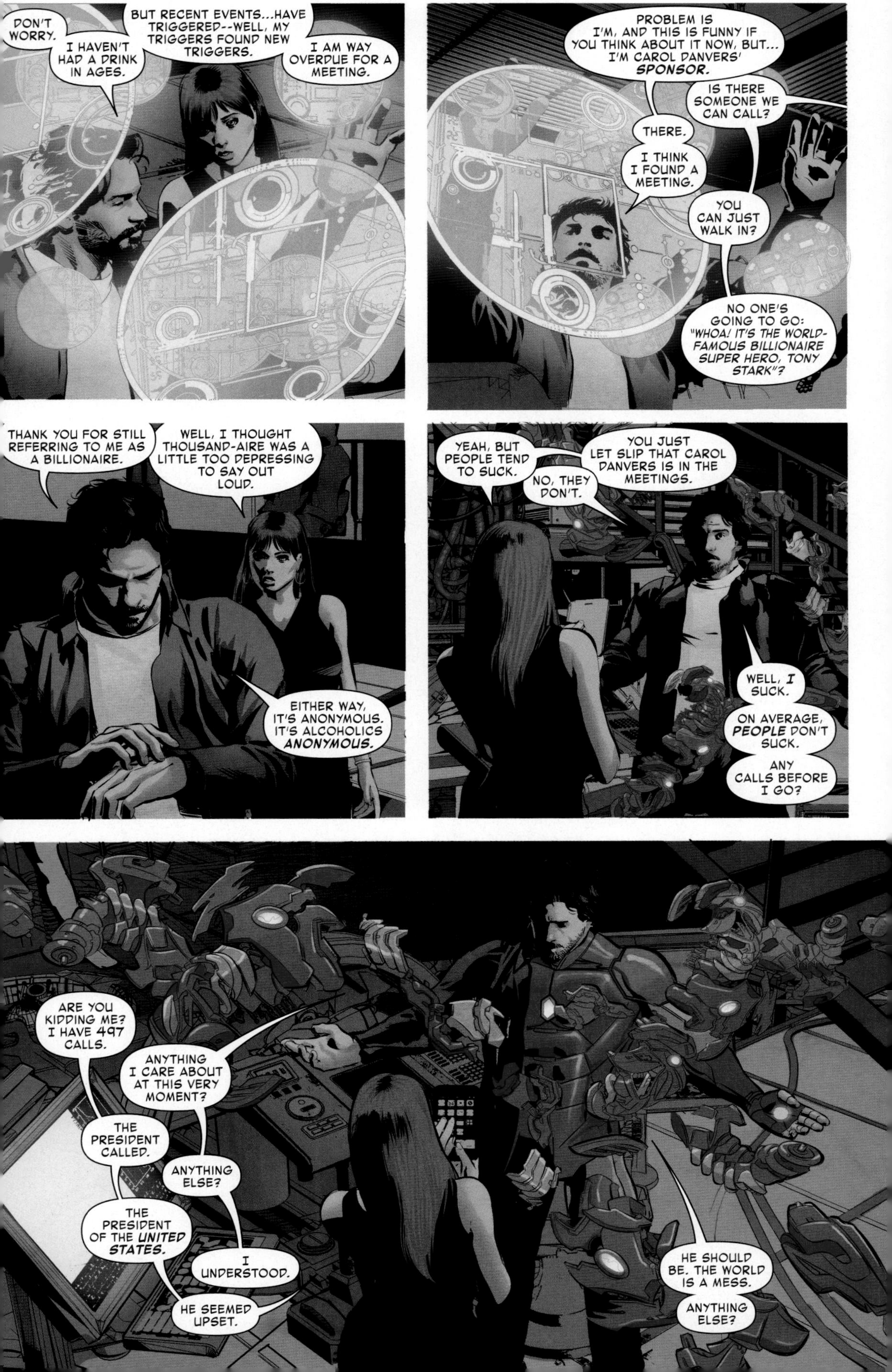
DON'T WORRY.
I HAVEN'T HAD A DRINK IN AGES.
BUT RECENT EVENTS...HAVE TRIGGERED--WELL, MY TRIGGERS FOUND NEW TRIGGERS.
I AM WAY OVERDUE FOR A MEETING.
PROBLEM IS I'M, AND THIS IS FUNNY IF YOU THINK ABOUT IT NOW, BUT... I'M CAROL DANVERS' SPONSOR.
IS THERE SOMEONE WE CAN CALL?
THERE.
I THINK I FOUND A MEETING.
YOU CAN JUST WALK IN?
NO ONE'S GOING TO GO: "WHOA! IT'S THE WORLD-FAMOUS BILLIONAIRE SUPER HERO, TONY STARK"?
THANK YOU FOR STILL REFERRING TO ME AS A BILLIONAIRE.
WELL, I THOUGHT THOUSAND-AIRE WAS A LITTLE TOO DEPRESSING TO SAY OUT LOUD.
EITHER WAY, IT'S ANONYMOUS. IT'S ALCOHOLICS ANONYMOUS.
YEAH, BUT PEOPLE TEND TO SUCK.
YOU JUST LET SLIP THAT CAROL DANVERS IS IN THE MEETINGS.
NO, THEY DON'T.
WELL, I SUCK.
ON AVERAGE, PEOPLE DON'T SUCK.
ANY CALLS BEFORE I GO?
ARE YOU KIDDING ME? I HAVE 497 CALLS.
ANYTHING I CARE ABOUT AT THIS VERY MOMENT?
THE PRESIDENT CALLED.
ANYTHING ELSE?
THE PRESIDENT OF THE UNITED STATES.
I UNDERSTOOD.
HE SEEMED UPSET.
HE SHOULD BE. THE WORLD IS A MESS.
ANYTHING ELSE?

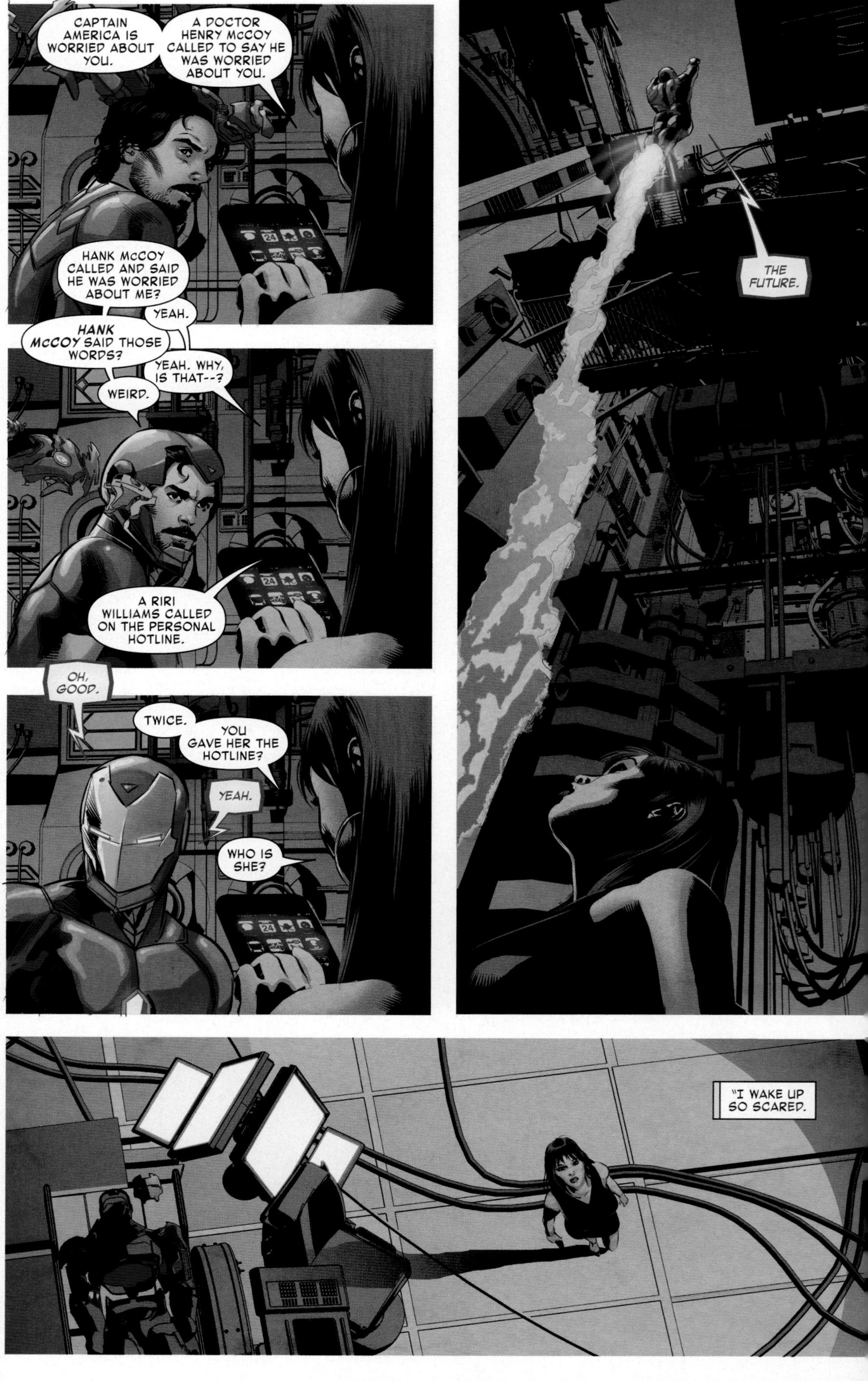
CAPTAIN AMERICA IS WORRIED ABOUT YOU.
A DOCTOR HENRY McCOY CALLED TO SAY HE WAS WORRIED ABOUT YOU.
HANK McCOY CALLED AND SAID HE WAS WORRIED ABOUT ME?
YEAH.
HANK McCOY SAID THOSE WORDS?
YEAH. WHY, IS THAT--?
WEIRD.
A RIRI WILLIAMS CALLED ON THE PERSONAL HOTLINE.
OH, GOOD.
TWICE.
YOU GAVE HER THE HOTLINE?
YEAH.
WHO IS SHE?
THE FUTURE.
"I WAKE UP SO SCARED.

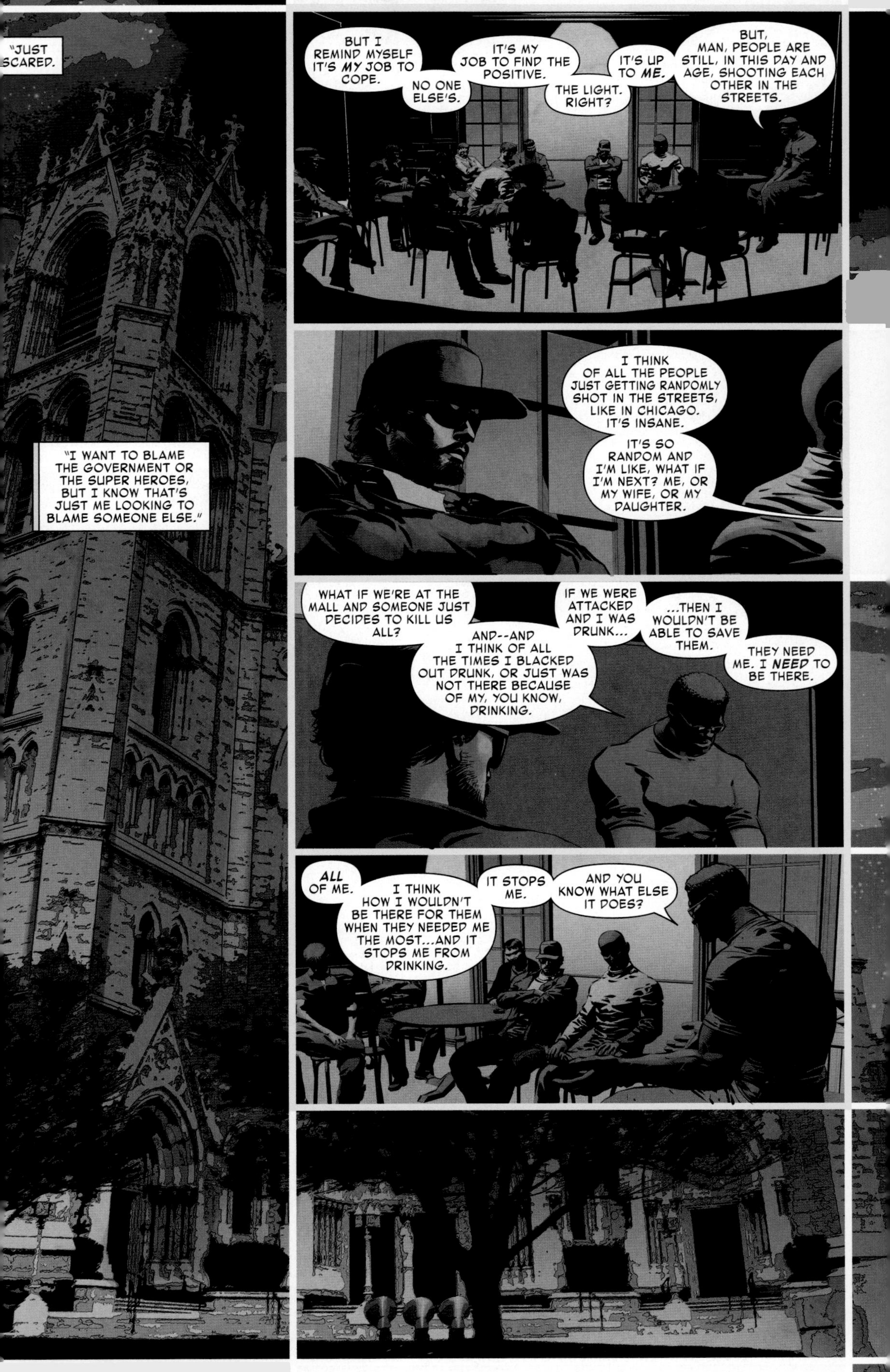
"JUST SCARED.
BUT I REMIND MYSELF IT'S MY JOB TO COPE.
NO ONE ELSE'S.
IT'S MY JOB TO FIND THE POSITIVE.
THE LIGHT. RIGHT?
IT'S UP TO ME.
BUT, MAN, PEOPLE ARE STILL, IN THIS DAY AND AGE, SHOOTING EACH OTHER IN THE STREETS.
"I WANT TO BLAME THE GOVERNMENT OR THE SUPER HEROES, BUT I KNOW THAT'S JUST ME LOOKING TO BLAME SOMEONE ELSE."
I THINK OF ALL THE PEOPLE JUST GETTING RANDOMLY SHOT IN THE STREETS, LIKE IN CHICAGO. IT'S INSANE.
IT'S SO RANDOM AND I'M LIKE, WHAT IF I'M NEXT? ME, OR MY WIFE, OR MY DAUGHTER.
WHAT IF WE'RE AT THE MALL AND SOMEONE JUST DECIDES TO KILL US ALL?
AND--AND I THINK OF ALL THE TIMES I BLACKED OUT DRUNK, OR JUST WAS NOT THERE BECAUSE OF MY, YOU KNOW, DRINKING.
IF WE WERE ATTACKED AND I WAS DRUNK...
...THEN I WOULDN'T BE ABLE TO SAVE THEM.
THEY NEED ME. I NEED TO BE THERE.
ALL OF ME.
I THINK HOW I WOULDN'T BE THERE FOR THEM WHEN THEY NEEDED ME THE MOST...AND IT STOPS ME FROM DRINKING.
IT STOPS ME.
AND YOU KNOW WHAT ELSE IT DOES?

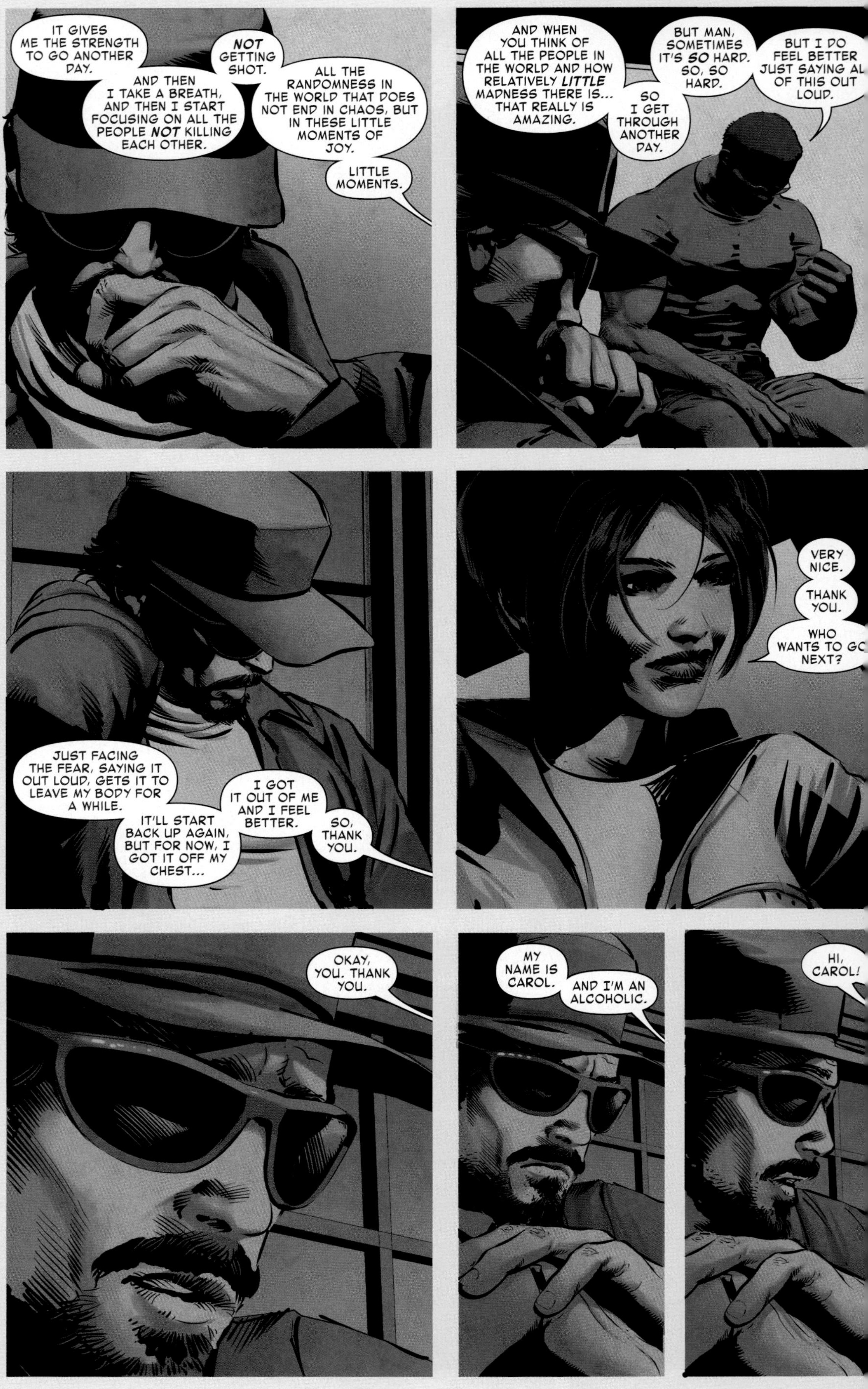

IT GIVES ME THE STRENGTH TO GO ANOTHER DAY.
AND THEN I TAKE A BREATH, AND THEN I START FOCUSING ON ALL THE PEOPLE NOT KILLING EACH OTHER.
NOT GETTING SHOT.
ALL THE RANDOMNESS IN THE WORLD THAT DOES NOT END IN CHAOS, BUT IN THESE LITTLE MOMENTS OF JOY.
LITTLE MOMENTS.
AND WHEN YOU THINK OF ALL THE PEOPLE IN THE WORLD AND HOW RELATIVELY LITTLE MADNESS THERE IS... THAT REALLY IS AMAZING.
SO I GET THROUGH ANOTHER DAY.
BUT MAN, SOMETIMES IT'S SO HARD. SO, SO HARD.
BUT I DO FEEL BETTER JUST SAYING AL OF THIS OUT LOUD.
JUST FACING THE FEAR, SAYING IT OUT LOUD, GETS IT TO LEAVE MY BODY FOR A WHILE.
IT'LL START BACK UP AGAIN, BUT FOR NOW, I GOT IT OFF MY CHEST...
I GOT IT OUT OF ME AND I FEEL BETTER.
SO, THANK YOU.
VERY NICE.
THANK YOU.
WHO WANTS TO GO NEXT?
OKAY, YOU. THANK YOU.
MY NAME IS CAROL.
AND I'M AN ALCOHOLIC.
HI, CAROL!

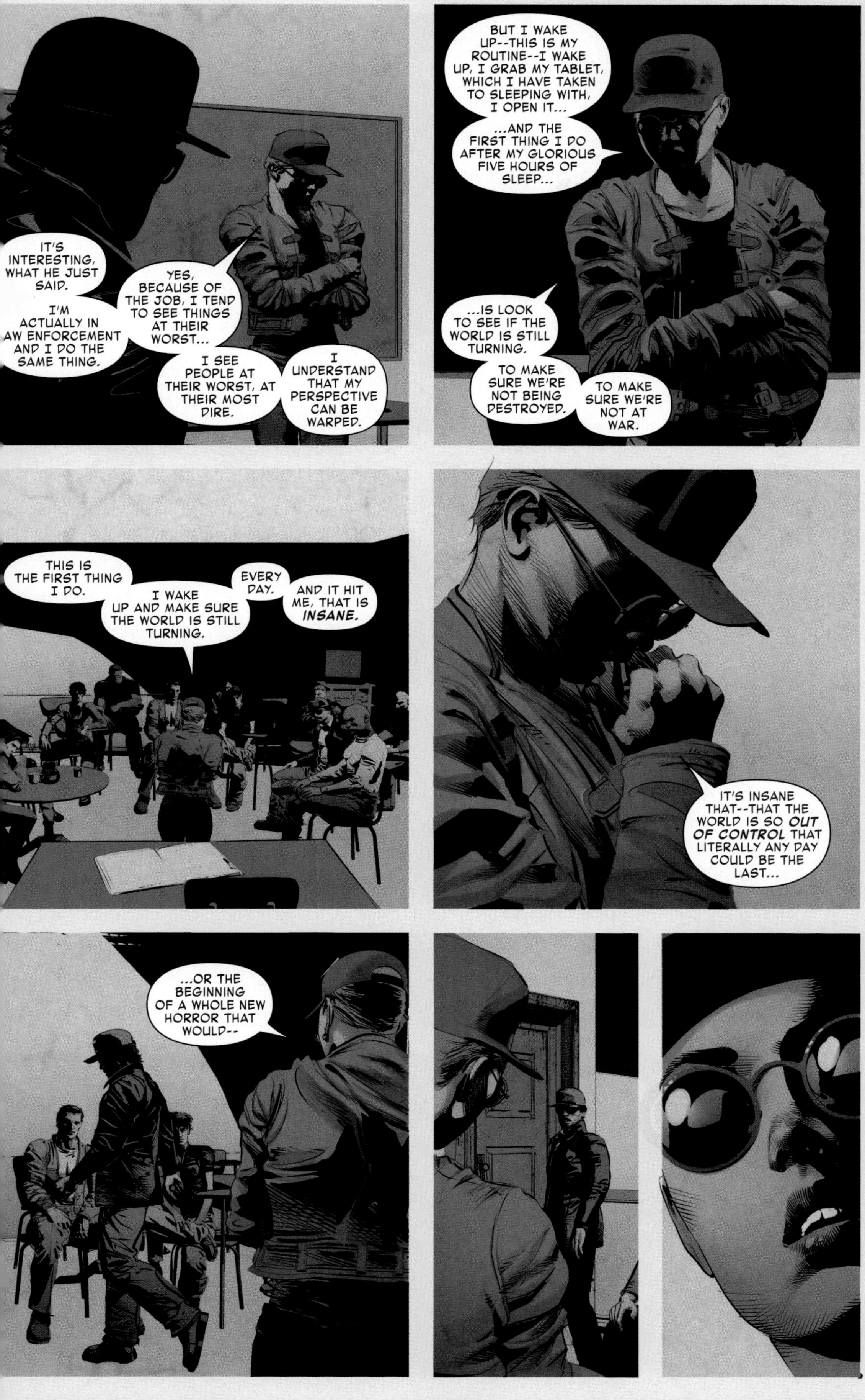
IT'S INTERESTING, WHAT HE JUST SAID.
I'M ACTUALLY IN AW ENFORCEMENT AND I DO THE SAME THING.
YES, BECAUSE OF THE JOB, I TEND TO SEE THINGS AT THEIR WORST...
I SEE PEOPLE AT THEIR WORST, AT THEIR MOST DIRE.
I UNDERSTAND THAT MY PERSPECTIVE CAN BE WARPED.
BUT I WAKE UP--THIS IS MY ROUTINE--I WAKE UP, I GRAB MY TABLET, WHICH I HAVE TAKEN TO SLEEPING WITH, I OPEN IT...
...AND THE FIRST THING I DO AFTER MY GLORIOUS FIVE HOURS OF SLEEP...
...IS LOOK TO SEE IF THE WORLD IS STILL TURNING.
TO MAKE SURE WE'RE NOT BEING DESTROYED.
TO MAKE SURE WE'RE NOT AT WAR.
THIS IS THE FIRST THING I DO.
I WAKE UP AND MAKE SURE THE WORLD IS STILL TURNING.
EVERY DAY.
AND IT HIT ME, THAT IS *INSANE.*
IT'S INSANE THAT--THAT THE WORLD IS SO *OUT OF CONTROL* THAT LITERALLY ANY DAY COULD BE THE LAST...
...OR THE BEGINNING OF A WHOLE NEW HORROR THAT WOULD--

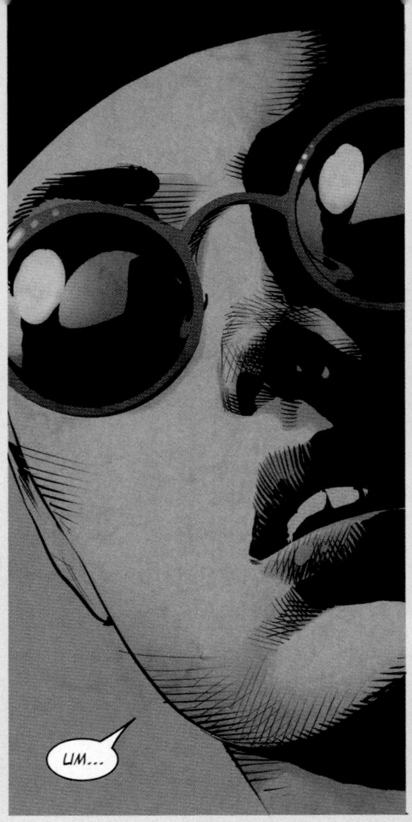
UM...

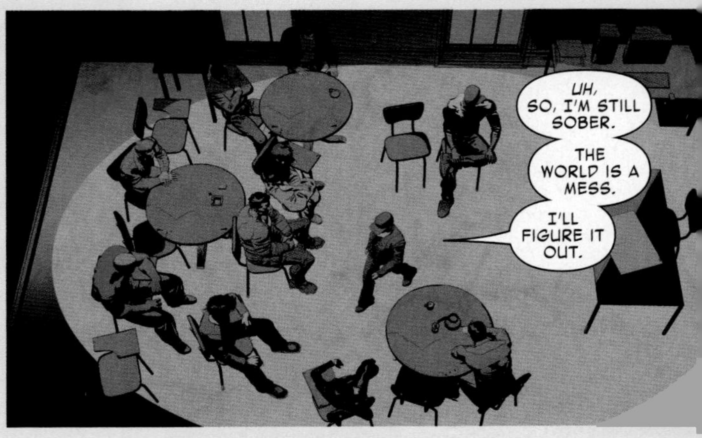
UH, SO, I'M STILL SOBER.
THE WORLD IS A MESS.
I'LL FIGURE IT OUT.

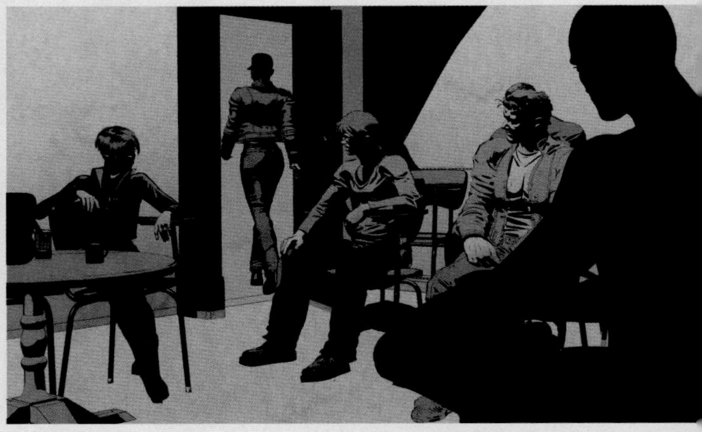

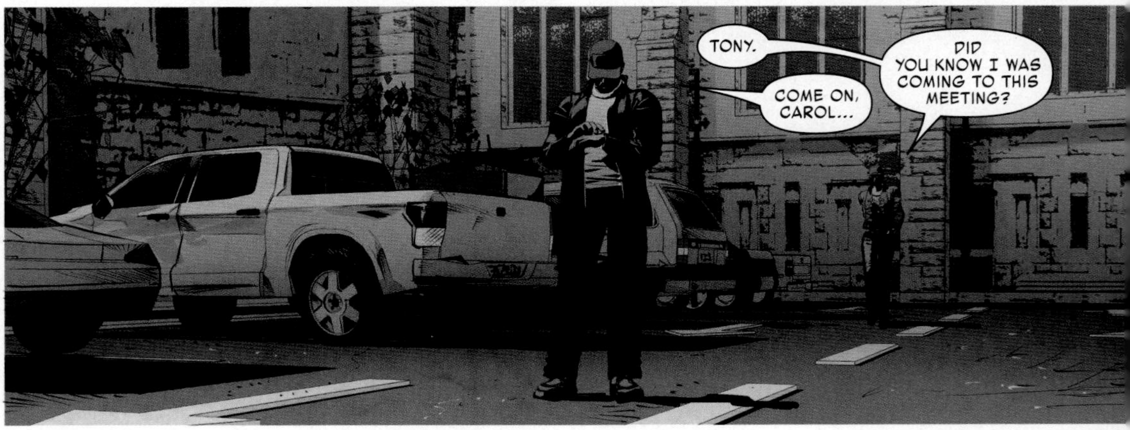
TONY.
DID YOU KNOW I WAS COMING TO THIS MEETING?
COME ON, CAROL...

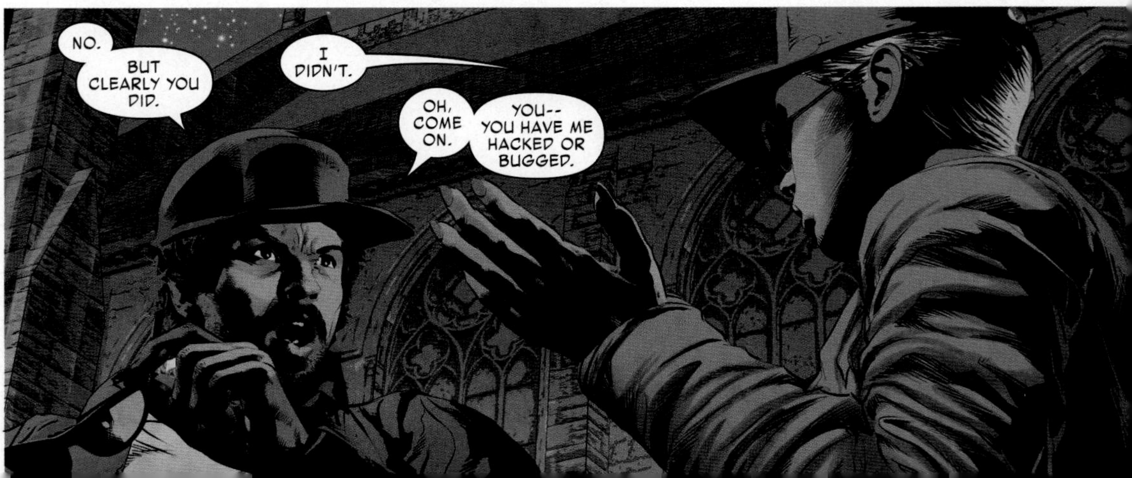
NO.
BUT CLEARLY YOU DID.
I DIDN'T.
OH, COME ON.
YOU-- YOU HAVE ME HACKED OR BUGGED.

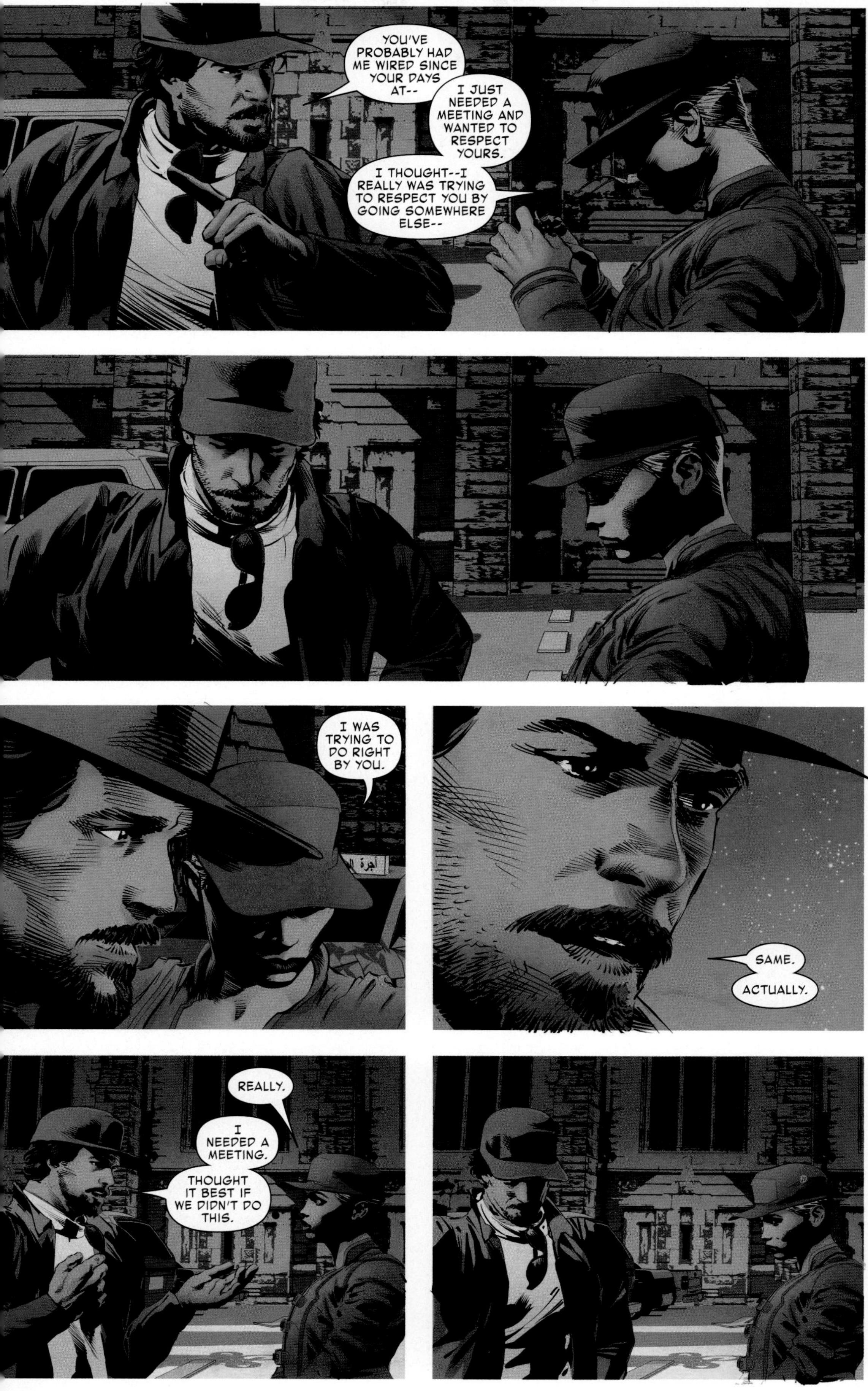
YOU'VE PROBABLY HAD ME WIRED SINCE YOUR DAYS AT--
I JUST NEEDED A MEETING AND WANTED TO RESPECT YOURS.
I THOUGHT--I REALLY WAS TRYING TO RESPECT YOU BY GOING SOMEWHERE ELSE--
I WAS TRYING TO DO RIGHT BY YOU.
SAME.
ACTUALLY.
REALLY.
I NEEDED A MEETING.
THOUGHT IT BEST IF WE DIDN'T DO THIS.

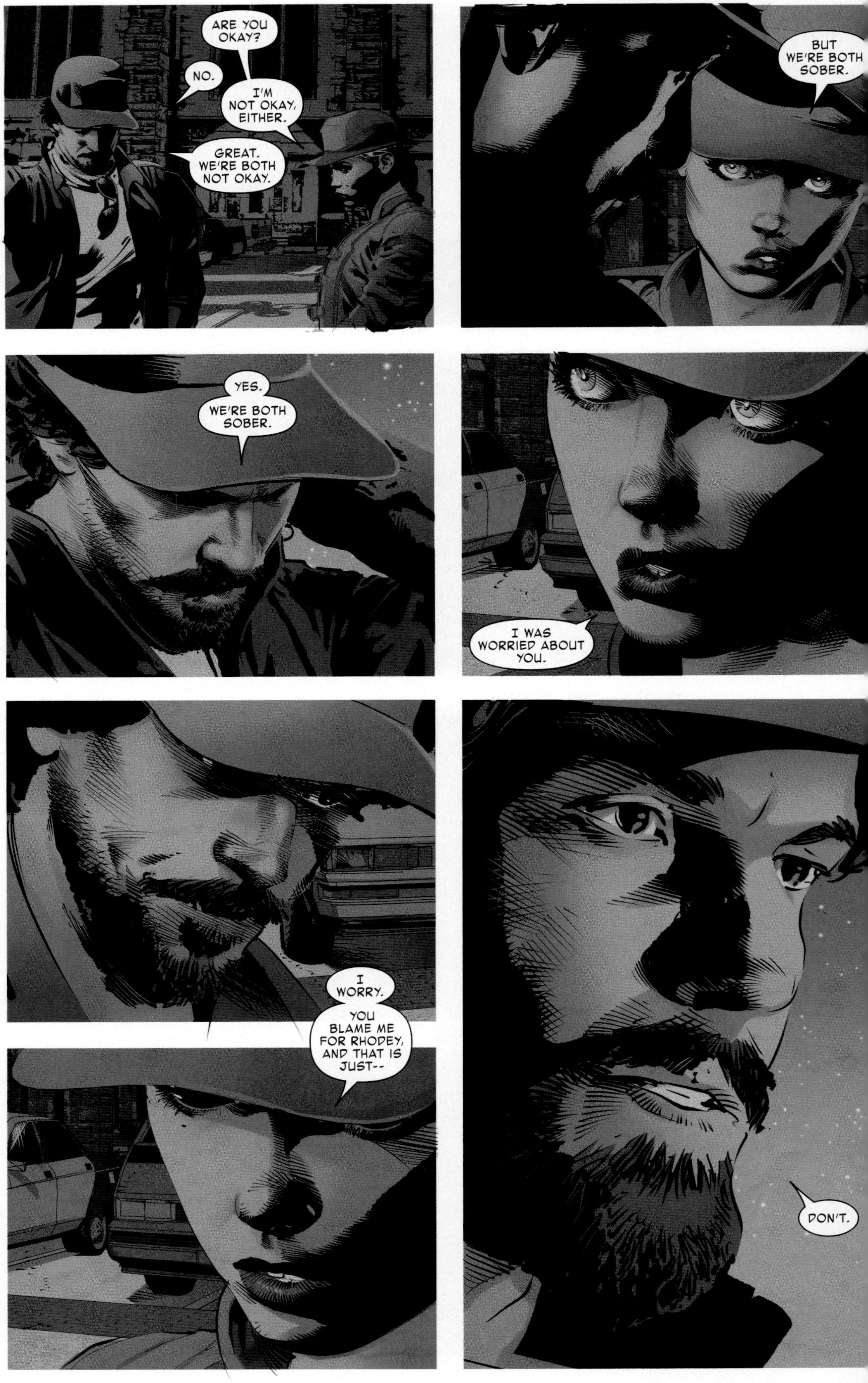
ARE YOU OKAY?
NO.
I'M NOT OKAY, EITHER.
GREAT. WE'RE BOTH NOT OKAY.
BUT WE'RE BOTH SOBER.
YES. WE'RE BOTH SOBER.
I WAS WORRIED ABOUT YOU.
I WORRY.
YOU BLAME ME FOR RHODEY, AND THAT IS JUST--
DON'T.

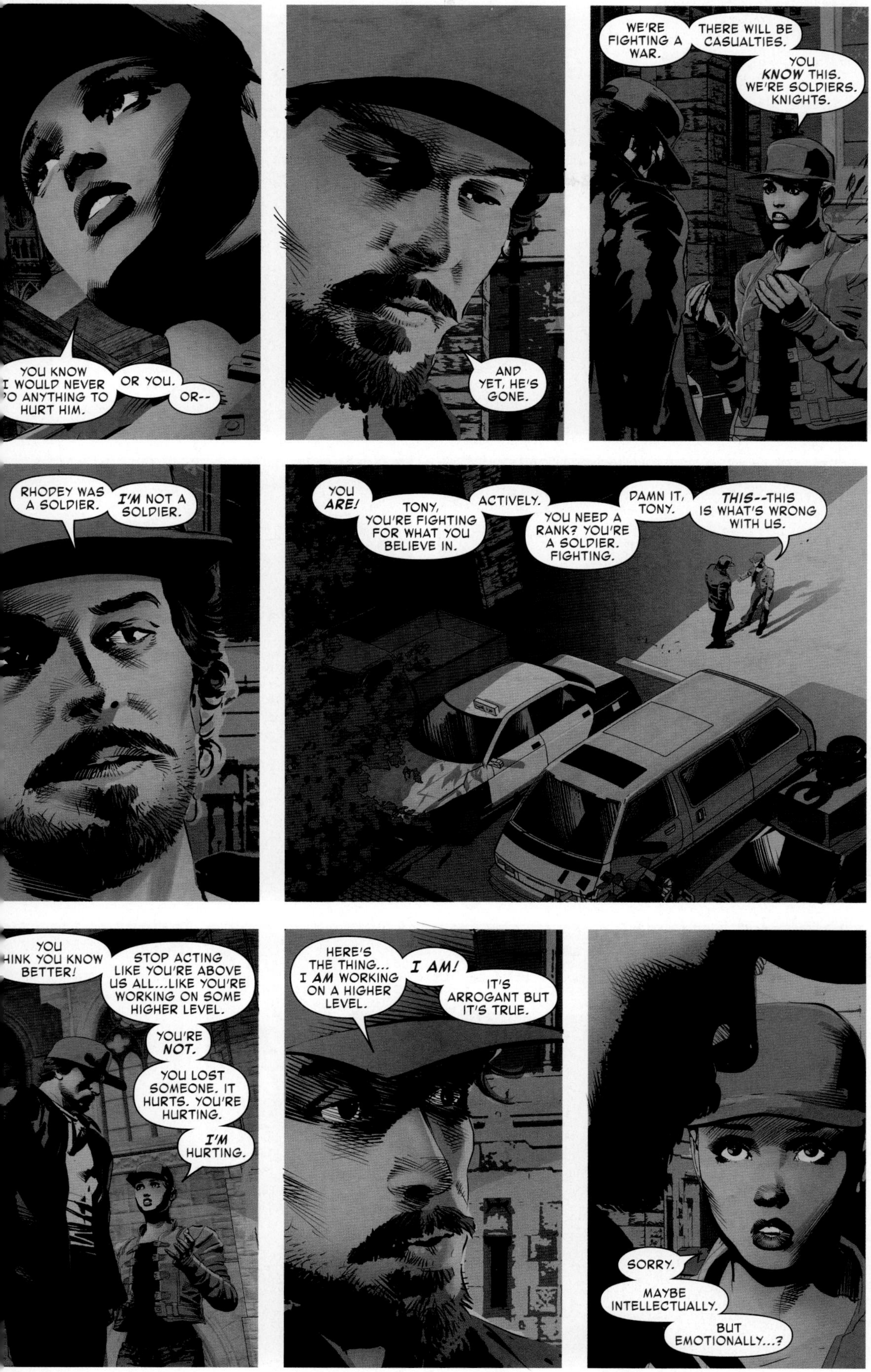
YOU KNOW I WOULD NEVER DO ANYTHING TO HURT HIM.
OR YOU.
OR--
AND YET, HE'S GONE.
WE'RE FIGHTING A WAR.
THERE WILL BE CASUALTIES.
YOU KNOW THIS. WE'RE SOLDIERS. KNIGHTS.
RHODEY WAS A SOLDIER.
I'M NOT A SOLDIER.
YOU ARE!
TONY, YOU'RE FIGHTING FOR WHAT YOU BELIEVE IN.
ACTIVELY.
YOU NEED A RANK? YOU'RE A SOLDIER. FIGHTING.
DAMN IT, TONY.
THIS--THIS IS WHAT'S WRONG WITH US.
YOU THINK YOU KNOW BETTER!
STOP ACTING LIKE YOU'RE ABOVE US ALL...LIKE YOU'RE WORKING ON SOME HIGHER LEVEL.
YOU'RE NOT.
YOU LOST SOMEONE. IT HURTS. YOU'RE HURTING.
I'M HURTING.
HERE'S THE THING... I AM WORKING ON A HIGHER LEVEL.
I AM!
IT'S ARROGANT BUT IT'S TRUE.
SORRY.
MAYBE INTELLECTUALLY.
BUT EMOTIONALLY...?

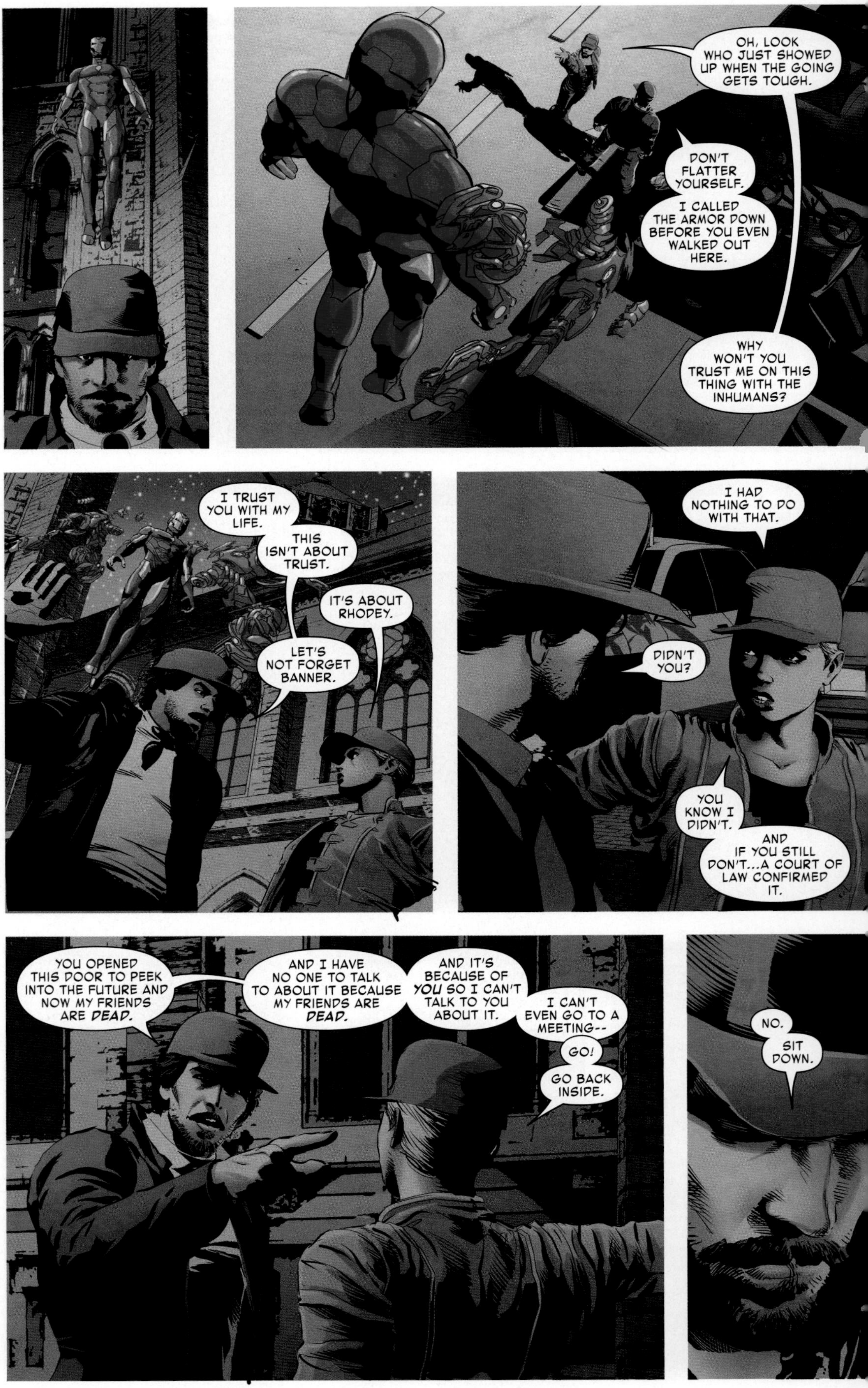
OH, LOOK WHO JUST SHOWED UP WHEN THE GOING GETS TOUGH.
DON'T FLATTER YOURSELF.
I CALLED THE ARMOR DOWN BEFORE YOU EVEN WALKED OUT HERE.
WHY WON'T YOU TRUST ME ON THIS THING WITH THE INHUMANS?
I TRUST YOU WITH MY LIFE.
THIS ISN'T ABOUT TRUST.
IT'S ABOUT RHODEY.
LET'S NOT FORGET BANNER.
I HAD NOTHING TO DO WITH THAT.
DIDN'T YOU?
YOU KNOW I DIDN'T.
AND IF YOU STILL DON'T...A COURT OF LAW CONFIRMED IT.
YOU OPENED THIS DOOR TO PEEK INTO THE FUTURE AND NOW MY FRIENDS ARE *DEAD.*
AND I HAVE NO ONE TO TALK TO ABOUT IT BECAUSE MY FRIENDS ARE *DEAD.*
AND IT'S BECAUSE OF *YOU* SO I CAN'T TALK TO YOU ABOUT IT.
I CAN'T EVEN GO TO A MEETING--
GO!
GO BACK INSIDE.
NO.
SIT DOWN.

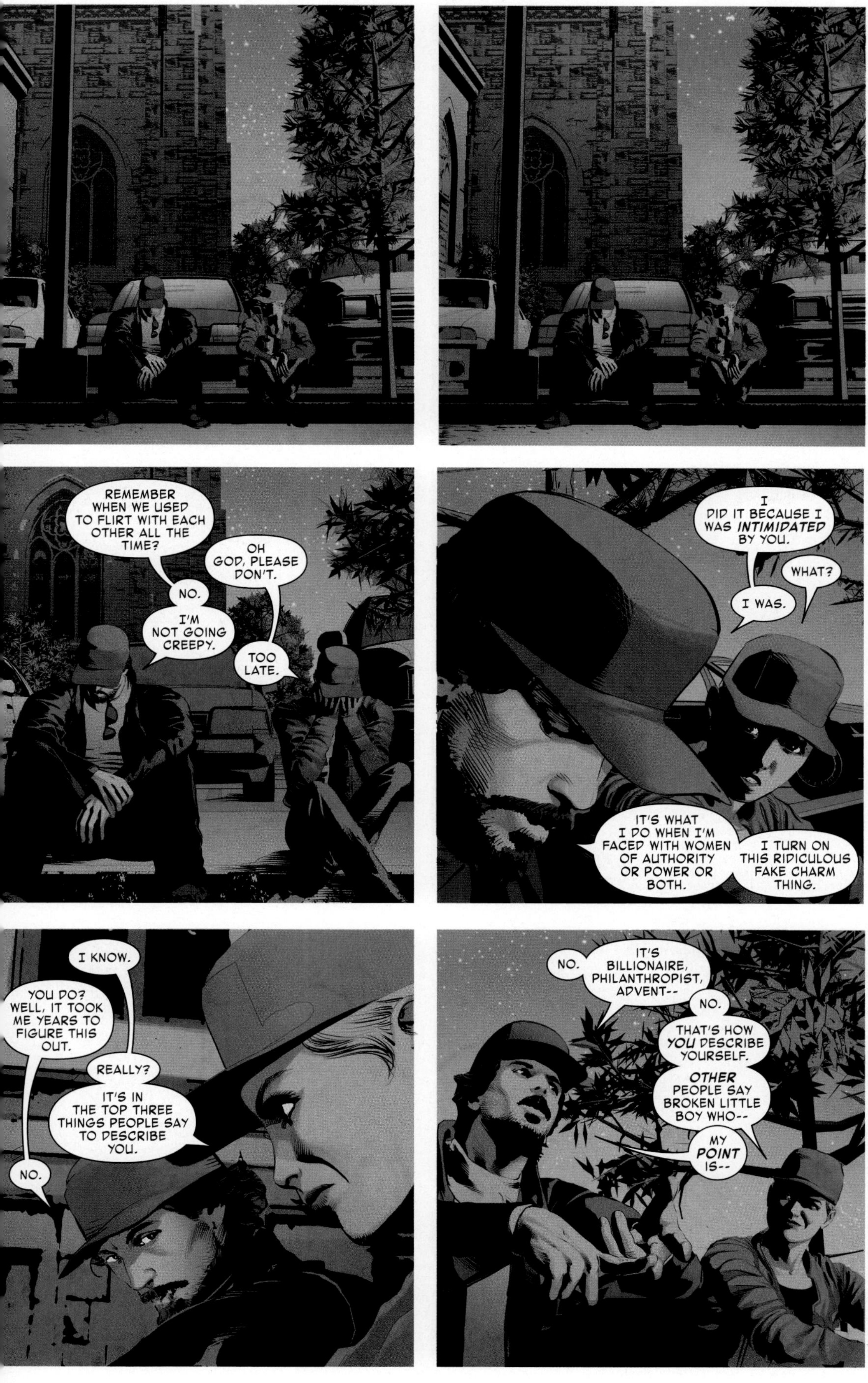
REMEMBER WHEN WE USED TO FLIRT WITH EACH OTHER ALL THE TIME?
OH GOD, PLEASE DON'T.
NO.
I'M NOT GOING CREEPY.
TOO LATE.
I DID IT BECAUSE I WAS *INTIMIDATED* BY YOU.
WHAT?
I WAS.
IT'S WHAT I DO WHEN I'M FACED WITH WOMEN OF AUTHORITY OR POWER OR BOTH.
I TURN ON THIS RIDICULOUS FAKE CHARM THING.
I KNOW.
YOU DO? WELL, IT TOOK ME YEARS TO FIGURE THIS OUT.
REALLY?
IT'S IN THE TOP THREE THINGS PEOPLE SAY TO DESCRIBE YOU.
NO.
NO.
IT'S BILLIONAIRE, PHILANTHROPIST, ADVENT--
NO.
THAT'S HOW *YOU* DESCRIBE YOURSELF.
OTHER PEOPLE SAY BROKEN LITTLE BOY WHO--
MY *POINT* IS--

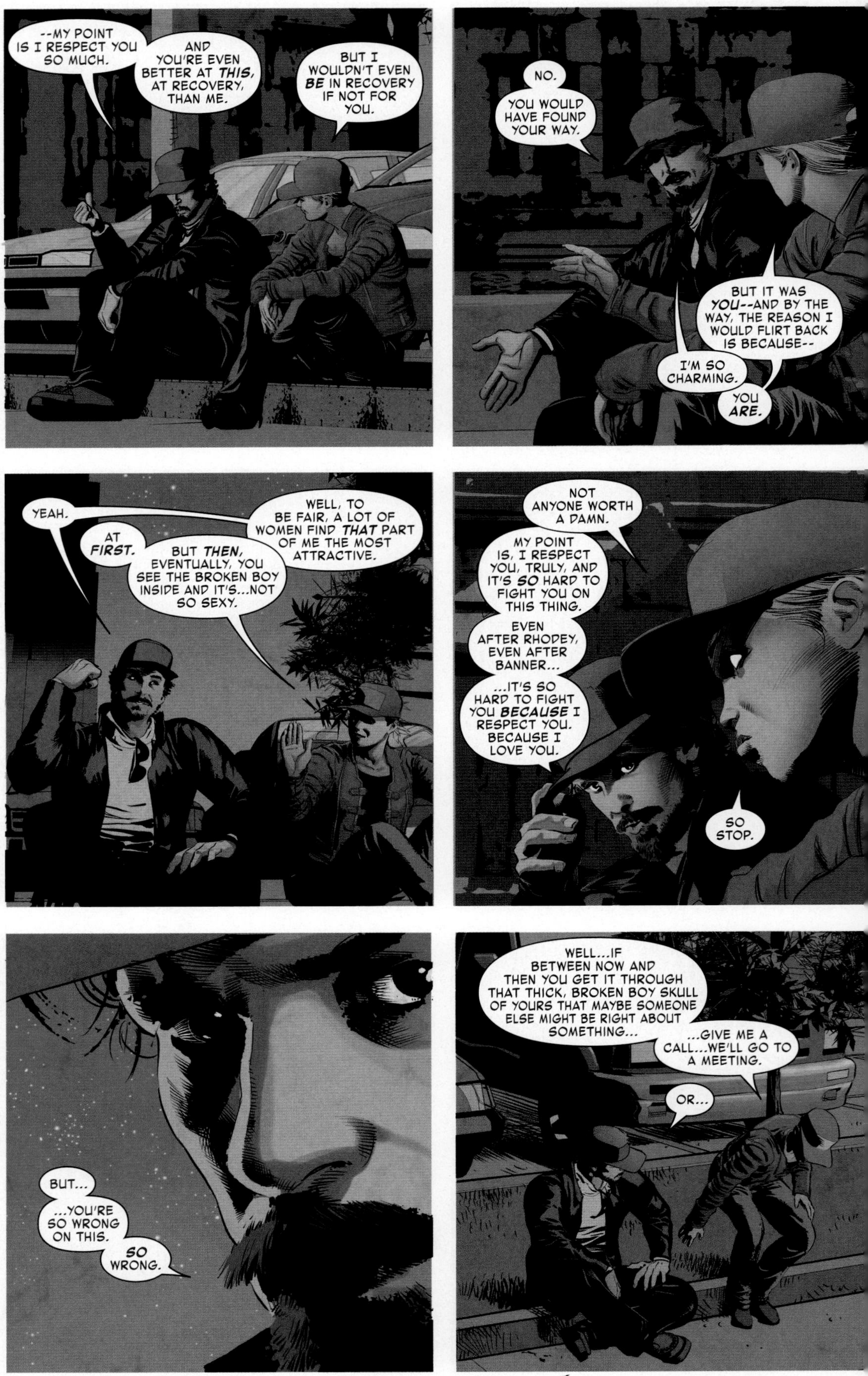
--MY POINT IS I RESPECT YOU SO MUCH.
AND YOU'RE EVEN BETTER AT THIS, AT RECOVERY, THAN ME.
BUT I WOULDN'T EVEN BE IN RECOVERY IF NOT FOR YOU.
NO.
YOU WOULD HAVE FOUND YOUR WAY.
BUT IT WAS YOU--AND BY THE WAY, THE REASON I WOULD FLIRT BACK IS BECAUSE--
I'M SO CHARMING.
YOU ARE.
WELL, TO BE FAIR, A LOT OF WOMEN FIND THAT PART OF ME THE MOST ATTRACTIVE.
YEAH.
AT FIRST.
BUT THEN, EVENTUALLY, YOU SEE THE BROKEN BOY INSIDE AND IT'S...NOT SO SEXY.
NOT ANYONE WORTH A DAMN.
MY POINT IS, I RESPECT YOU, TRULY, AND IT'S SO HARD TO FIGHT YOU ON THIS THING.
EVEN AFTER RHODEY, EVEN AFTER BANNER...
...IT'S SO HARD TO FIGHT YOU BECAUSE I RESPECT YOU. BECAUSE I LOVE YOU.
SO STOP.
BUT...
...YOU'RE SO WRONG ON THIS.
SO WRONG.
WELL...IF BETWEEN NOW AND THEN YOU GET IT THROUGH THAT THICK, BROKEN BOY SKULL OF YOURS THAT MAYBE SOMEONE ELSE MIGHT BE RIGHT ABOUT SOMETHING...
...GIVE ME A CALL...WE'LL GO TO A MEETING.
OR...

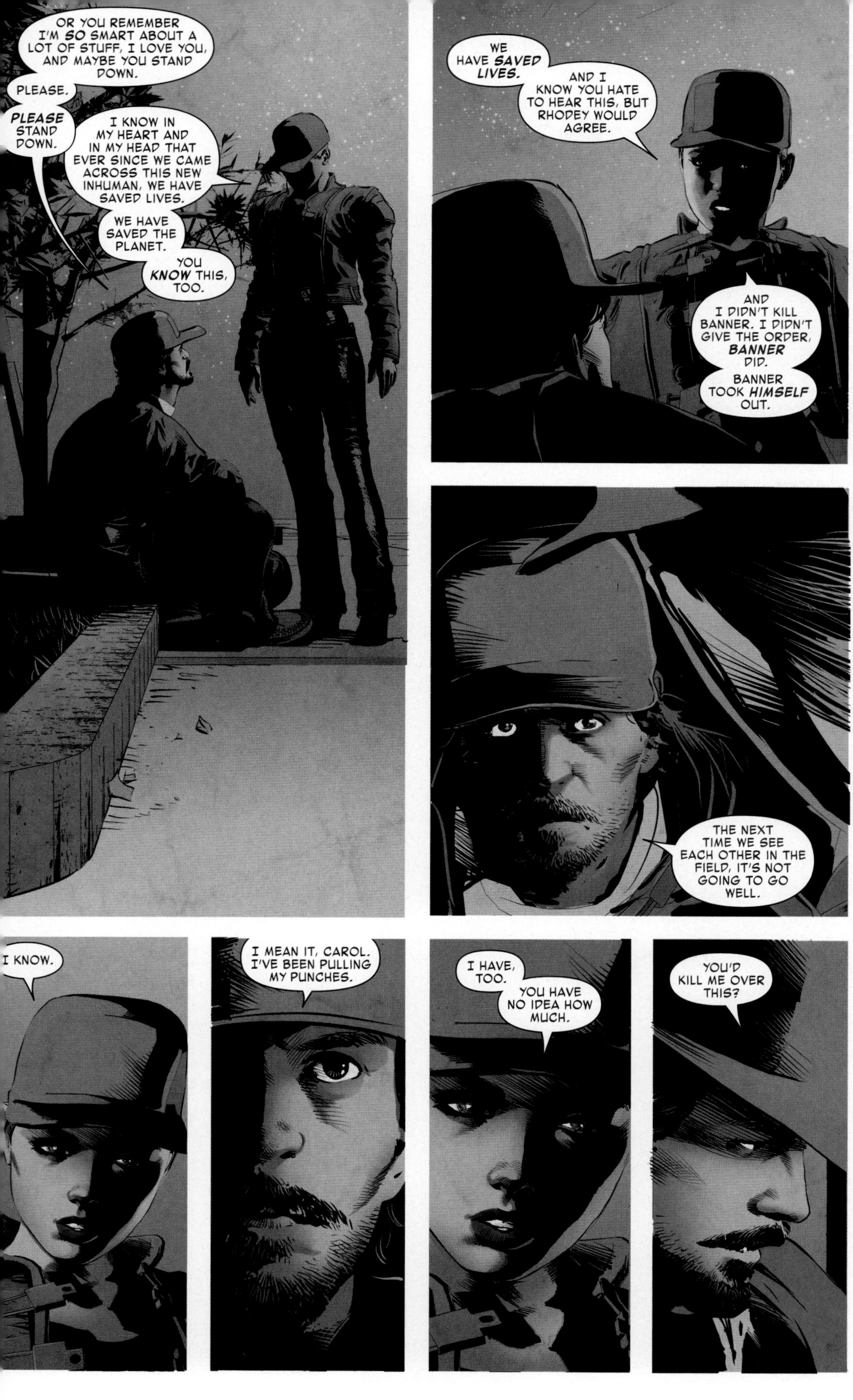
OR YOU REMEMBER I'M SO SMART ABOUT A LOT OF STUFF, I LOVE YOU, AND MAYBE YOU STAND DOWN.
PLEASE.
PLEASE STAND DOWN.
I KNOW IN MY HEART AND IN MY HEAD THAT EVER SINCE WE CAME ACROSS THIS NEW INHUMAN, WE HAVE SAVED LIVES.
WE HAVE SAVED THE PLANET.
YOU KNOW THIS, TOO.
WE HAVE SAVED LIVES.
AND I KNOW YOU HATE TO HEAR THIS, BUT RHODEY WOULD AGREE.
AND I DIDN'T KILL BANNER. I DIDN'T GIVE THE ORDER, BANNER DID.
BANNER TOOK HIMSELF OUT.
THE NEXT TIME WE SEE EACH OTHER IN THE FIELD, IT'S NOT GOING TO GO WELL.
I KNOW.
I MEAN IT, CAROL. I'VE BEEN PULLING MY PUNCHES.
I HAVE, TOO.
YOU HAVE NO IDEA HOW MUCH.
YOU'D KILL ME OVER THIS?

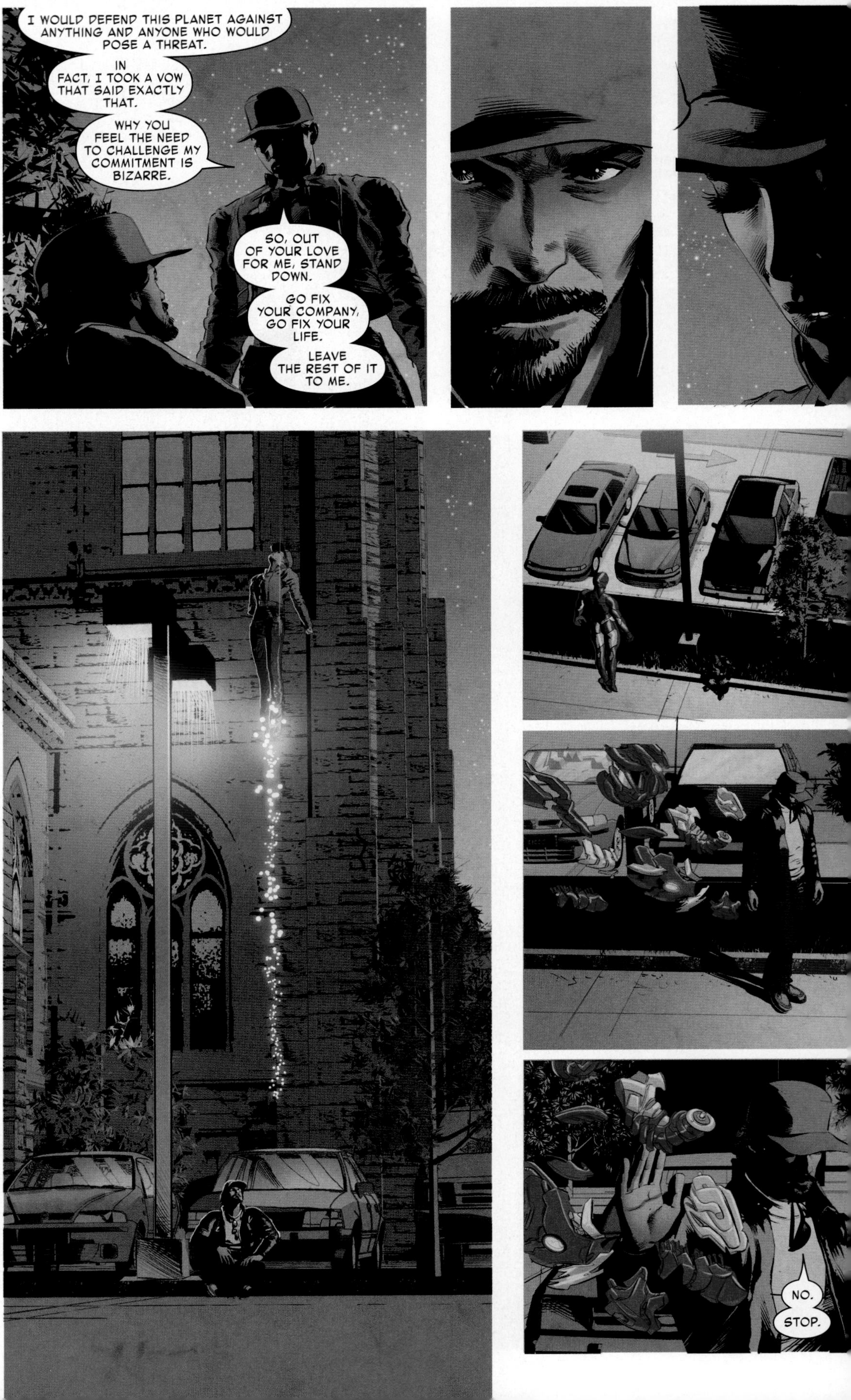

I WOULD DEFEND THIS PLANET AGAINST ANYTHING AND ANYONE WHO WOULD POSE A THREAT.
IN FACT, I TOOK A VOW THAT SAID EXACTLY THAT.
WHY YOU FEEL THE NEED TO CHALLENGE MY COMMITMENT IS BIZARRE.
SO, OUT OF YOUR LOVE FOR ME, STAND DOWN.
GO FIX YOUR COMPANY, GO FIX YOUR LIFE.
LEAVE THE REST OF IT TO ME.
NO.
STOP.

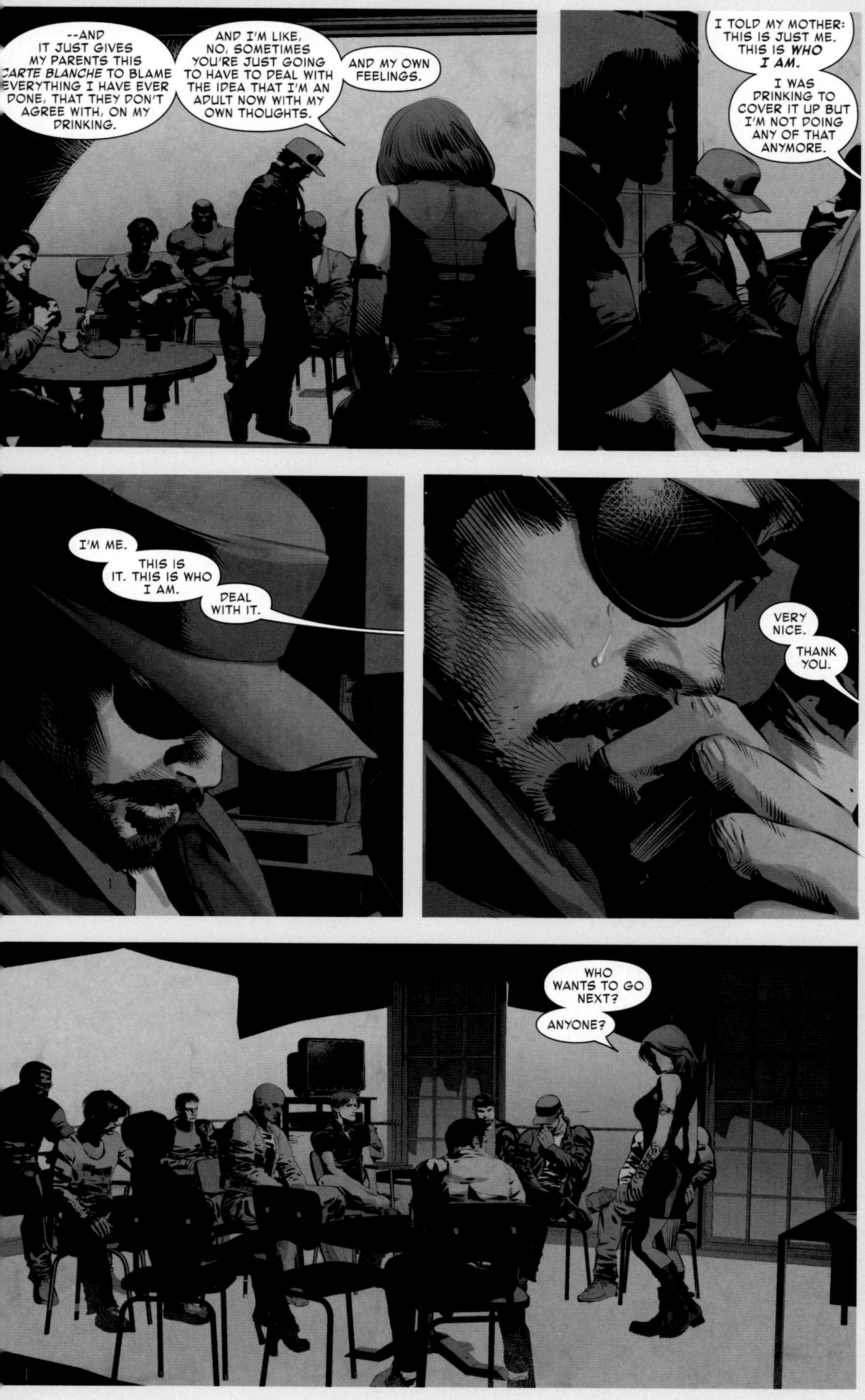
--AND IT JUST GIVES MY PARENTS THIS CARTE BLANCHE TO BLAME EVERYTHING I HAVE EVER DONE, THAT THEY DON'T AGREE WITH, ON MY DRINKING.
AND I'M LIKE, NO, SOMETIMES YOU'RE JUST GOING TO HAVE TO DEAL WITH THE IDEA THAT I'M AN ADULT NOW WITH MY OWN THOUGHTS.
AND MY OWN FEELINGS.
I TOLD MY MOTHER: THIS IS JUST ME. THIS IS WHO I AM.
I WAS DRINKING TO COVER IT UP BUT I'M NOT DOING ANY OF THAT ANYMORE.
I'M ME.
THIS IS IT. THIS IS WHO I AM.
DEAL WITH IT.
VERY NICE.
THANK YOU.
WHO WANTS TO GO NEXT?
ANYONE?

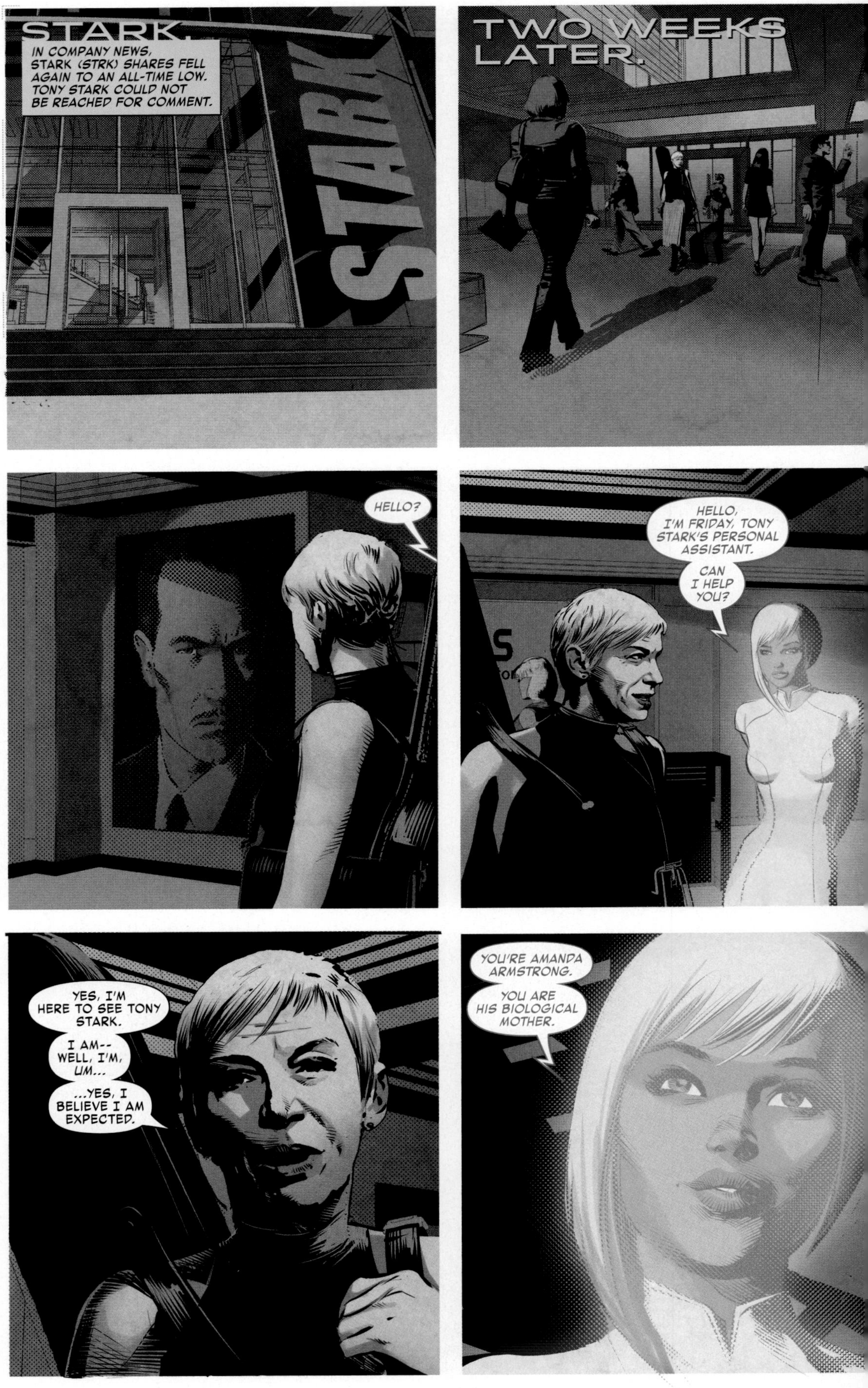
STARK.
IN COMPANY NEWS, STARK (STRK) SHARES FELL AGAIN TO AN ALL-TIME LOW. TONY STARK COULD NOT BE REACHED FOR COMMENT.
STARK
TWO WEEKS LATER.
HELLO?
HELLO, I'M FRIDAY, TONY STARK'S PERSONAL ASSISTANT.
CAN I HELP YOU?
YES, I'M HERE TO SEE TONY STARK.
I AM-- WELL, I'M, UM...
...YES, I BELIEVE I AM EXPECTED.
YOU'RE AMANDA ARMSTRONG.
YOU ARE HIS BIOLOGICAL MOTHER.

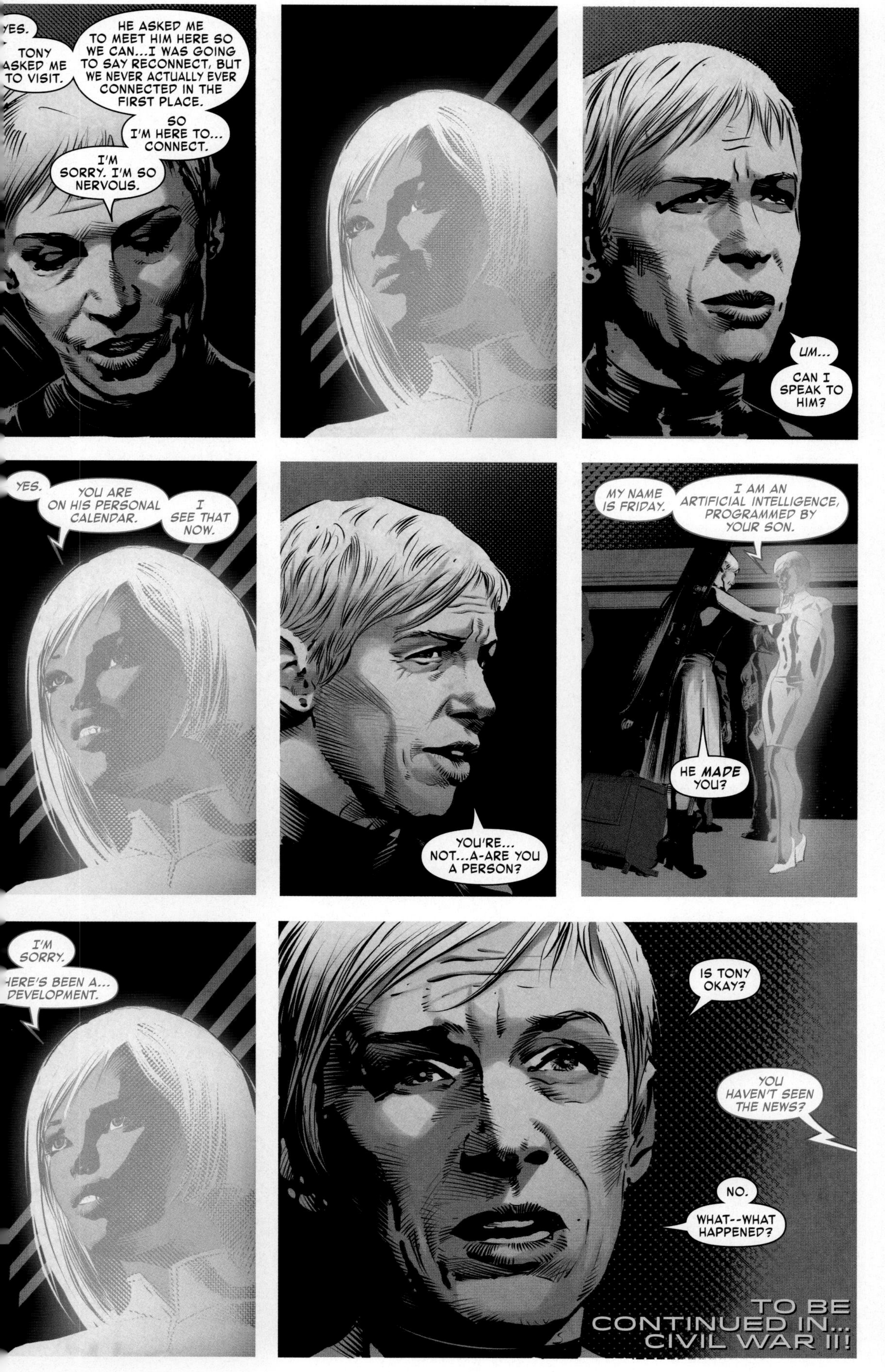
YES.
TONY ASKED ME TO VISIT.
HE ASKED ME TO MEET HIM HERE SO WE CAN...I WAS GOING TO SAY RECONNECT, BUT WE NEVER ACTUALLY EVER CONNECTED IN THE FIRST PLACE.
SO I'M HERE TO... CONNECT.
I'M SORRY. I'M SO NERVOUS.
UM...
CAN I SPEAK TO HIM?
YES.
YOU ARE ON HIS PERSONAL CALENDAR.
I SEE THAT NOW.
YOU'RE... NOT...A-ARE YOU A PERSON?
MY NAME IS FRIDAY.
I AM AN ARTIFICIAL INTELLIGENCE, PROGRAMMED BY YOUR SON.
HE MADE YOU?
I'M SORRY.
HERE'S BEEN A... DEVELOPMENT.
IS TONY OKAY?
YOU HAVEN'T SEEN THE NEWS?
NO.
WHAT--WHAT HAPPENED?
TO BE CONTINUED IN... CIVIL WAR II!

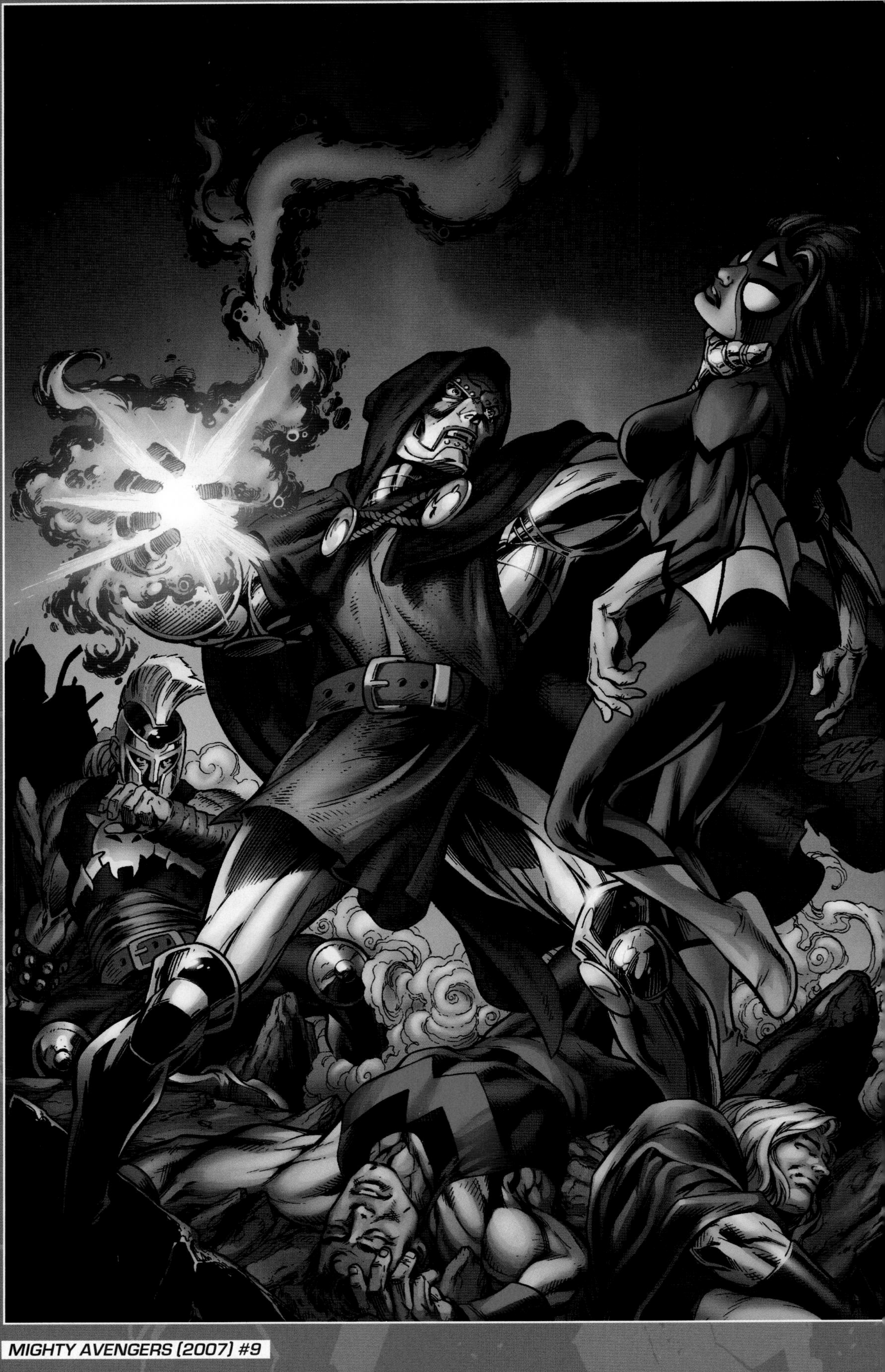

MIGHTY AVENGERS (2007) #9

AND THERE CAME A DAY, A DAY UNLIKE ANY OTHER, WHEN EARTH'S MIGHTIEST HEROES FOUND
THEMSELVES UNITED AGAINST A COMMON THREAT! ON THAT DAY, THE AVENGERS WERE BORN,
TO FIGHT THE FOES NO SINGLE SUPER HERO COULD WITHSTAND!

THE MIGHTY AVENGERS

PREVIOUSLY...

THE MIGHTY AVENGERS BATTLE THE ENTIRE POPULATION OF NEW YORK
CITY AS ITS CITIZENS ARE TRANSFORMED INTO SYMBIOTES AFTER A
MYSTERIOUS VIRUS DROPS FROM A SATELLITE IN ORBIT ABOVE THE
EARTH. WHEN IRON MAN INVESTIGATES THE SATELLITE'S ORIGIN, HE
DISCOVERS THAT IT BELONGS TO NONE OTHER THAN LATVERIAN
MONARCH VICTOR VON DOOM.

IRON MAN GATHERS THE AVENGERS AND HIS AGENTS OF S.H.I.E.L.D.
AND BRINGS THE FIGHT TO LATVERIA...

BRIAN MICHAEL BENDIS
WRITER

MARK BAGLEY
PENCILER

**DANNY MIKI & CRIME LAB STUDIOS'
ALLEN MARTINEZ & VICTOR OLAZABA**
INKERS

JUSTIN PONSOR
COLORIST

MARKO DJURDJEVIC
ARTIST, YEAR 1211

ARTMONKEYS' DAVE LANPHEAR
LETTERER

MARK BAGLEY
WITH **JOHN DELL** (#9), **DANNY MIKI** (#10-11) & **JASON KEITH** (#9-11)
COVER ART

MOLLY LAZER
ASSOCIATE EDITOR

TOM BREVOORT
EDITOR

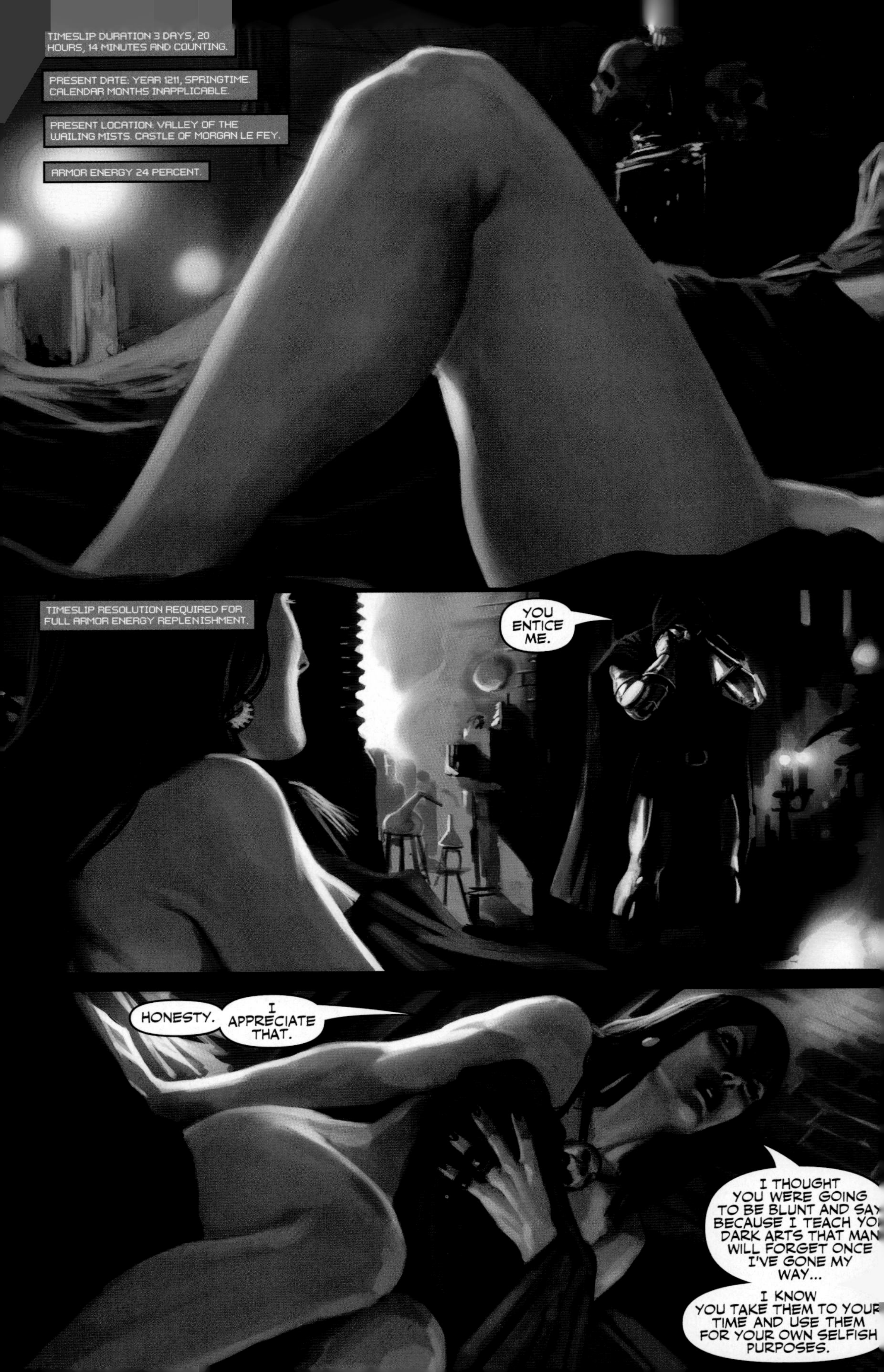
TIMESLIP DURATION 3 DAYS, 20 HOURS, 14 MINUTES AND COUNTING.
PRESENT DATE: YEAR 1211, SPRINGTIME. CALENDAR MONTHS INAPPLICABLE.
PRESENT LOCATION: VALLEY OF THE WAILING MISTS. CASTLE OF MORGAN LE FEY.
ARMOR ENERGY 24 PERCENT.
TIMESLIP RESOLUTION REQUIRED FOR FULL ARMOR ENERGY REPLENISHMENT.
YOU ENTICE ME.
HONESTY.
I APPRECIATE THAT.
I THOUGHT YOU WERE GOING TO BE BLUNT AND SAY BECAUSE I TEACH YOU DARK ARTS THAT MAN WILL FORGET ONCE I'VE GONE MY WAY...
I KNOW YOU TAKE THEM TO YOUR TIME AND USE THEM FOR YOUR OWN SELFISH PURPOSES.

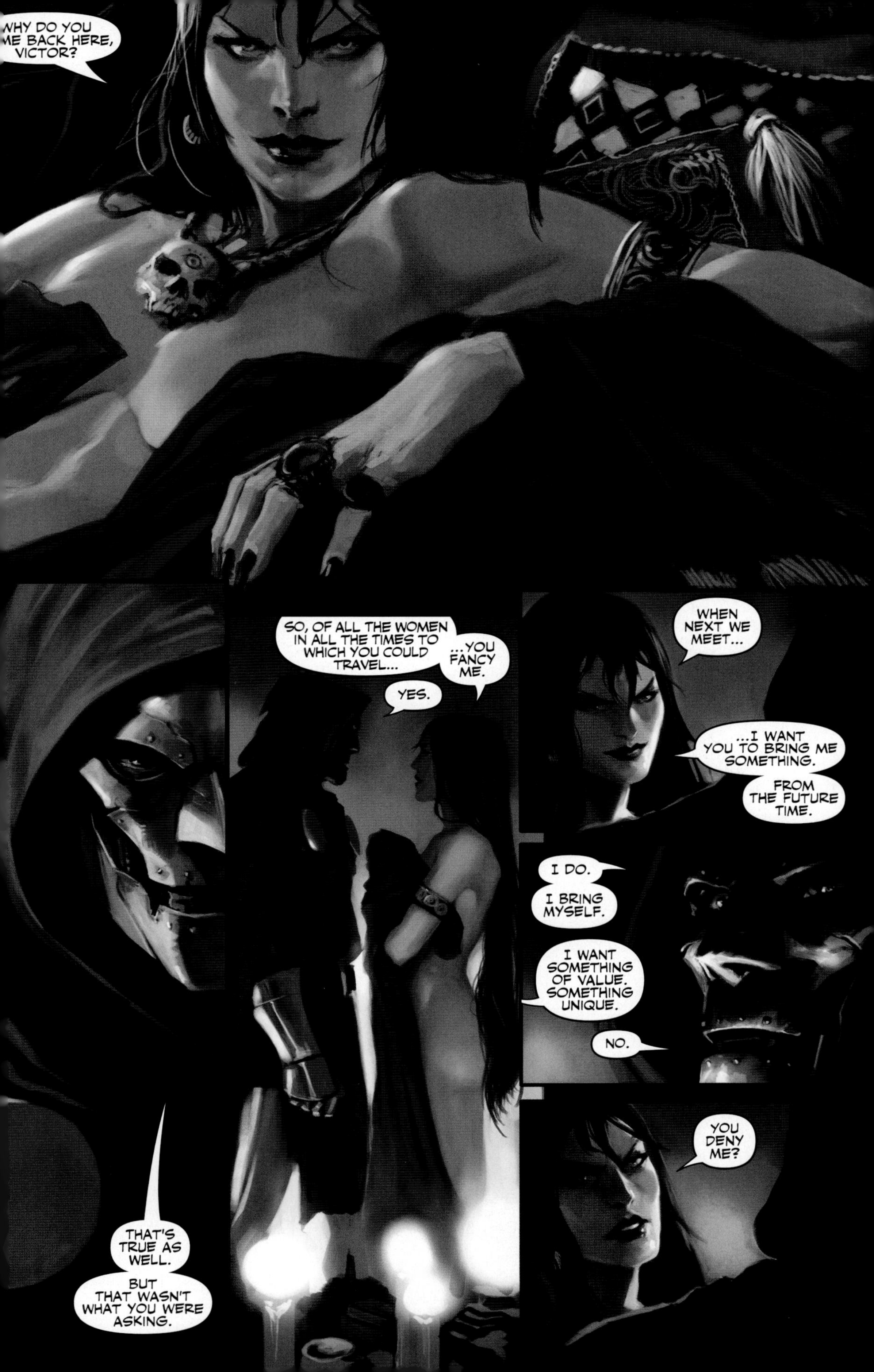
WHY DO YOU ME BACK HERE, VICTOR?
SO, OF ALL THE WOMEN IN ALL THE TIMES TO WHICH YOU COULD TRAVEL...
...YOU FANCY ME.
YES.
THAT'S TRUE AS WELL.
BUT THAT WASN'T WHAT YOU WERE ASKING.
WHEN NEXT WE MEET...
...I WANT YOU TO BRING ME SOMETHING.
FROM THE FUTURE TIME.
I DO.
I BRING MYSELF.
I WANT SOMETHING OF VALUE. SOMETHING UNIQUE.
NO.
YOU DENY ME?

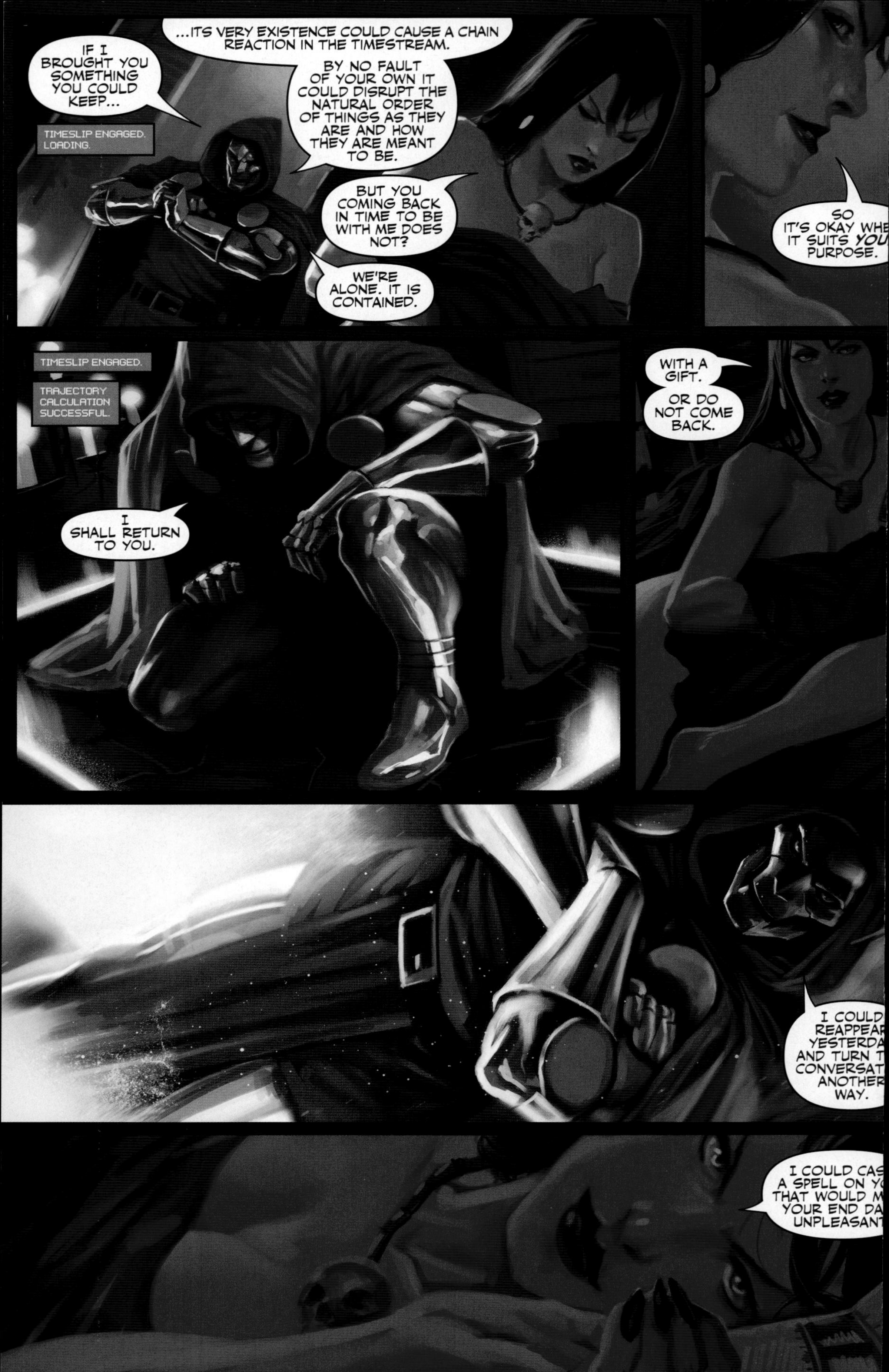
IF I BROUGHT YOU SOMETHING YOU COULD KEEP...
TIMESLIP ENGAGED. LOADING.
...ITS VERY EXISTENCE COULD CAUSE A CHAIN REACTION IN THE TIMESTREAM.
BY NO FAULT OF YOUR OWN IT COULD DISRUPT THE NATURAL ORDER OF THINGS AS THEY ARE AND HOW THEY ARE MEANT TO BE.
BUT YOU COMING BACK IN TIME TO BE WITH ME DOES NOT?
WE'RE ALONE. IT IS CONTAINED.
SO IT'S OKAY WHE IT SUITS YOU PURPOSE.
TIMESLIP ENGAGED.
TRAJECTORY CALCULATION SUCCESSFUL.
I SHALL RETURN TO YOU.
WITH A GIFT.
OR DO NOT COME BACK.
I COULD REAPPEAR YESTERDA AND TURN T CONVERSAT ANOTHER WAY.
I COULD CAS A SPELL ON YO THAT WOULD M YOUR END DA UNPLEASANT

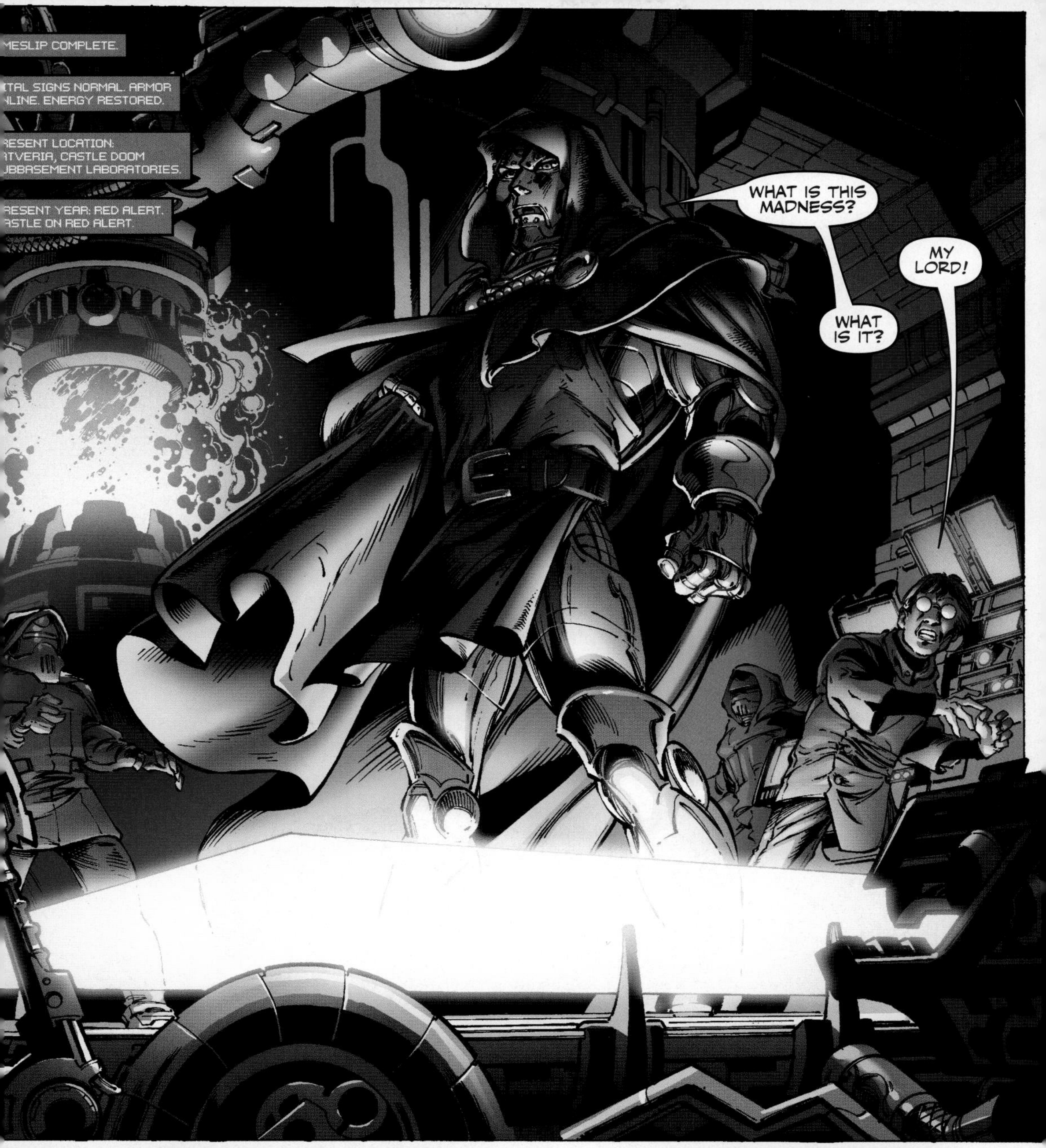
MESLIP COMPLETE.
TAL SIGNS NORMAL. ARMOR
NLINE. ENERGY RESTORED.
RESENT LOCATION:
TVERIA, CASTLE DOOM
UBBASEMENT LABORATORIES.
RESENT YEAR: RED ALERT.
ASTLE ON RED ALERT.
WHAT IS THIS MADNESS?
WHAT IS IT?
MY LORD!

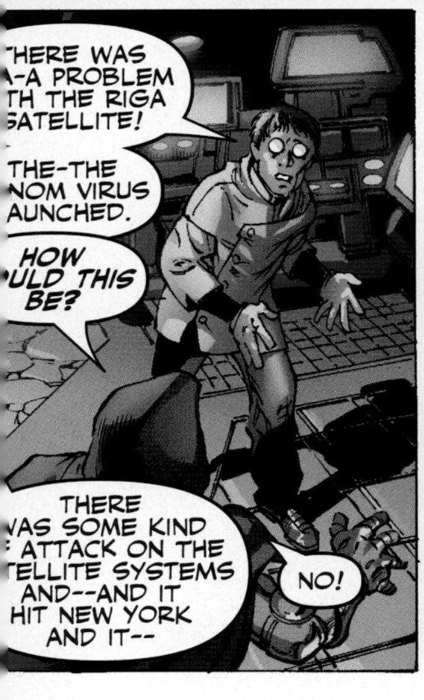
THERE WAS A-A PROBLEM TH THE RIGA SATELLITE!
THE-THE NOM VIRUS AUNCHED.
HOW ULD THIS BE?
THERE WAS SOME KIND F ATTACK ON THE TELLITE SYSTEMS AND--AND IT HIT NEW YORK AND IT--
NO!

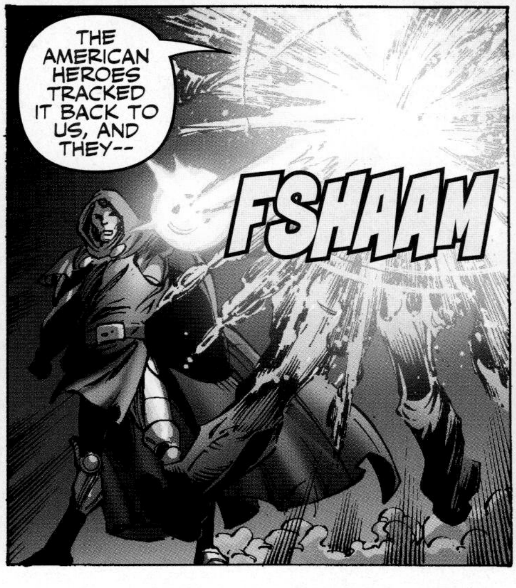
THE AMERICAN HEROES TRACKED IT BACK TO US, AND THEY--
FSHAAM

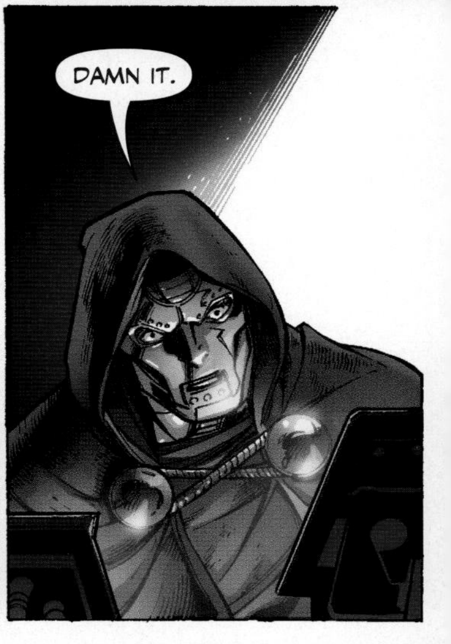
DAMN IT.

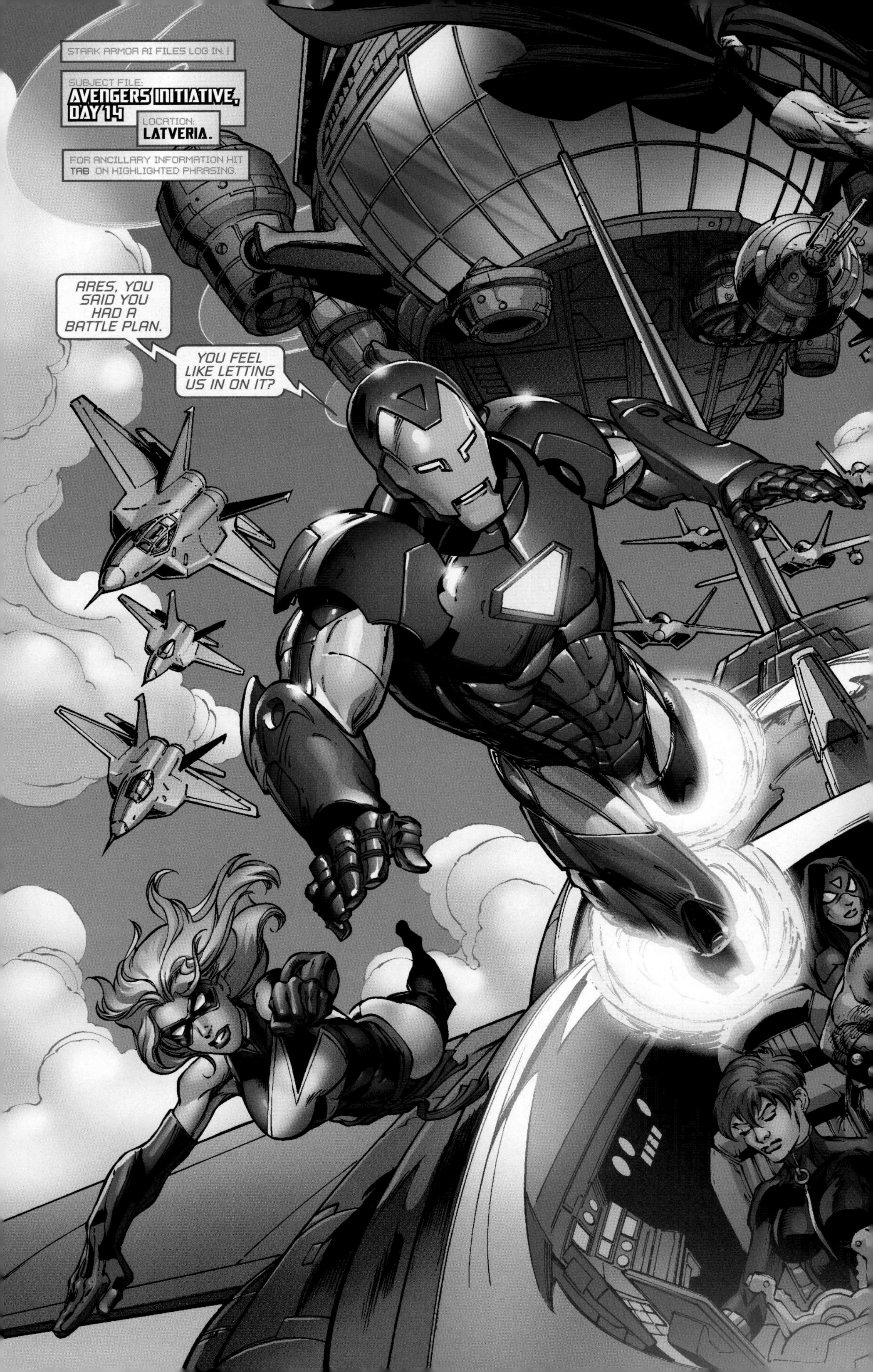
STARK ARMOR AI FILES LOG IN. |
SUBJECT FILE:
AVENGERS INITIATIVE, DAY 14
LOCATION:
LATVERIA.
FOR ANCILLARY INFORMATION HIT TAB ON HIGHLIGHTED PHRASING.
ARES, YOU SAID YOU HAD A BATTLE PLAN.
YOU FEEL LIKE LETTING US IN ON IT?

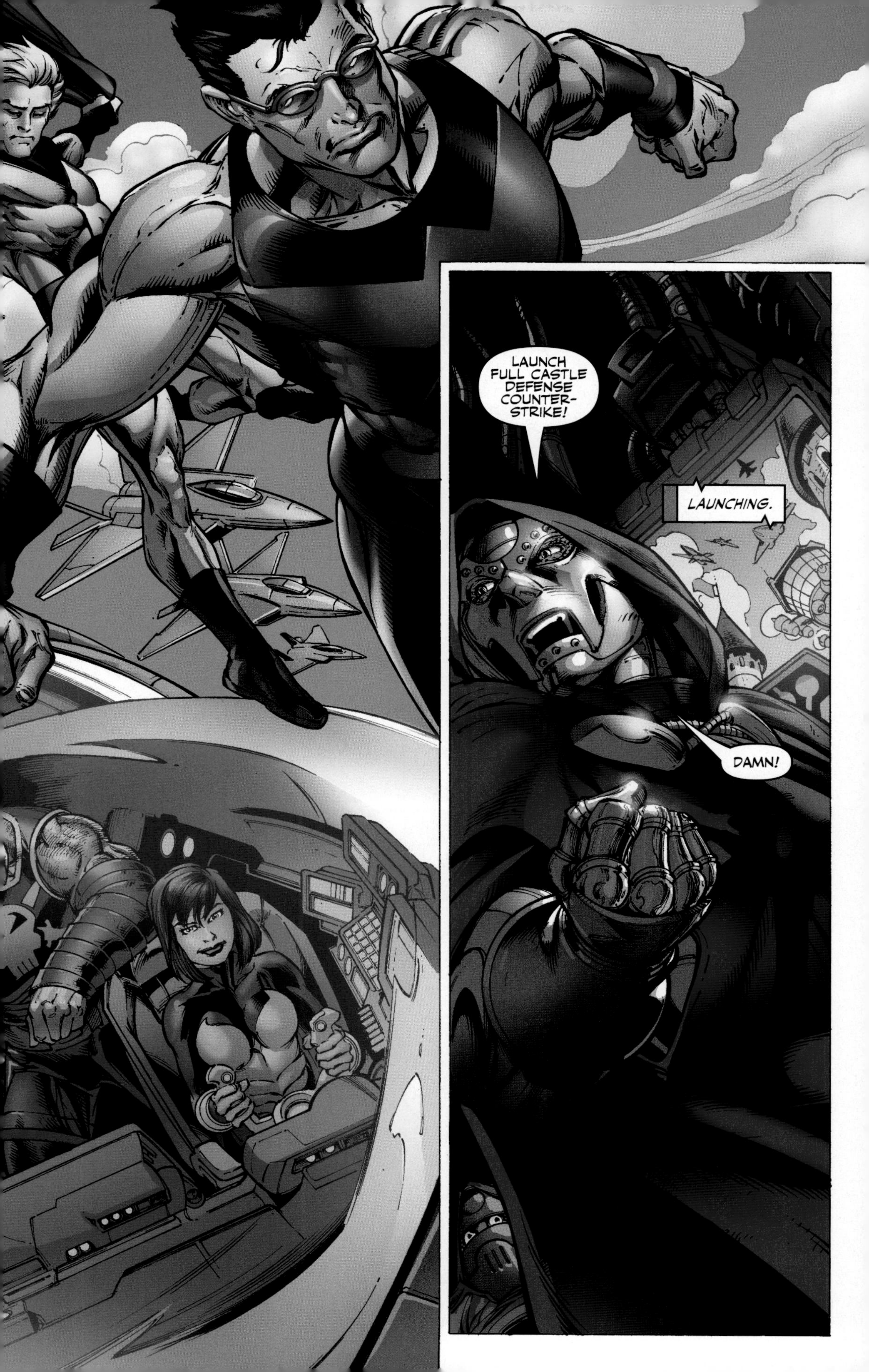
LAUNCH FULL CASTLE DEFENSE COUNTER-STRIKE!
LAUNCHING.
DAMN!

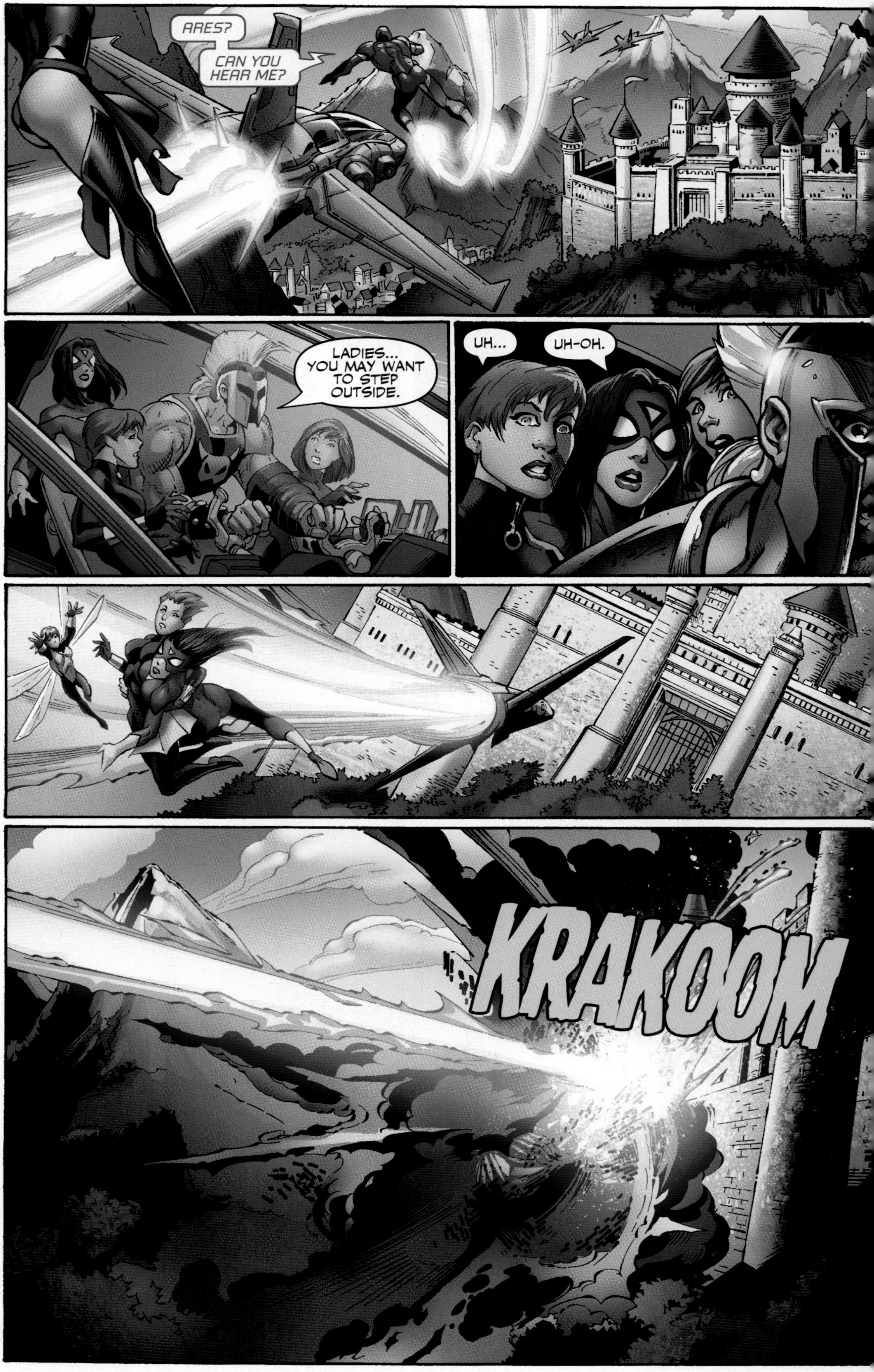
ARES?
CAN YOU HEAR ME?
LADIES... YOU MAY WANT TO STEP OUTSIDE.
UH...
UH-OH.
KRAKOOM

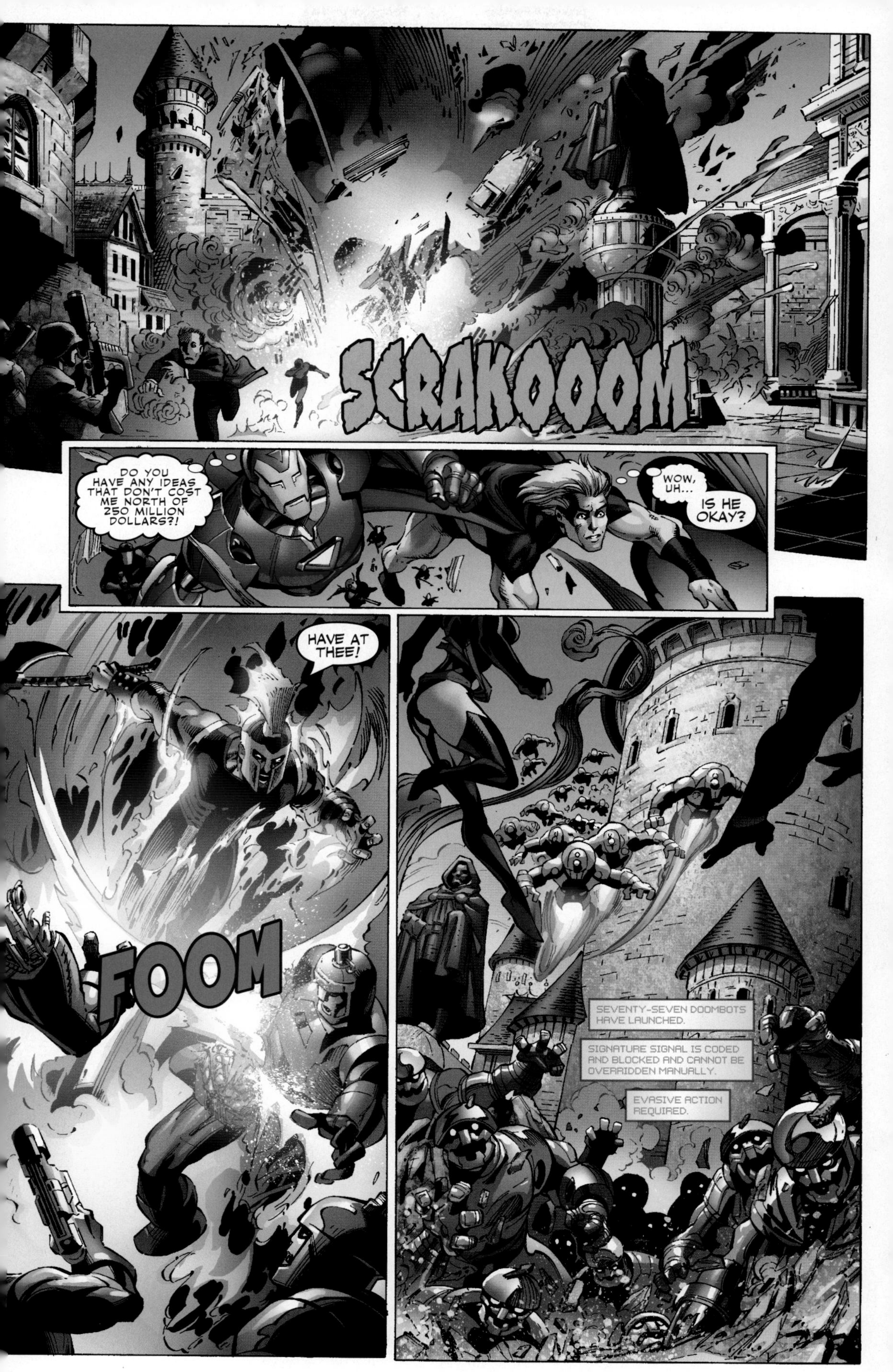
SCRAKOOOM
DO YOU HAVE ANY IDEAS THAT DON'T COST ME NORTH OF 250 MILLION DOLLARS?!
WOW, UH...
IS HE OKAY?
HAVE AT THEE!
FOOM
SEVENTY-SEVEN DOOMBOTS HAVE LAUNCHED.
SIGNATURE SIGNAL IS CODED AND BLOCKED AND CANNOT BE OVERRIDDEN MANUALLY.
EVASIVE ACTION REQUIRED.

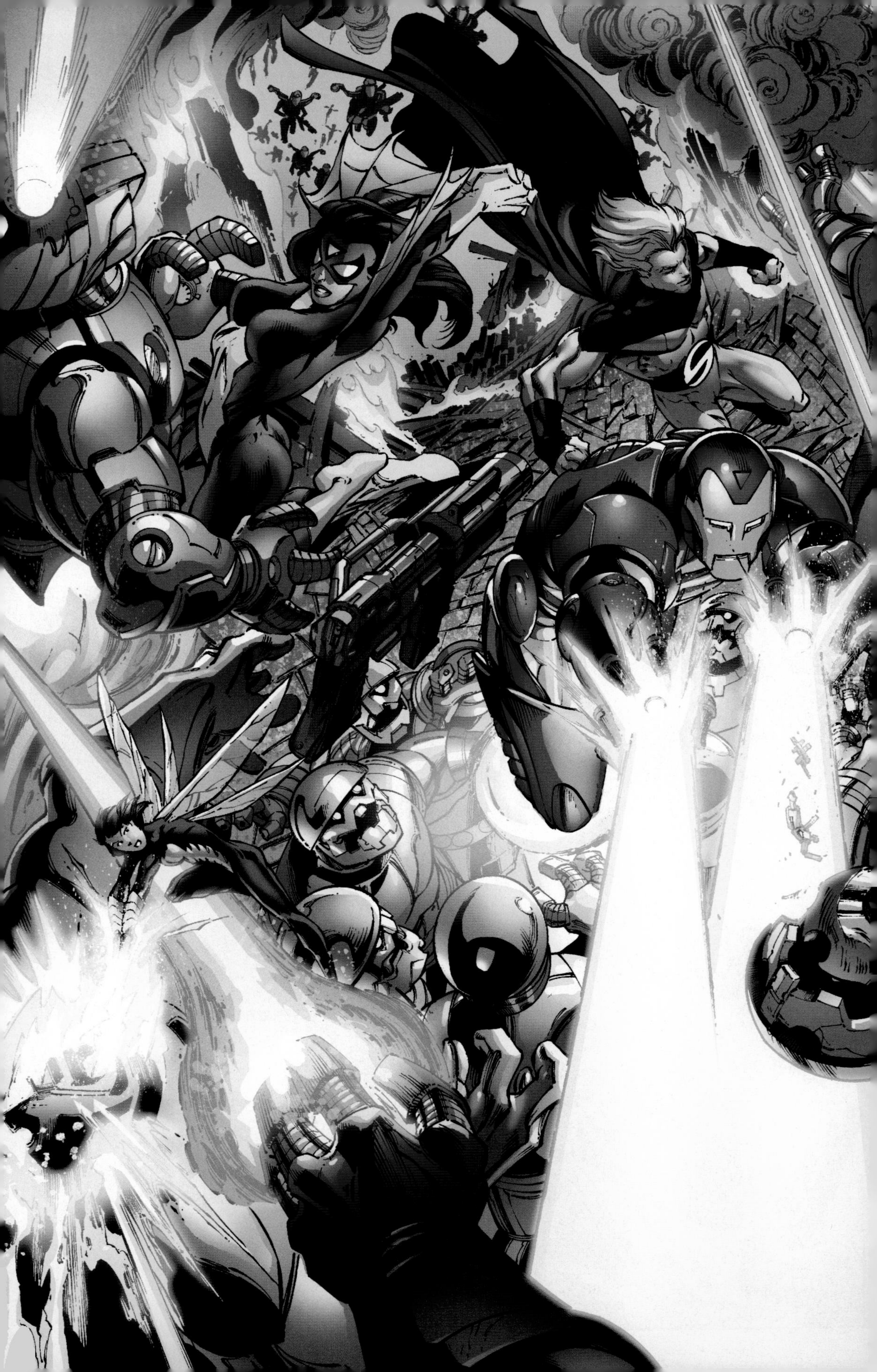

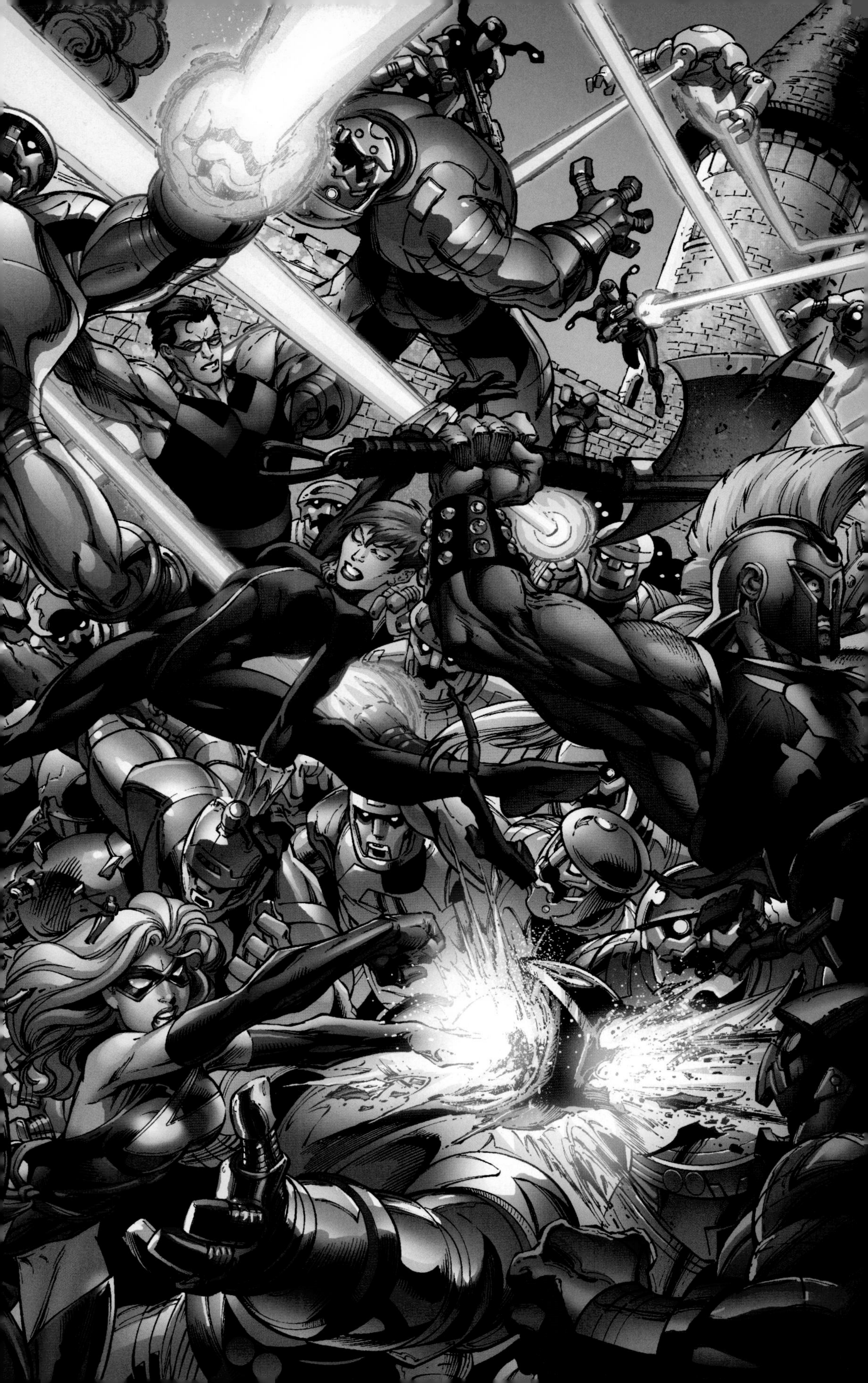

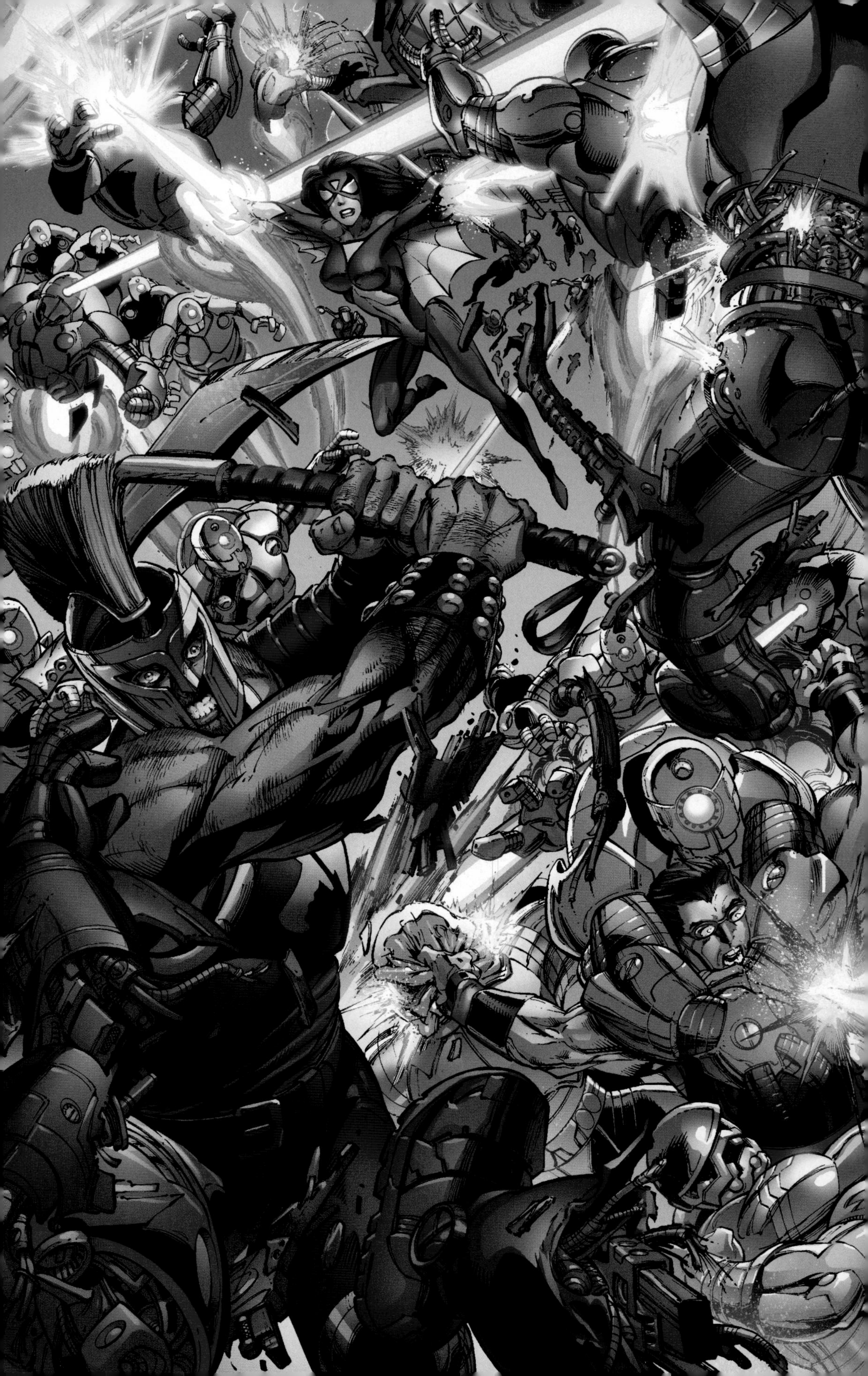

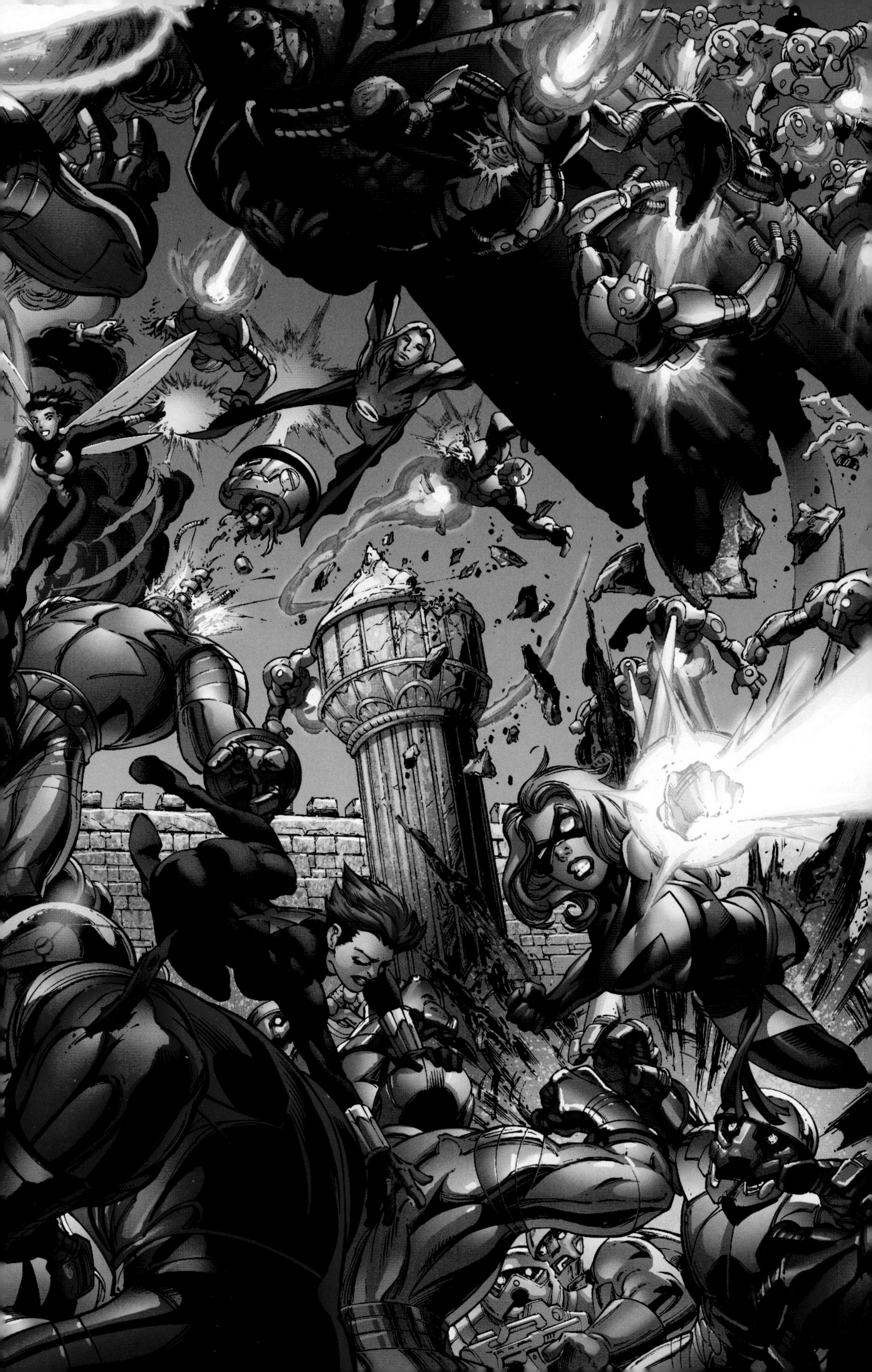

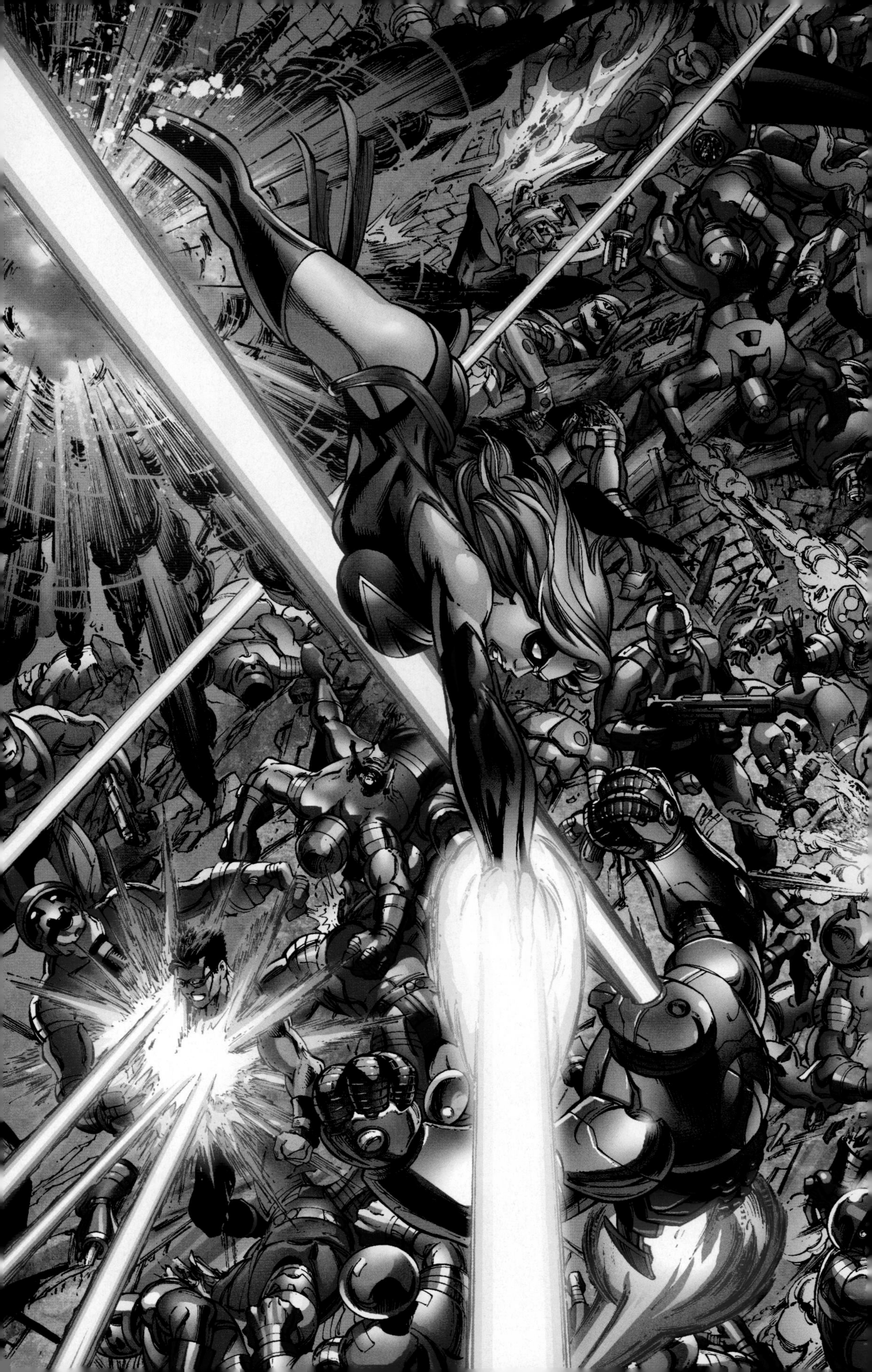

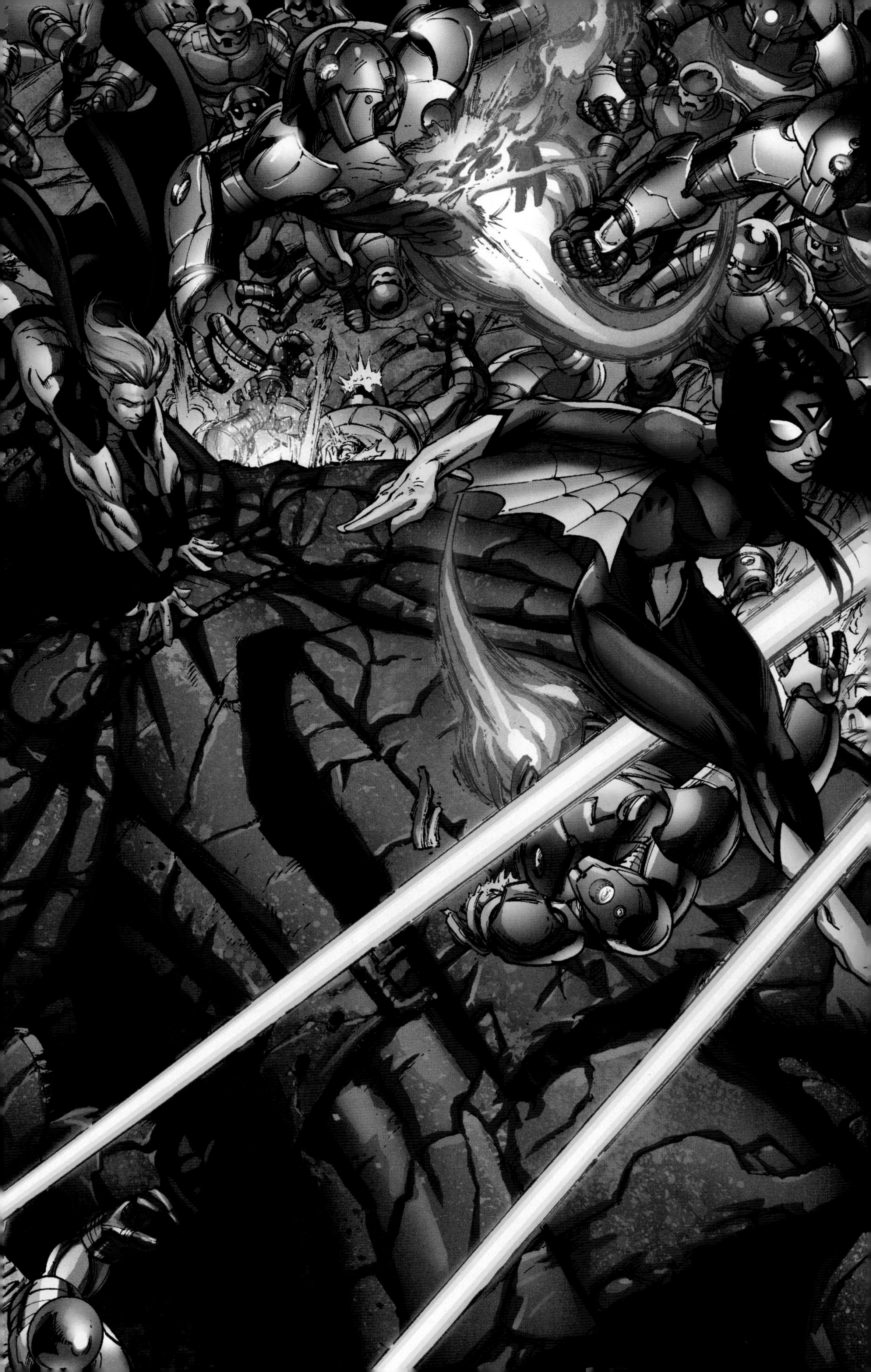

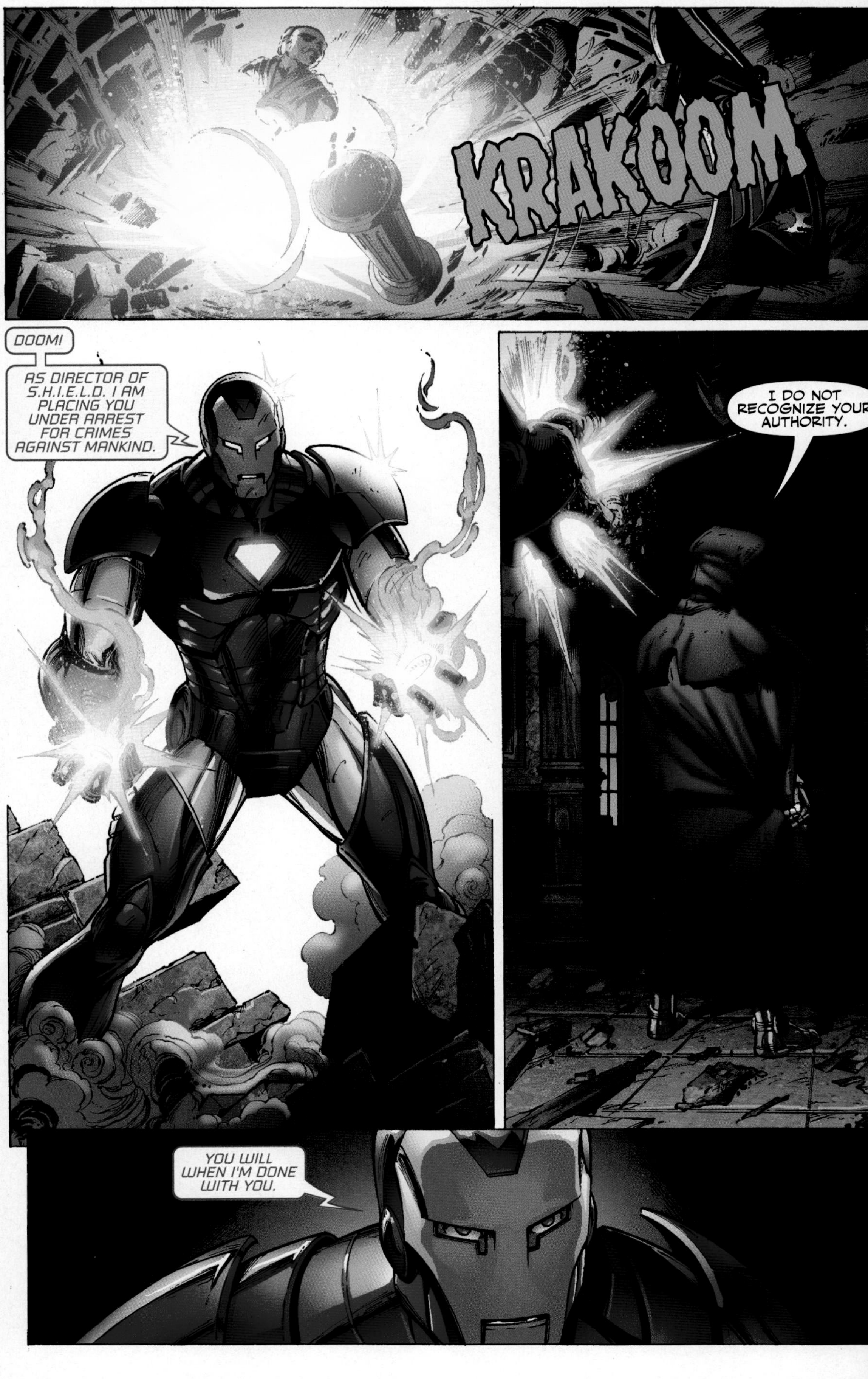
KRAKOOM
DOOM!
AS DIRECTOR OF S.H.I.E.L.D. I AM PLACING YOU UNDER ARREST FOR CRIMES AGAINST MANKIND.
I DO NOT RECOGNIZE YOUR AUTHORITY.
YOU WILL WHEN I'M DONE WITH YOU.

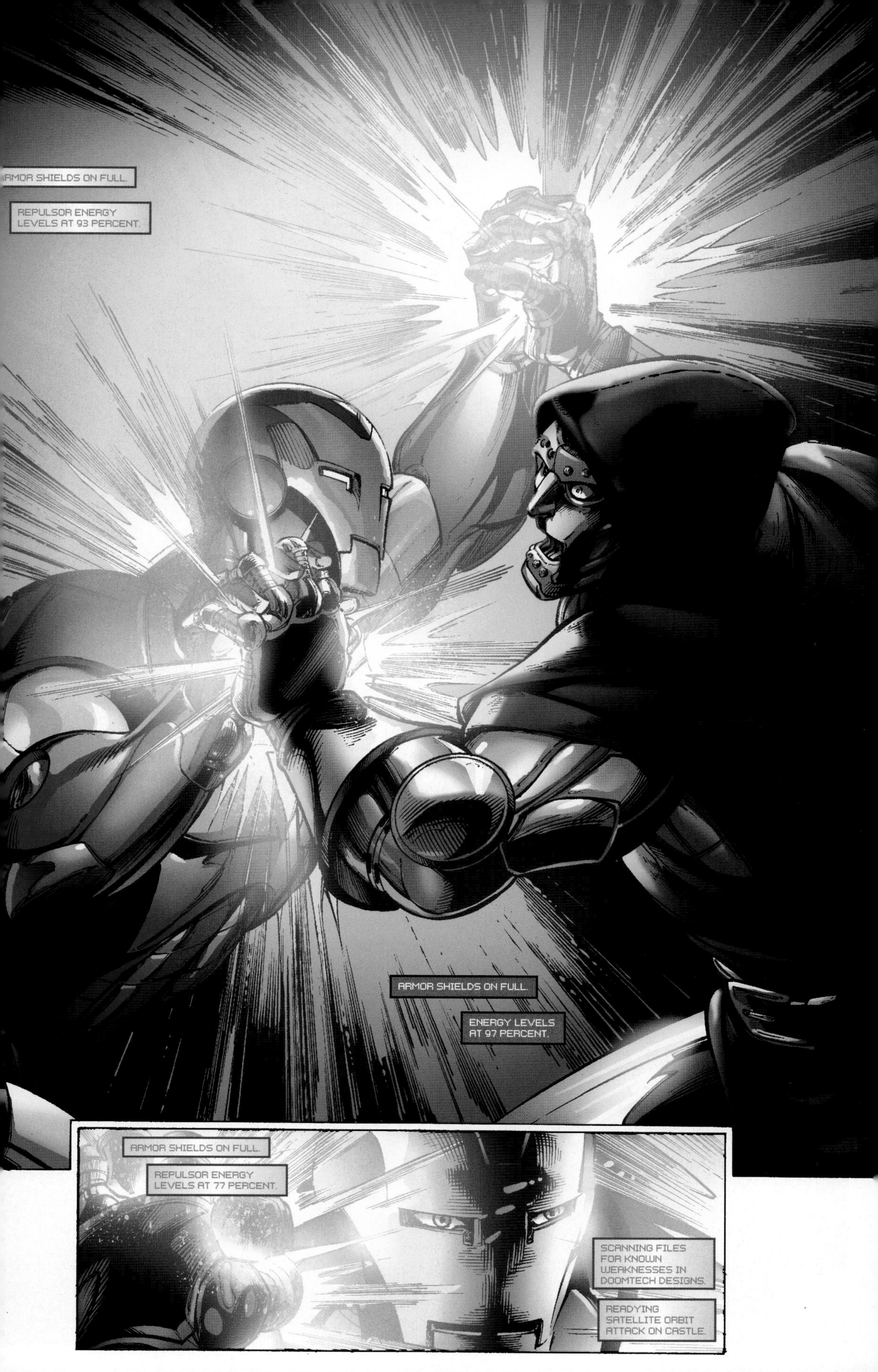
ARMOR SHIELDS ON FULL.
REPULSOR ENERGY LEVELS AT 93 PERCENT.
ARMOR SHIELDS ON FULL.
ENERGY LEVELS AT 97 PERCENT.
ARMOR SHIELDS ON FULL.
REPULSOR ENERGY LEVELS AT 77 PERCENT.
SCANNING FILES FOR KNOWN WEAKNESSES IN DOOMTECH DESIGNS.
READYING SATELLITE ORBIT ATTACK ON CASTLE.

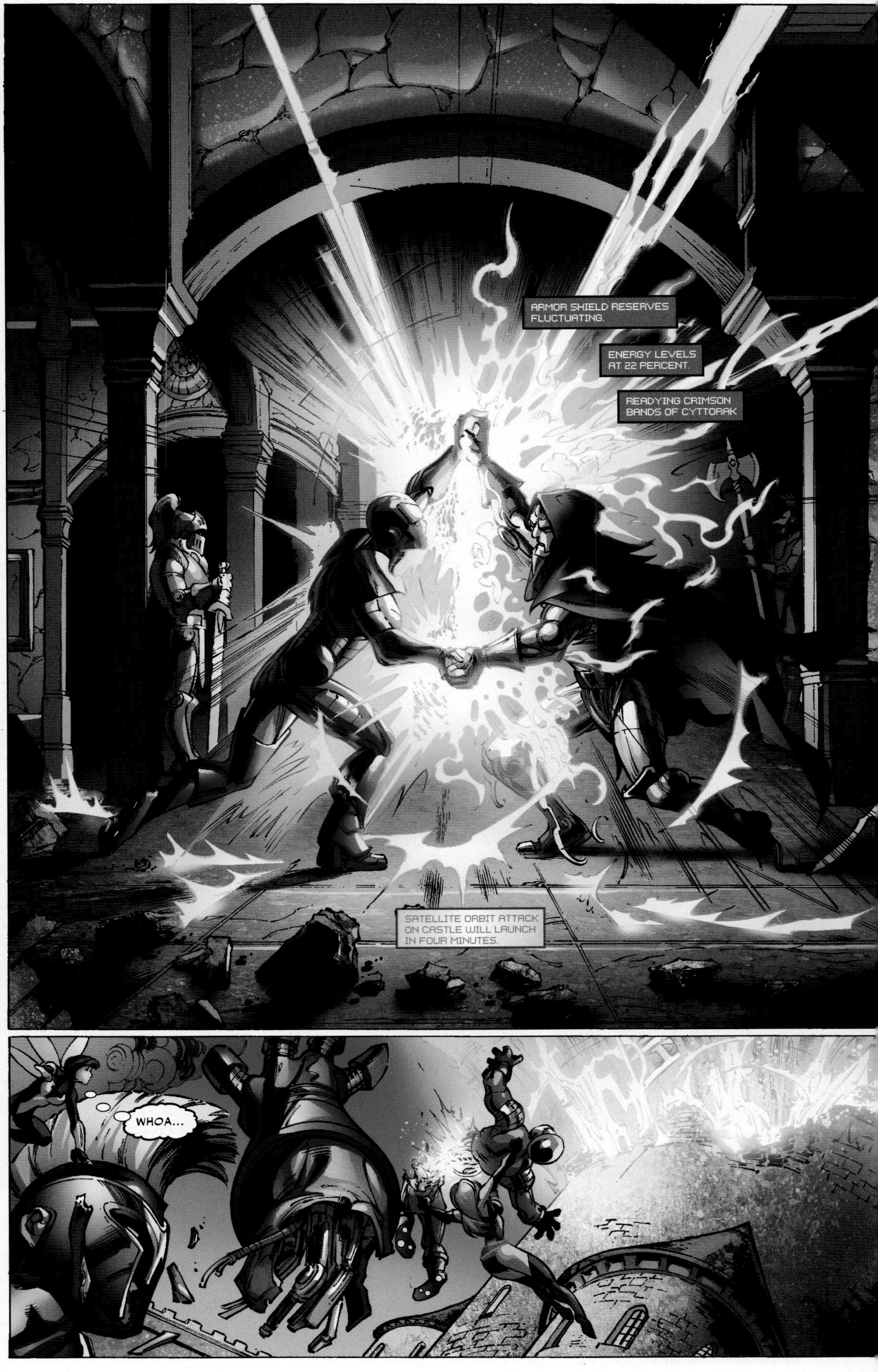
ARMOR SHIELD RESERVES FLUCTUATING.
ENERGY LEVELS AT 22 PERCENT.
READYING CRIMSON BANDS OF CYTTORAK
SATELLITE ORBIT ATTACK ON CASTLE WILL LAUNCH IN FOUR MINUTES.
WHOA...

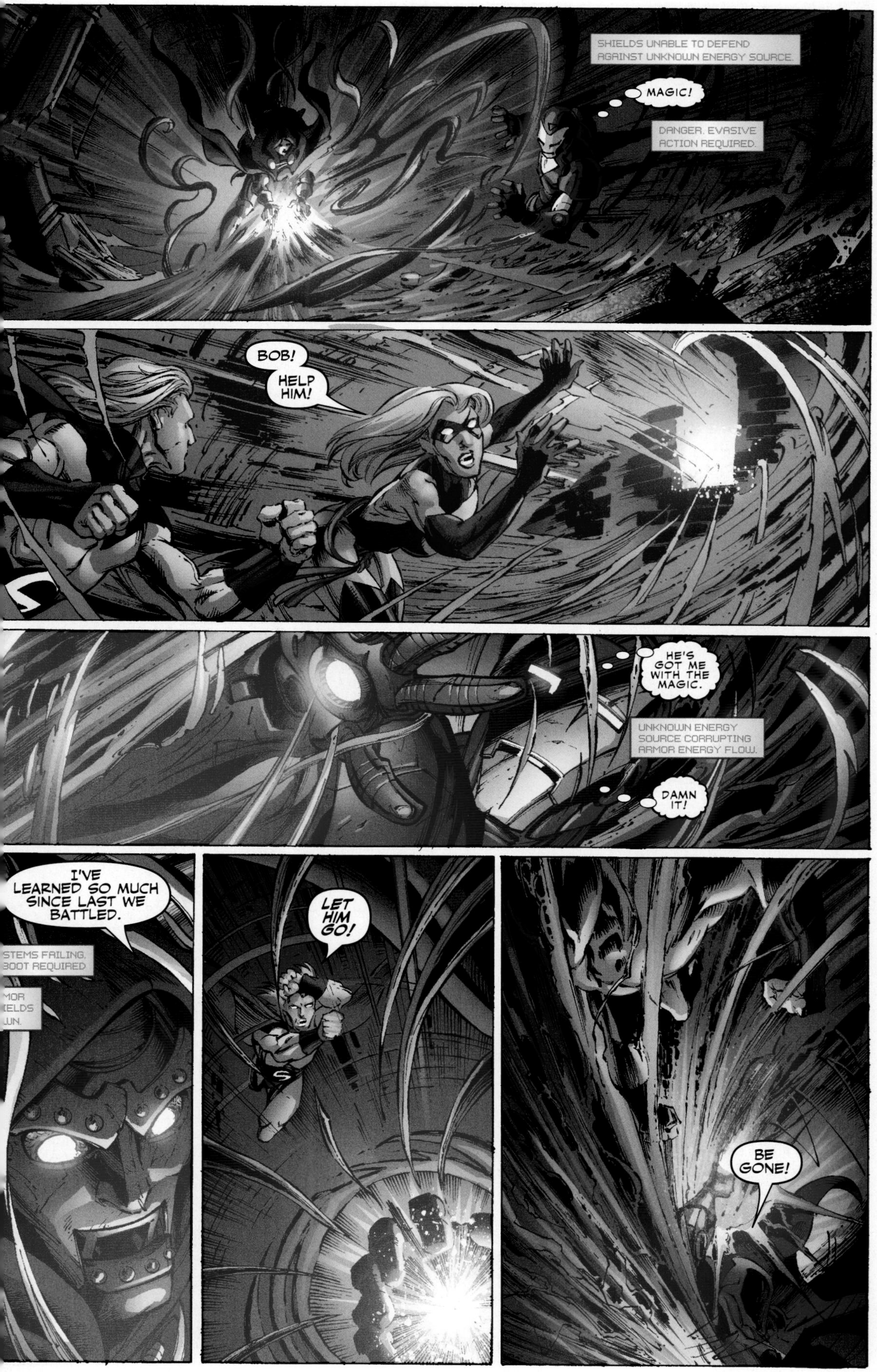
SHIELDS UNABLE TO DEFEND AGAINST UNKNOWN ENERGY SOURCE.
MAGIC!
DANGER. EVASIVE ACTION REQUIRED.
BOB! HELP HIM!
HE'S GOT ME WITH THE MAGIC.
UNKNOWN ENERGY SOURCE CORRUPTING ARMOR ENERGY FLOW.
DAMN IT!
I'VE LEARNED SO MUCH SINCE LAST WE BATTLED.
STEMS FAILING. BOOT REQUIRED
LET HIM GO!
BE GONE!

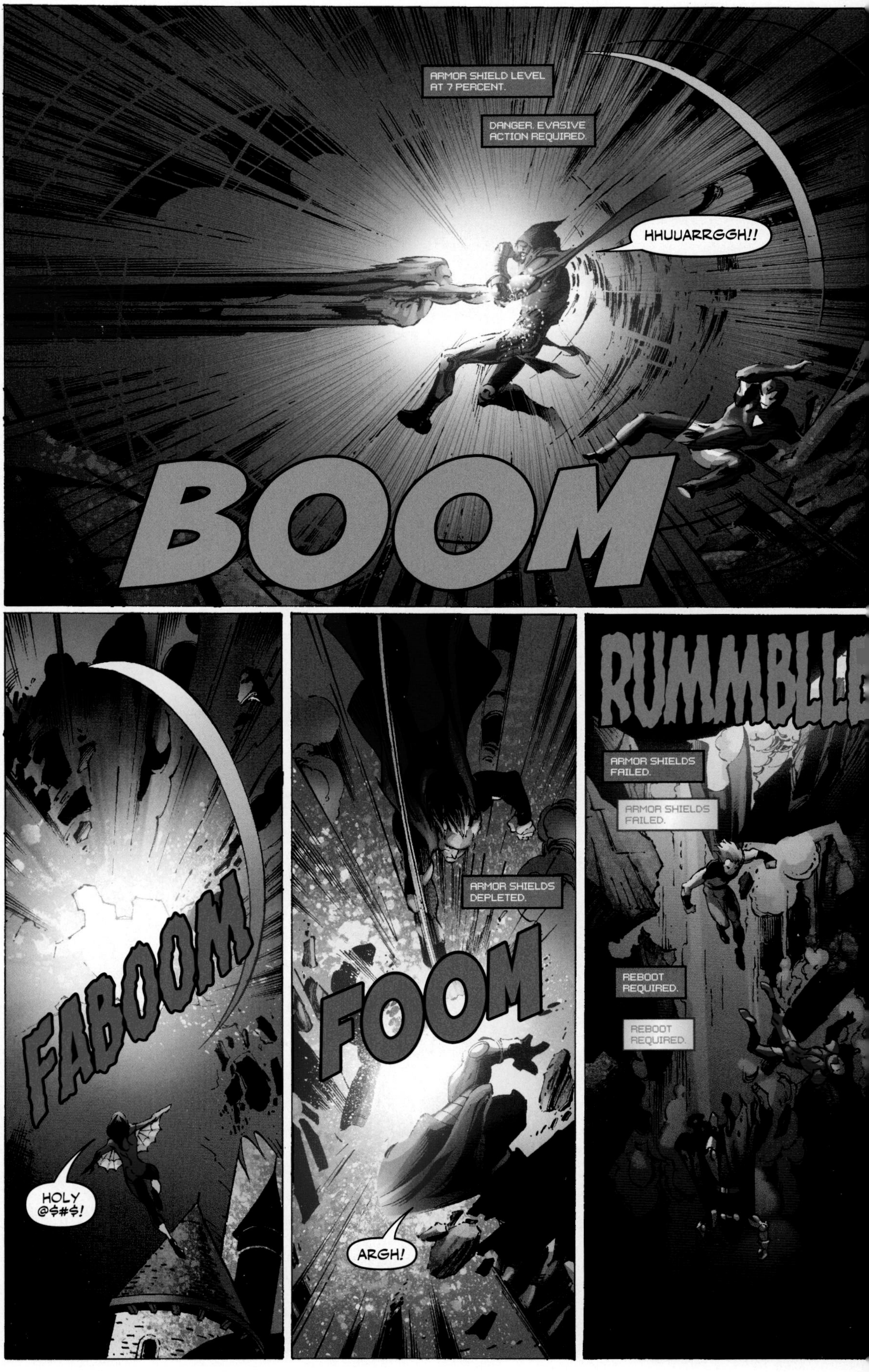
ARMOR SHIELD LEVEL AT 7 PERCENT.
DANGER. EVASIVE ACTION REQUIRED.
HHUUARRGGH!!
BOOM
FABOOM
HOLY @$#$!
ARMOR SHIELDS DEPLETED.
FOOM
ARGH!
RUMMBLLE
ARMOR SHIELDS FAILED.
ARMOR SHIELDS FAILED.
REBOOT REQUIRED.
REBOOT REQUIRED.

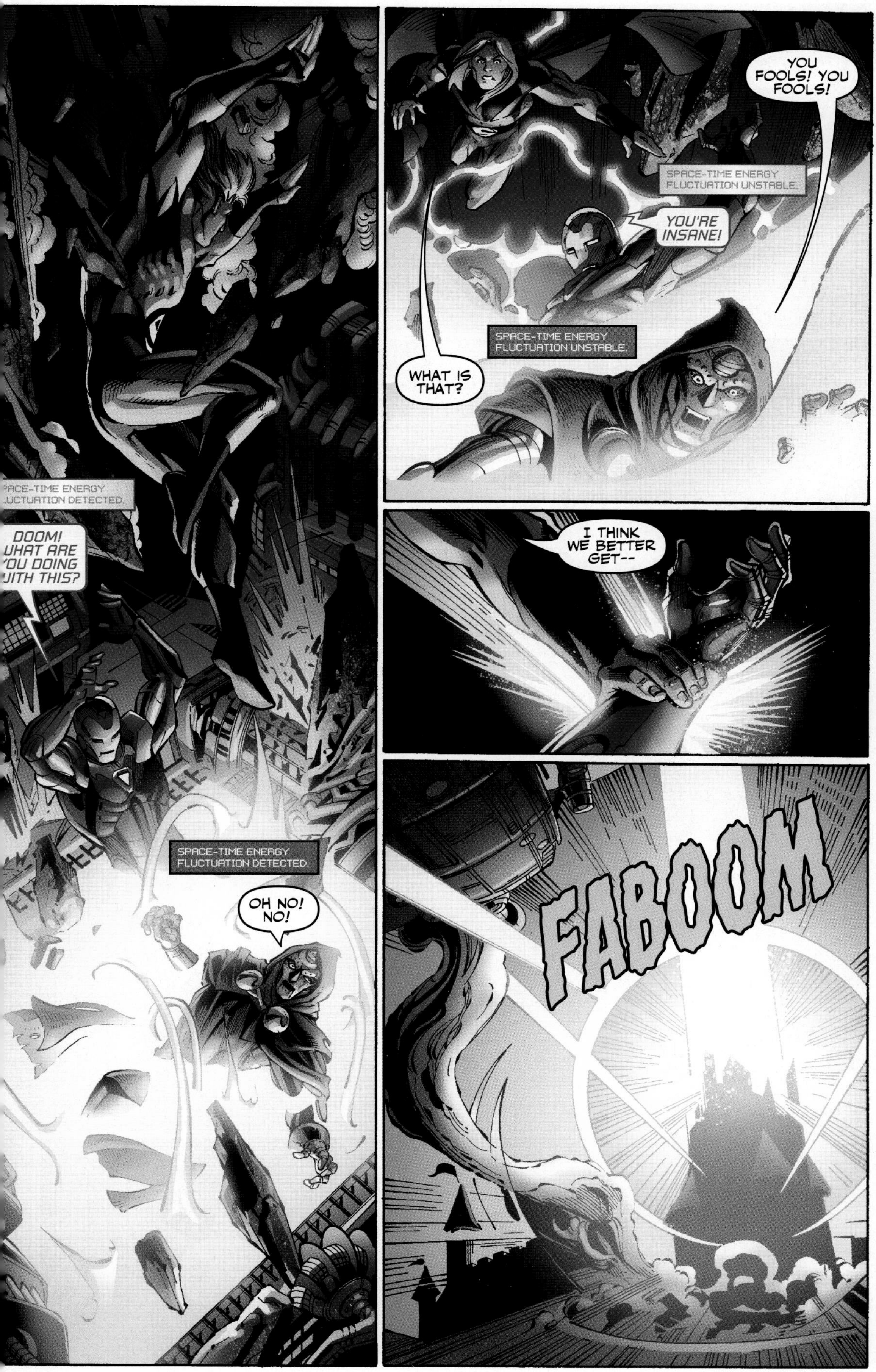
SPACE-TIME ENERGY FLUCTUATION DETECTED.
DOOM! WHAT ARE YOU DOING WITH THIS?
SPACE-TIME ENERGY FLUCTUATION DETECTED.
OH NO! NO!
YOU FOOLS! YOU FOOLS!
SPACE-TIME ENERGY FLUCTUATION UNSTABLE.
YOU'RE INSANE!
SPACE-TIME ENERGY FLUCTUATION UNSTABLE.
WHAT IS THAT?
I THINK WE BETTER GET--
FABOOM

HA HA! NOW *THAT* WAS A BATTLE!

WELL, AT LEAST WE KNOW WHAT IT TAKES TO MAKE HIM HAPPY.

EVERYONE OKAY?

PEACHY!

OH NO!

TONY!

I GOT A BAD FEELING ABOUT THIS.

UH, WHAT'S THAT GLOWING THING?

TONY!

COMMANDER HILL, YOU UP THERE? IS TONY ONLINE?

THIS IS HILL. HE'S--OH, HE'S OFF THE GRID.

UH-OH...

HOW ABOUT THE SENTRY OR DOOM?

WE--THE GUYS ARE TELLING ME THERE'S A MASSIVE FLUCTUATION.

THEY'RE HAVING TROUBLE GETTING EVERYTHING OFF THE SATELLITES.

OH NO.

IS THAT--

WHAT IS IT? WHAT'S DOWN THERE?

WHAT IS IT?

WHOA!

BACK! EVERYBODY *BACK!*

WHAT IS THAT?

IT'S DOOM'S @#$% TIME PLATFORM.

IF TONY AND BOB AND DOOM WERE DOWN THERE WHEN THE THING WENT OFF...

IF IT'S BROKEN LIKE THAT...

THEN THEY'RE *WHAT?* LO SOMEWHE IN TIME

THAT WOULD BE THE GOOD NEWS...

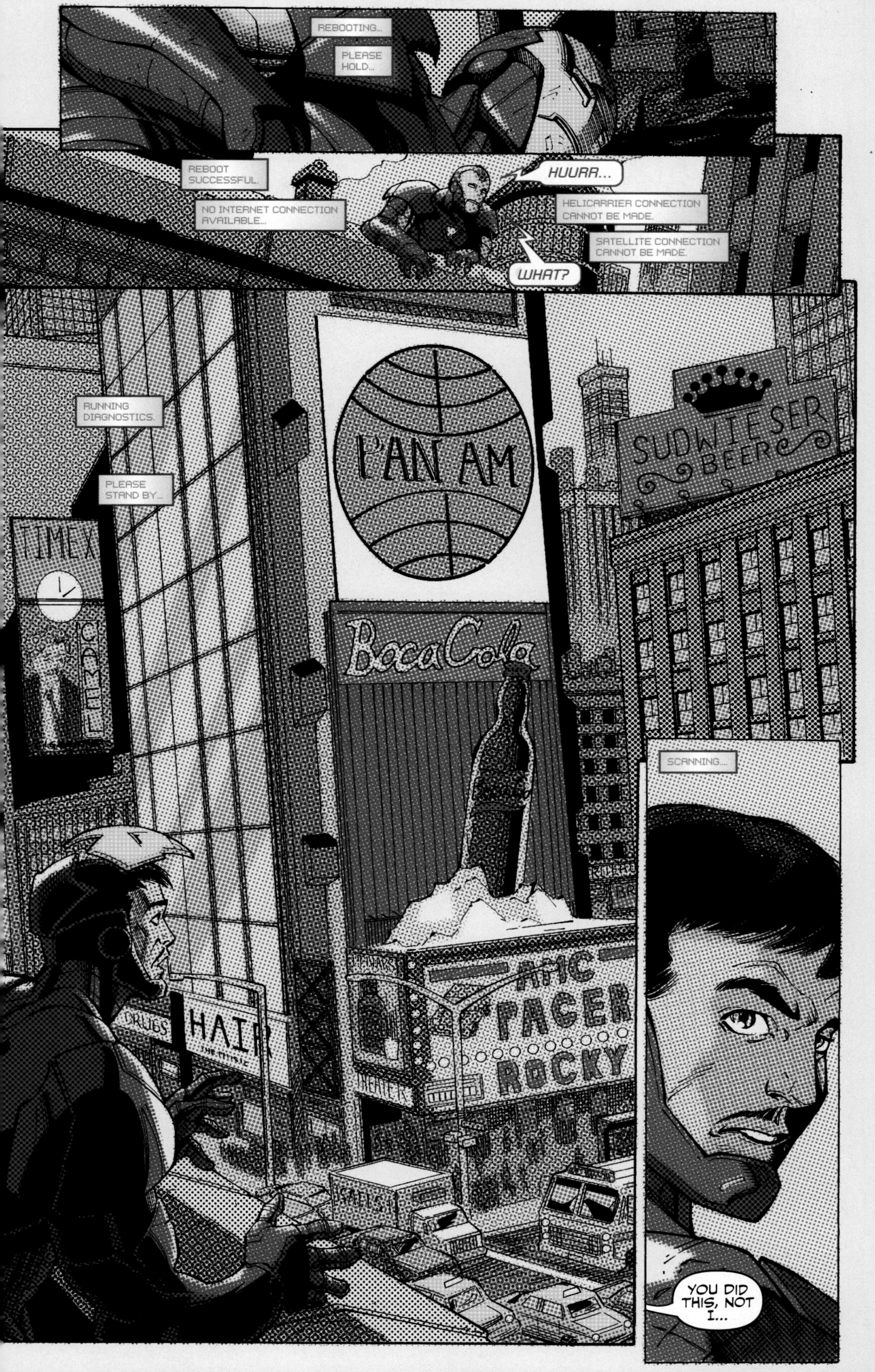
REBOOTING...
PLEASE HOLD...
REBOOT SUCCESSFUL.
NO INTERNET CONNECTION AVAILABLE...
HUURR...
HELICARRIER CONNECTION CANNOT BE MADE.
SATELLITE CONNECTION CANNOT BE MADE.
WHAT?
RUNNING DIAGNOSTICS.
PLEASE STAND BY...
PAN AM
SUDWIESER BEER
TIMEX
CAMEL
Boca Cola
HAIR
DRUGS
THEATER
AMC PACER ROCKY
SCANNING...
YOU DID THIS, NOT I...

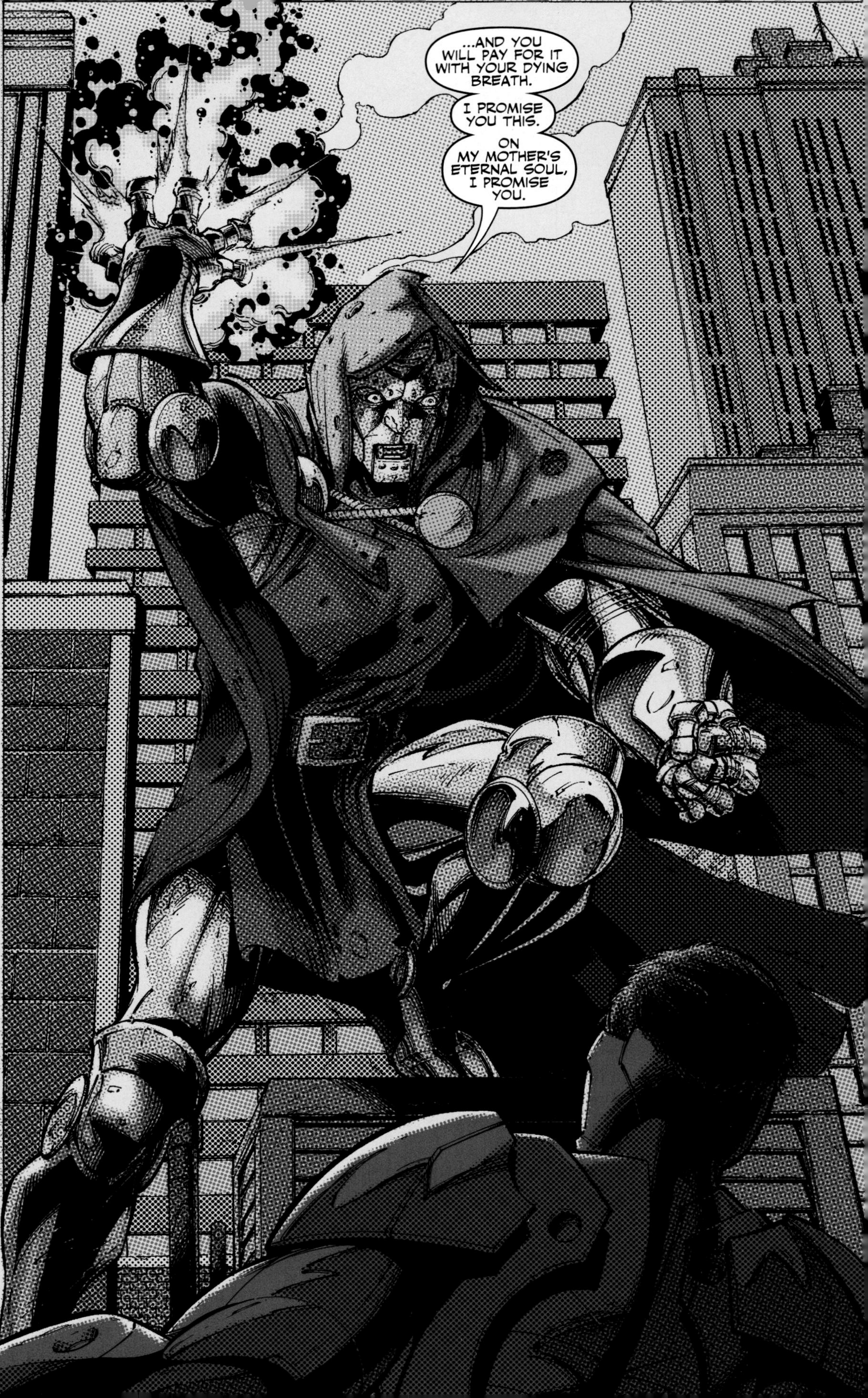
...AND YOU WILL PAY FOR IT WITH YOUR DYING BREATH.
I PROMISE YOU THIS.
ON MY MOTHER'S ETERNAL SOUL, I PROMISE YOU.

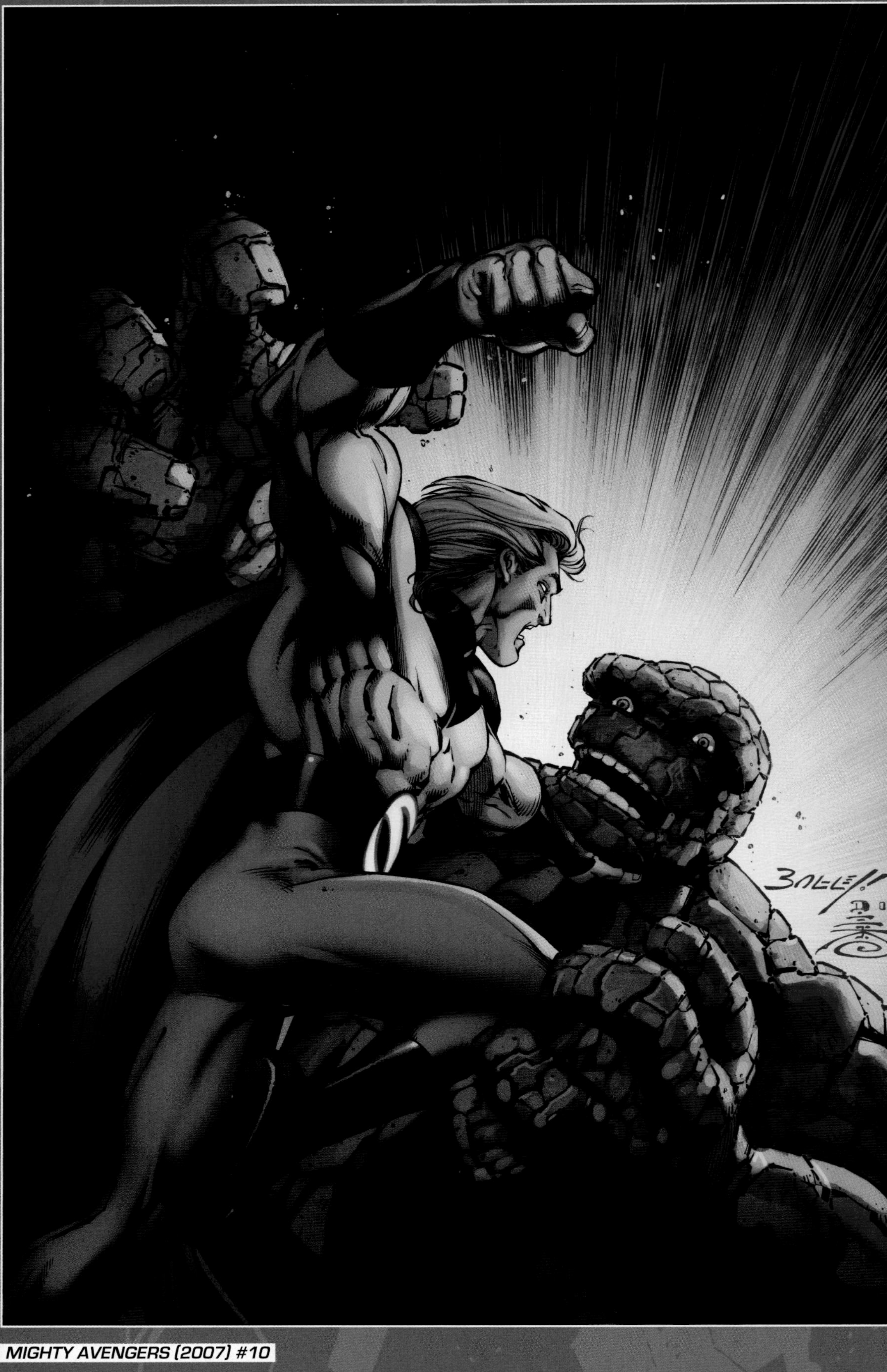

MIGHTY AVENGERS (2007) #10

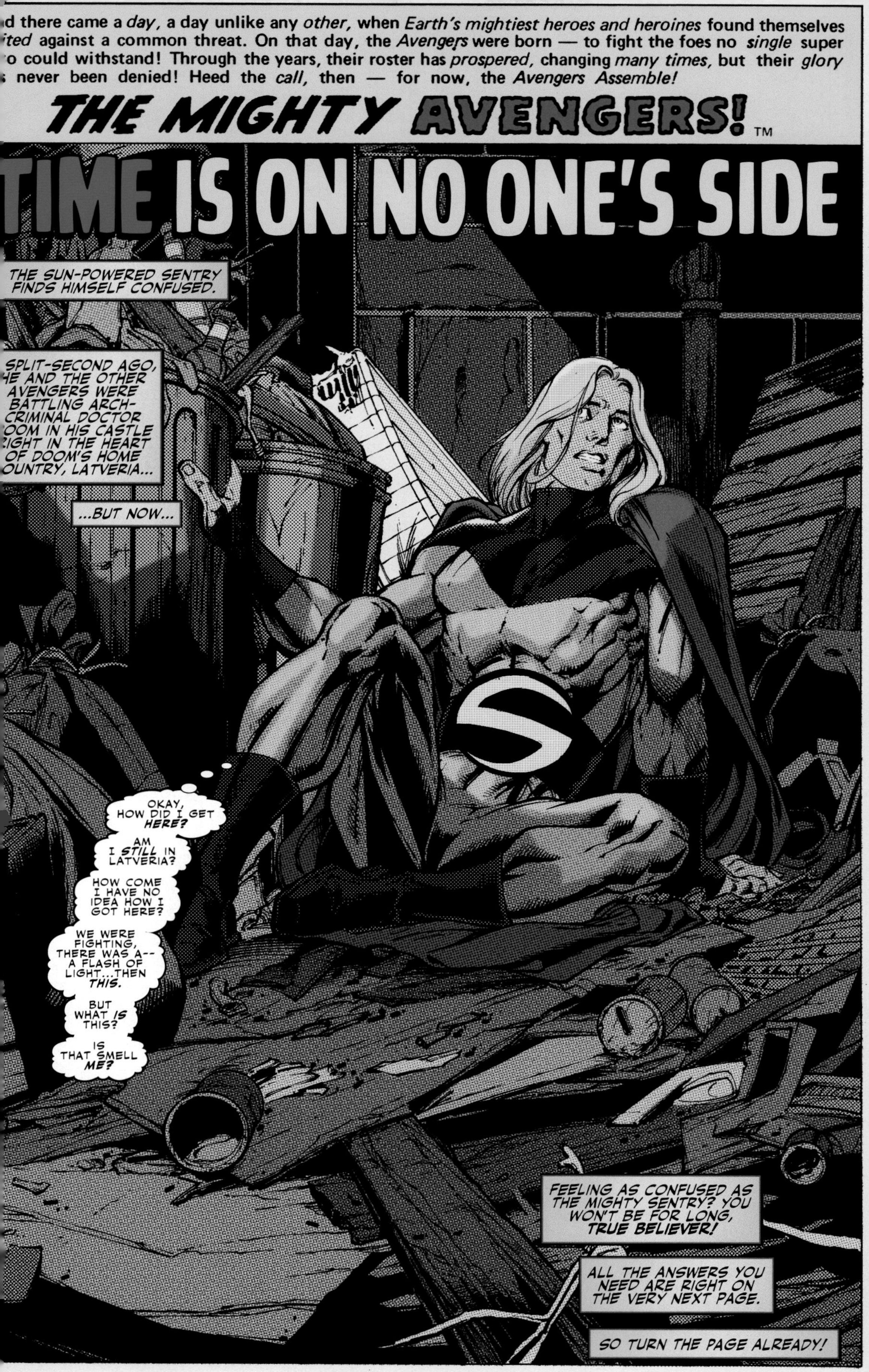

d there came a day, a day unlike any other, when Earth's mightiest heroes and heroines found themselves ited against a common threat. On that day, the Avengers were born — to fight the foes no single super o could withstand! Through the years, their roster has prospered, changing many times, but their glory never been denied! Heed the call, then — for now, the Avengers Assemble!
THE MIGHTY AVENGERS!™
TIME IS ON NO ONE'S SIDE
THE SUN-POWERED SENTRY FINDS HIMSELF CONFUSED.
SPLIT-SECOND AGO, HE AND THE OTHER AVENGERS WERE BATTLING ARCH-CRIMINAL DOCTOR OOM IN HIS CASTLE IGHT IN THE HEART OF DOOM'S HOME OUNTRY, LATVERIA...
...BUT NOW...
OKAY, HOW DID I GET HERE?
AM I STILL IN LATVERIA?
HOW COME I HAVE NO IDEA HOW I GOT HERE?
WE WERE FIGHTING, THERE WAS A-- A FLASH OF LIGHT...THEN THIS.
BUT WHAT IS THIS?
IS THAT SMELL ME?
FEELING AS CONFUSED AS THE MIGHTY SENTRY? YOU WON'T BE FOR LONG, TRUE BELIEVER!
ALL THE ANSWERS YOU NEED ARE RIGHT ON THE VERY NEXT PAGE.
SO TURN THE PAGE ALREADY!

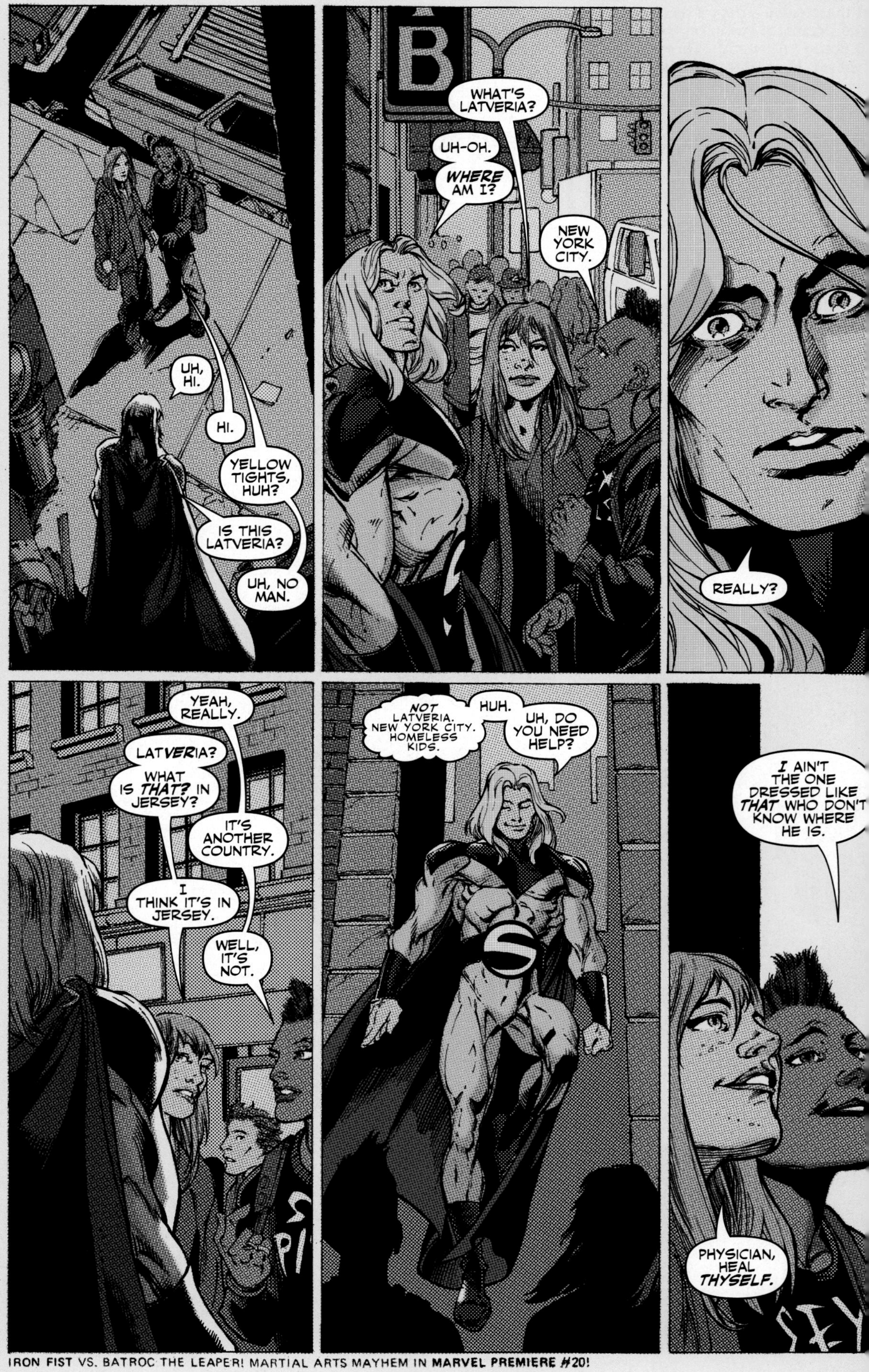
UH, HI.
HI.
YELLOW TIGHTS, HUH?
IS THIS LATVERIA?
UH, NO MAN.
WHAT'S LATVERIA?
UH-OH.
WHERE AM I?
NEW YORK CITY.
REALLY?
YEAH, REALLY.
LATVERIA?
WHAT IS THAT? IN JERSEY?
IT'S ANOTHER COUNTRY.
I THINK IT'S IN JERSEY.
WELL, IT'S NOT.
NOT LATVERIA. NEW YORK CITY. HOMELESS KIDS.
HUH.
UH, DO YOU NEED HELP?
I AIN'T THE ONE DRESSED LIKE THAT WHO DON'T KNOW WHERE HE IS.
PHYSICIAN, HEAL THYSELF.

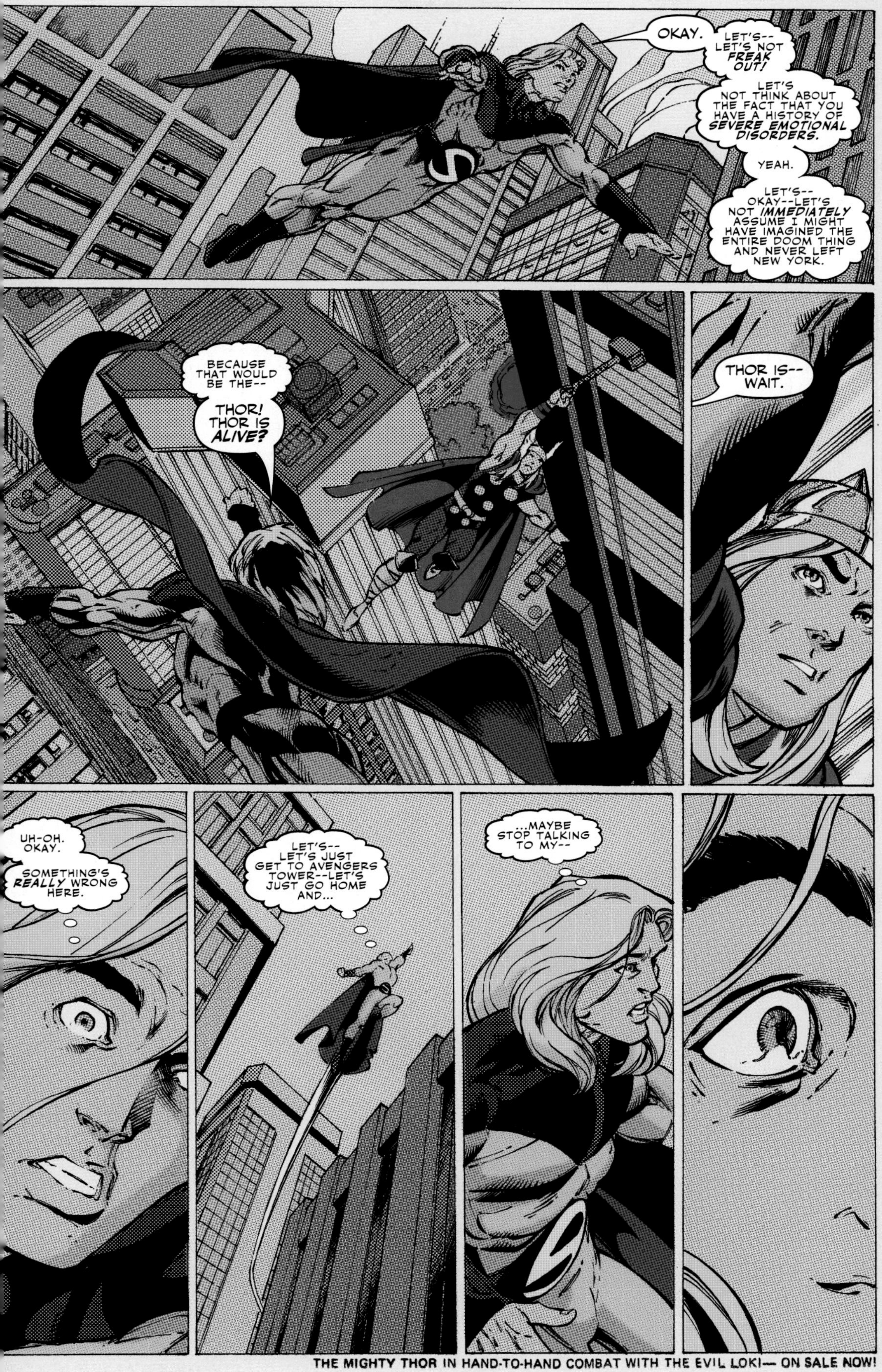
OKAY.
LET'S-- LET'S NOT FREAK OUT!
LET'S NOT THINK ABOUT THE FACT THAT YOU HAVE A HISTORY OF SEVERE EMOTIONAL DISORDERS.
YEAH.
LET'S-- OKAY--LET'S NOT IMMEDIATELY ASSUME I MIGHT HAVE IMAGINED THE ENTIRE DOOM THING AND NEVER LEFT NEW YORK.
BECAUSE THAT WOULD BE THE--
THOR! THOR IS ALIVE?
THOR IS-- WAIT.
UH-OH. OKAY.
SOMETHING'S REALLY WRONG HERE.
LET'S-- LET'S JUST GET TO AVENGERS TOWER--LET'S JUST GO HOME AND...
...MAYBE STOP TALKING TO MY--

THE MIGHTY THOR IN HAND-TO-HAND COMBAT WITH THE EVIL LOKI— ON SALE NOW!

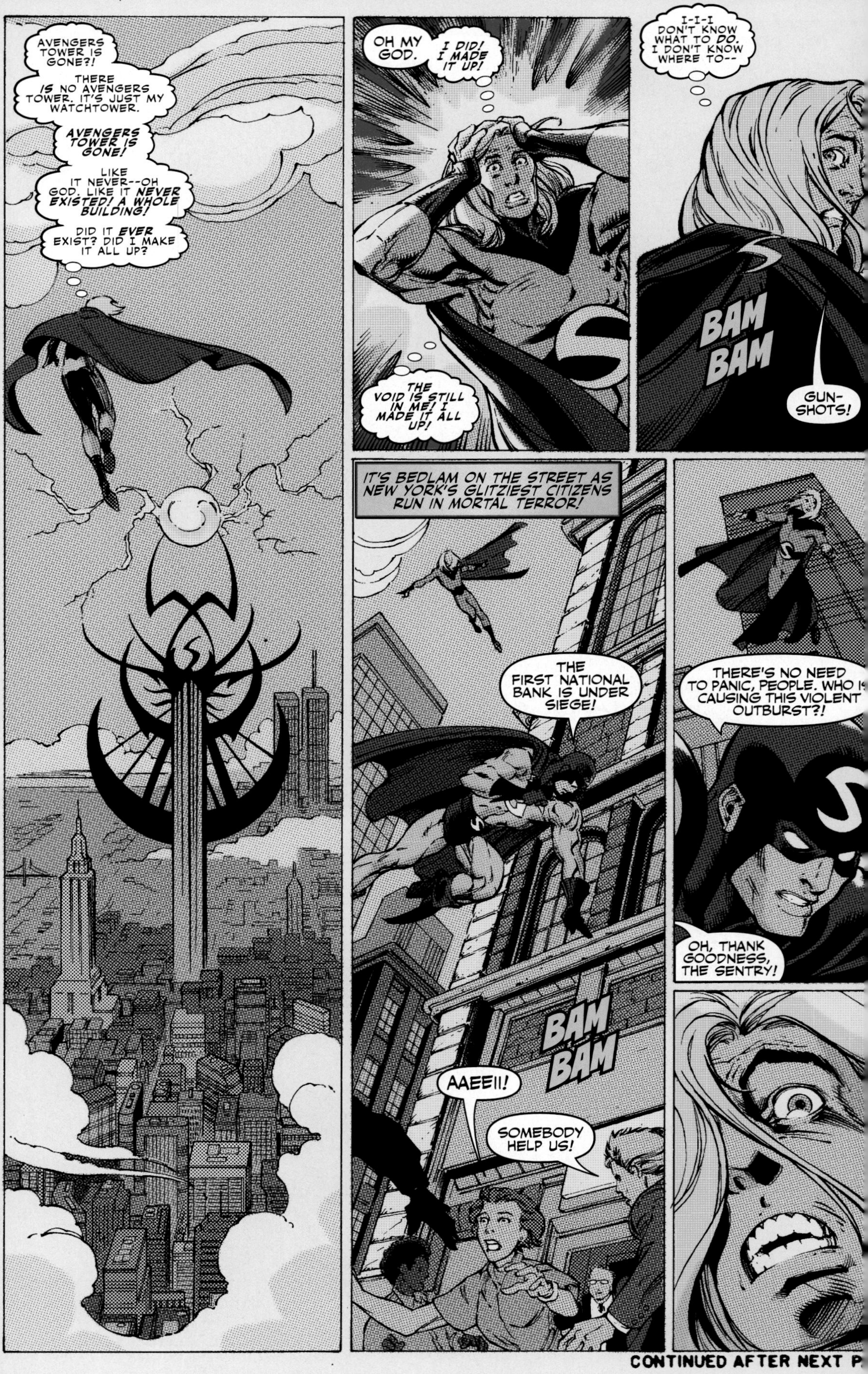
AVENGERS TOWER IS GONE?!
THERE *IS* NO AVENGERS TOWER. IT'S JUST MY WATCHTOWER.
AVENGERS TOWER IS GONE!
LIKE IT NEVER--OH GOD. LIKE IT *NEVER EXISTED! A WHOLE BUILDING!*
DID IT *EVER* EXIST? DID I MAKE IT ALL UP?
OH MY GOD.
I DID! I MADE IT UP!
THE VOID IS STILL IN ME! I MADE IT ALL UP!
I-I-I DON'T KNOW WHAT TO *DO*. I DON'T KNOW WHERE TO--
BAM BAM
GUN-SHOTS!
IT'S BEDLAM ON THE STREET AS NEW YORK'S GLITZIEST CITIZENS RUN IN MORTAL TERROR!
THE FIRST NATIONAL BANK IS UNDER SIEGE!
BAM BAM
AAEEII!
SOMEBODY HELP US!
THERE'S NO NEED TO PANIC, PEOPLE. WHO IS CAUSING THIS VIOLENT OUTBURST?!
OH, THANK GOODNESS, THE SENTRY!

CONTINUED AFTER NEXT P

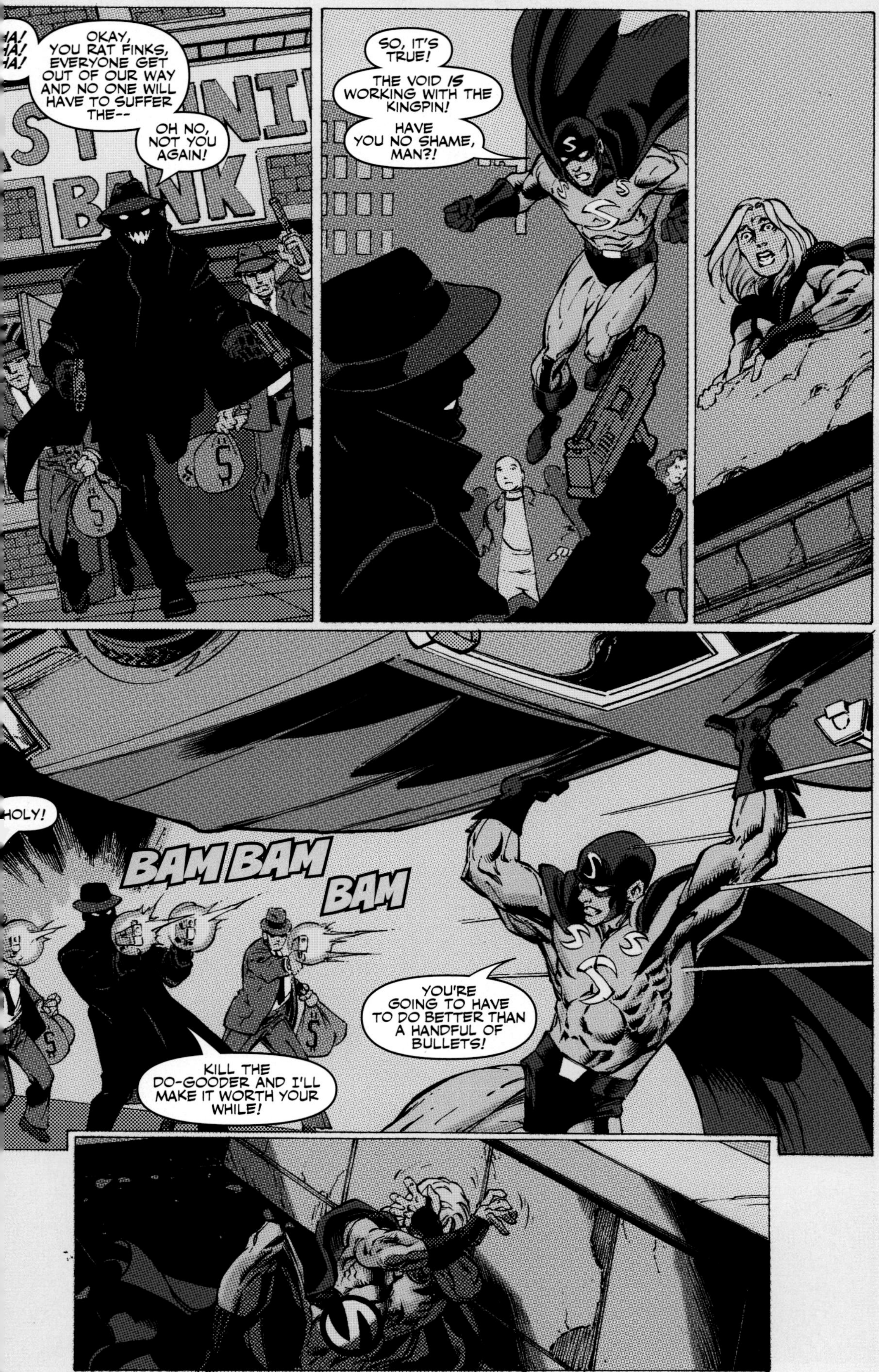
HA! HA! HA!
OKAY, YOU RAT FINKS, EVERYONE GET OUT OF OUR WAY AND NO ONE WILL HAVE TO SUFFER THE--
OH NO, NOT YOU AGAIN!
BANK
SO, IT'S TRUE!
THE VOID IS WORKING WITH THE KINGPIN!
HAVE YOU NO SHAME, MAN?!
HOLY!
BAM BAM BAM
YOU'RE GOING TO HAVE TO DO BETTER THAN A HANDFUL OF BULLETS!
KILL THE DO-GOODER AND I'LL MAKE IT WORTH YOUR WHILE!

'T'S IT LIKE TO BE A LIVING VAMPIRE? FIND OUT IN THE PAGES OF FEAR— 'CAUSE **ONLY** MORBIUS KNOWS!

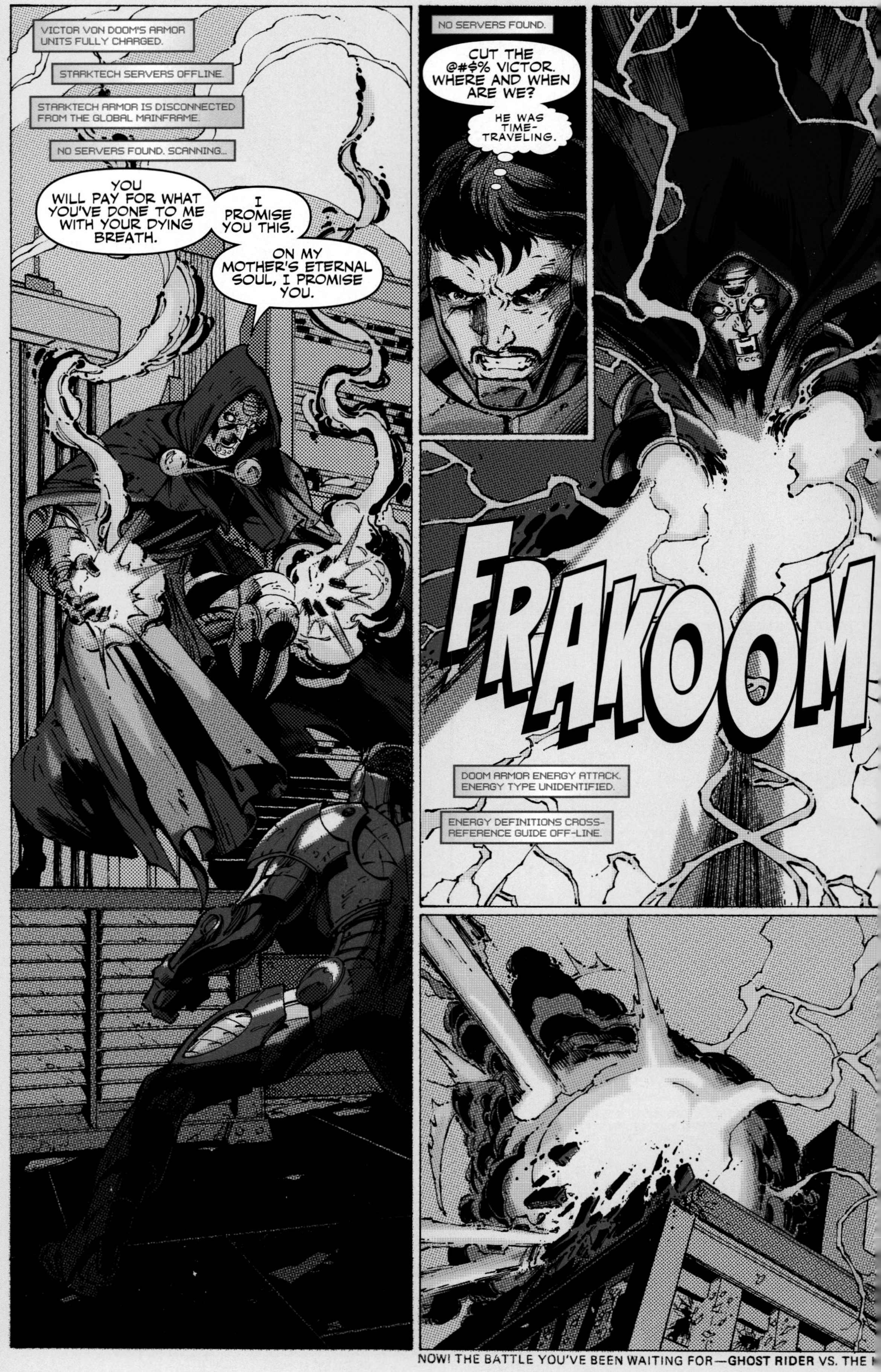
VICTOR VON DOOM'S ARMOR UNITS FULLY CHARGED.
STARKTECH SERVERS OFFLINE.
STARKTECH ARMOR IS DISCONNECTED FROM THE GLOBAL MAINFRAME.
NO SERVERS FOUND. SCANNING...
YOU WILL PAY FOR WHAT YOU'VE DONE TO ME WITH YOUR DYING BREATH.
I PROMISE YOU THIS.
ON MY MOTHER'S ETERNAL SOUL, I PROMISE YOU.
NO SERVERS FOUND.
CUT THE @#$% VICTOR. WHERE AND WHEN ARE WE?
HE WAS TIME-TRAVELING.
FRAKOOM
DOOM ARMOR ENERGY ATTACK. ENERGY TYPE UNIDENTIFIED.
ENERGY DEFINITIONS CROSS-REFERENCE GUIDE OFF-LINE.

NOW! THE BATTLE YOU'VE BEEN WAITING FOR—**GHOST RIDER** VS. THE

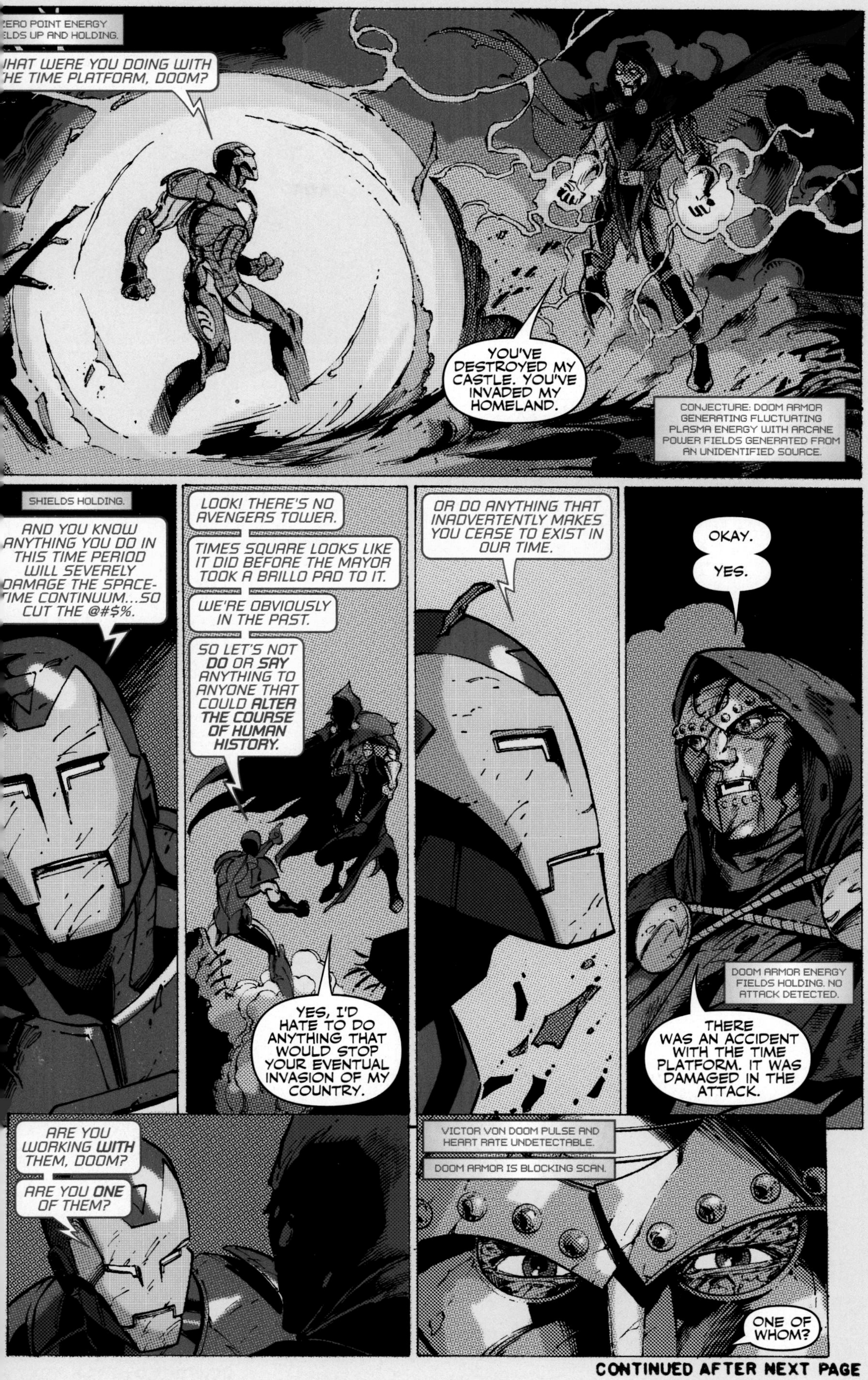

ZERO POINT ENERGY FIELDS UP AND HOLDING.
WHAT WERE YOU DOING WITH THE TIME PLATFORM, DOOM?
YOU'VE DESTROYED MY CASTLE. YOU'VE INVADED MY HOMELAND.
CONJECTURE: DOOM ARMOR GENERATING FLUCTUATING PLASMA ENERGY WITH ARCANE POWER FIELDS GENERATED FROM AN UNIDENTIFIED SOURCE.
SHIELDS HOLDING.
AND YOU KNOW ANYTHING YOU DO IN THIS TIME PERIOD WILL SEVERELY DAMAGE THE SPACE-TIME CONTINUUM...SO CUT THE @#$%.
LOOK! THERE'S NO AVENGERS TOWER.
TIMES SQUARE LOOKS LIKE IT DID BEFORE THE MAYOR TOOK A BRILLO PAD TO IT.
WE'RE OBVIOUSLY IN THE PAST.
SO LET'S NOT **DO** OR **SAY** ANYTHING TO ANYONE THAT COULD **ALTER THE COURSE OF HUMAN HISTORY.**
YES, I'D HATE TO DO ANYTHING THAT WOULD STOP YOUR EVENTUAL INVASION OF MY COUNTRY.
OR DO ANYTHING THAT INADVERTENTLY MAKES YOU CEASE TO EXIST IN OUR TIME.
OKAY.
YES.
DOOM ARMOR ENERGY FIELDS HOLDING. NO ATTACK DETECTED.
THERE WAS AN ACCIDENT WITH THE TIME PLATFORM. IT WAS DAMAGED IN THE ATTACK.
ARE YOU WORKING **WITH** THEM, DOOM?
ARE YOU **ONE** OF THEM?
VICTOR VON DOOM PULSE AND HEART RATE UNDETECTABLE.
DOOM ARMOR IS BLOCKING SCAN.
ONE OF WHOM?

CONTINUED AFTER NEXT PAGE

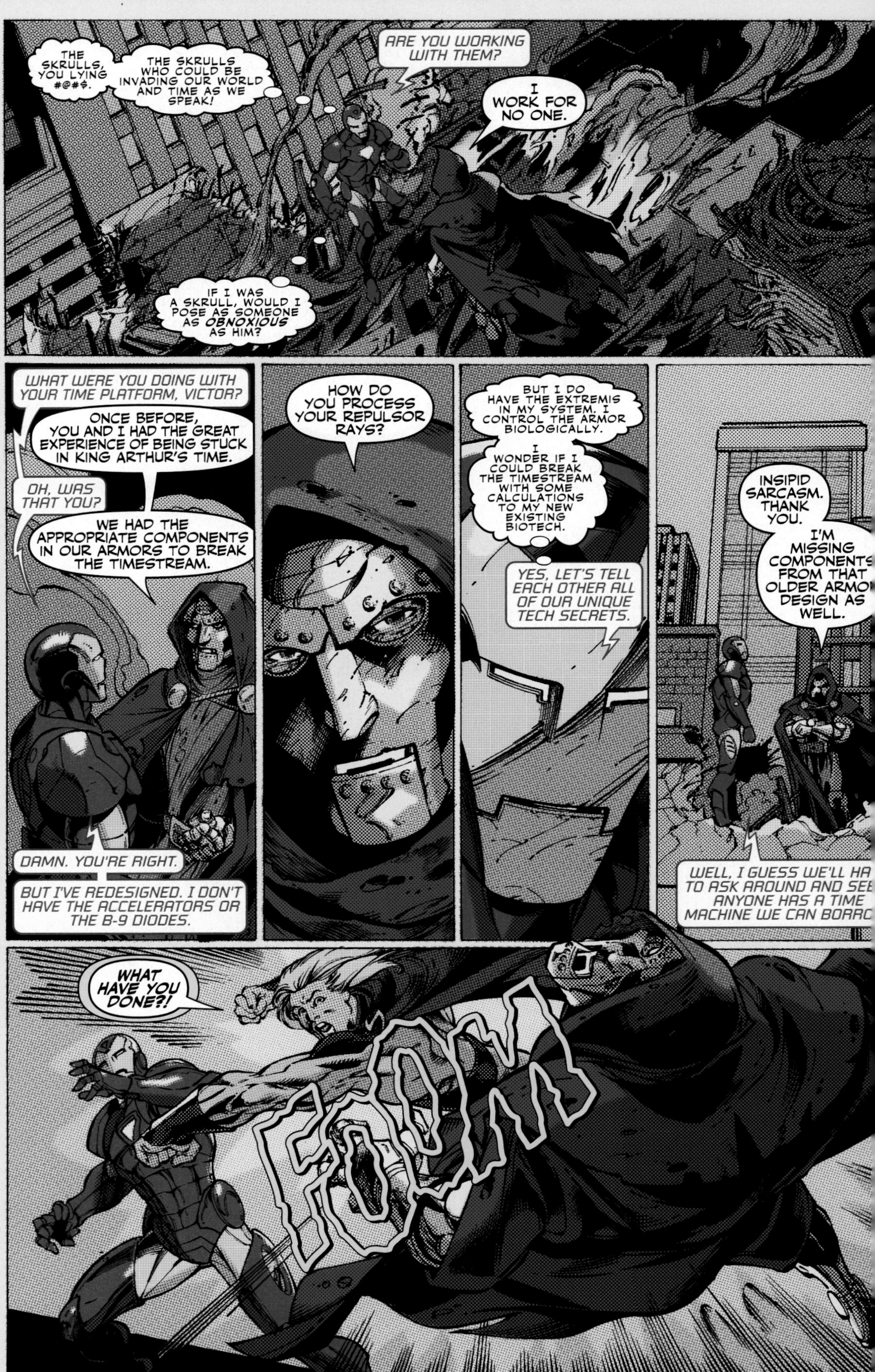
THE SKRULLS, YOU LYING #@#$.
THE SKRULLS WHO COULD BE INVADING OUR WORLD AND TIME AS WE SPEAK!
ARE YOU WORKING WITH THEM?
I WORK FOR NO ONE.
IF I WAS A SKRULL, WOULD I POSE AS SOMEONE AS OBNOXIOUS AS HIM?
WHAT WERE YOU DOING WITH YOUR TIME PLATFORM, VICTOR?
ONCE BEFORE, YOU AND I HAD THE GREAT EXPERIENCE OF BEING STUCK IN KING ARTHUR'S TIME.
OH, WAS THAT YOU?
WE HAD THE APPROPRIATE COMPONENTS IN OUR ARMORS TO BREAK THE TIMESTREAM.
DAMN. YOU'RE RIGHT.
BUT I'VE REDESIGNED. I DON'T HAVE THE ACCELERATORS OR THE B-9 DIODES.
HOW DO YOU PROCESS YOUR REPULSOR RAYS?
BUT I DO HAVE THE EXTREMIS IN MY SYSTEM. I CONTROL THE ARMOR BIOLOGICALLY.
I WONDER IF I COULD BREAK THE TIMESTREAM WITH SOME CALCULATIONS TO MY NEW EXISTING BIOTECH.
YES, LET'S TELL EACH OTHER ALL OF OUR UNIQUE TECH SECRETS.
INSIPID SARCASM. THANK YOU.
I'M MISSING COMPONENTS FROM THAT OLDER ARMO DESIGN AS WELL.
WELL, I GUESS WE'LL HA TO ASK AROUND AND SEE ANYONE HAS A TIME MACHINE WE CAN BORRO
WHAT HAVE YOU DONE?!
FOOM

CONTINUED AFTER NEXT P

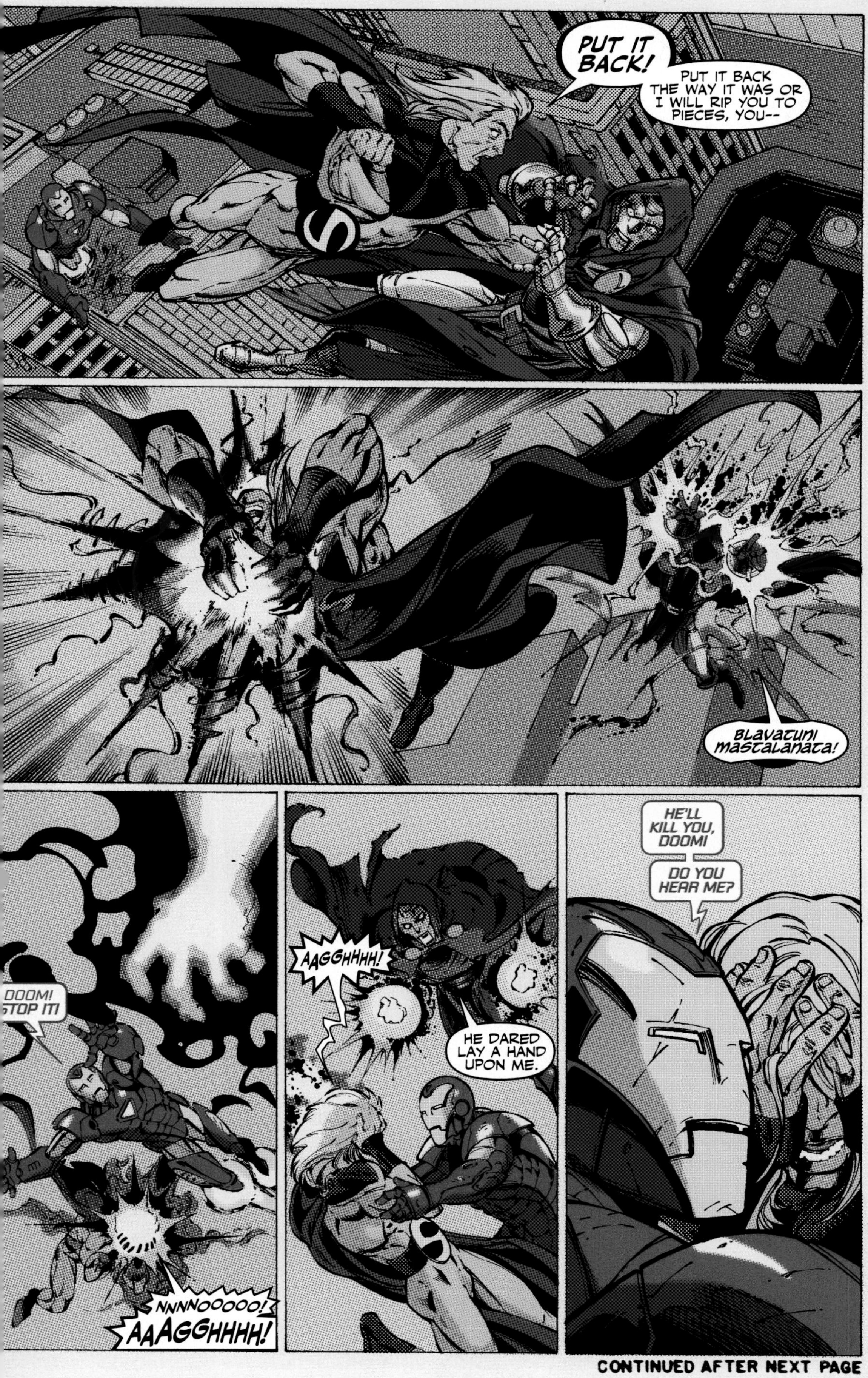

PUT IT BACK!
PUT IT BACK THE WAY IT WAS OR I WILL RIP YOU TO PIECES, YOU--
BLAVATUNI MASTALANATA!
DOOM! STOP IT!
NNNNOOOOO! AAAGGHHHH!
AAGGHHHH!
HE DARED LAY A HAND UPON ME.
HE'LL KILL YOU, DOOM!
DO YOU HEAR ME?

CONTINUED AFTER NEXT PAGE

HE REACTED TOO STRONGLY TO THAT SPIRIT REVERSAL SPELL.

HE'S NOT A WELL MAN.

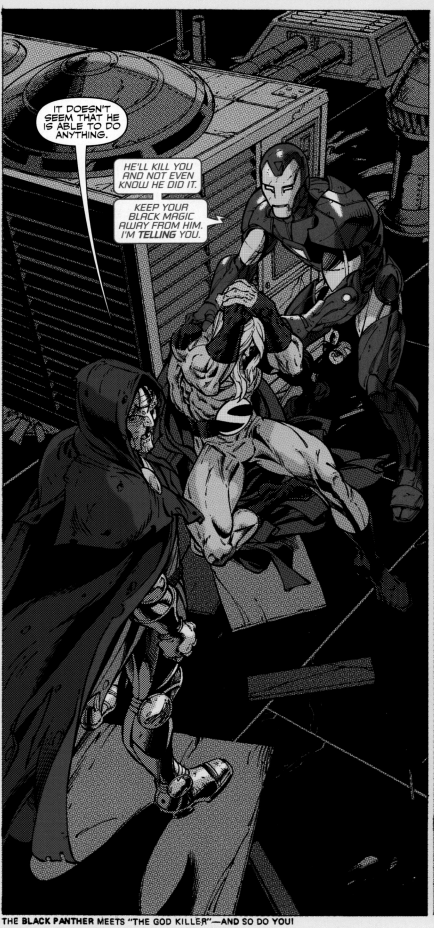

IT DOESN'T SEEM THAT HE IS ABLE TO DO ANYTHING.

HE'LL KILL YOU AND NOT EVEN KNOW HE DID IT.

KEEP YOUR BLACK MAGIC AWAY FROM HIM. I'M *TELLING* YOU.

WE'RE-- WE'RE IN THE *PAST?*

EVERYTHING IS FINE, BOB.

DON' FREAK ON M NOW

I-- I SAW MYSELF.

THE **BLACK PANTHER** MEETS "THE GOD KILLER"—AND SO DO YOU!

THANK YOU, DOCTOR.

YOU OKAY, BOB?

WHERE *ARE* WE? WHO-- WHAT'S GOING *ON*?

LISTEN TO ME AND LISTEN GOOD...

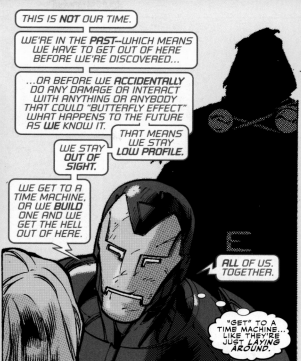

THIS IS *NOT* OUR TIME.

WE'RE IN THE *PAST*--WHICH MEANS WE HAVE TO GET OUT OF HERE BEFORE WE'RE DISCOVERED...

...OR BEFORE WE *ACCIDENTALLY* DO ANY DAMAGE OR INTERACT WITH ANYTHING OR ANYBODY THAT COULD "BUTTERFLY EFFECT" WHAT HAPPENS TO THE FUTURE AS *WE* KNOW IT.

WE STAY *OUT OF SIGHT.*

THAT MEANS WE STAY *LOW PROFILE.*

WE GET TO A TIME MACHINE, OR WE *BUILD* ONE AND WE GET THE HELL OUT OF HERE.

ALL OF US. TOGETHER.

"GET" TO A TIME MACHINE... LIKE THEY'RE JUST *LAYING AROUND.*

H NO.

DID YOU *TALK* TO YOURSELF?

NO.

DID YOUR OTHER SELF *SEE* YOU?

NO, NO I DON'T *THINK* SO.

DON'T THINK SO OR DON'T *KNOW* SO?

I DON'T THINK SO.

I-- I WANT TO GET *OUT* OF HERE.

WE ALL DO. RIGHT, DOCTOR?

IS HE INSANE?

WHO HAS A TIME MACHINE IN THIS ERA OTHER THAN YOU?

ONLY ONE MAN.

DAREDEVIL JOINS THE WORLD'S GREATEST NON-TEAM--IN GIANT-SIZE DEFENDERS #3!

OH, YEAH. BECAUSE OF THAT THING WITH THE PIRATES.

REGARDLESS. IT'S IN THERE.

LET'S GO.

I WANT TO GET OUT OF HERE.

WE CAN'T JUST GO IN.

REED RICHARDS HAS ONE?

YES.

HOW DO YOU KNOW?

HE **TOOK** IT FROM ME.

IT'S THE BAXTER BUILDING. IT'S AS FORTIFIED AND SECURE AS ANYTHING ANYWHERE **IN THE WORLD** IS FORTIFIED AND SECURE.

HE'S YOUR FRIEND. YOU COULD GET IN.

I COULD.

BUT THEN REED WOULD **KNOW** I WAS HERE AND THE **POINT** OF ALL THIS IS THAT WE DON'T WANT THEM **KNOWING** WE'RE HERE BECAUSE IT'LL CHANGE THE COURSE OF HUMAN HISTORY.

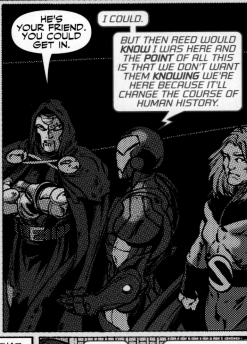

ONE WOULD ARGUE THAT A MAN LIKE REED RICHARDS, LIKE YOU, LIKE MYSELF, HAS SEEN AND DONE SO MUCH...

...THAT A TIME-SPACE EVENT LIKE THIS WOULDN'T MATTER AS IT WOULD TO A COMMON PERSON WHO HAS HAD NO EXPERIENCE IN SUCH THINGS.

MAYBE.

BUT THAT'S AN AWFUL **BIG** GAMBLE.

I'D HATE TO BE WRONG AND WE GET BACK HOME AND THE APES HAVE TAKEN OVER BECAUSE OF SOMETHING WE SAID OR DID HERE.

I DON'T DISAGREE.

DOCTOR DOOM HAS SEEN "PLANET OF THE APES?" THAT IS HARD TO PICTURE.

I-- I WANT TO GO HOME.

CONTINUED AFTER NEXT PA

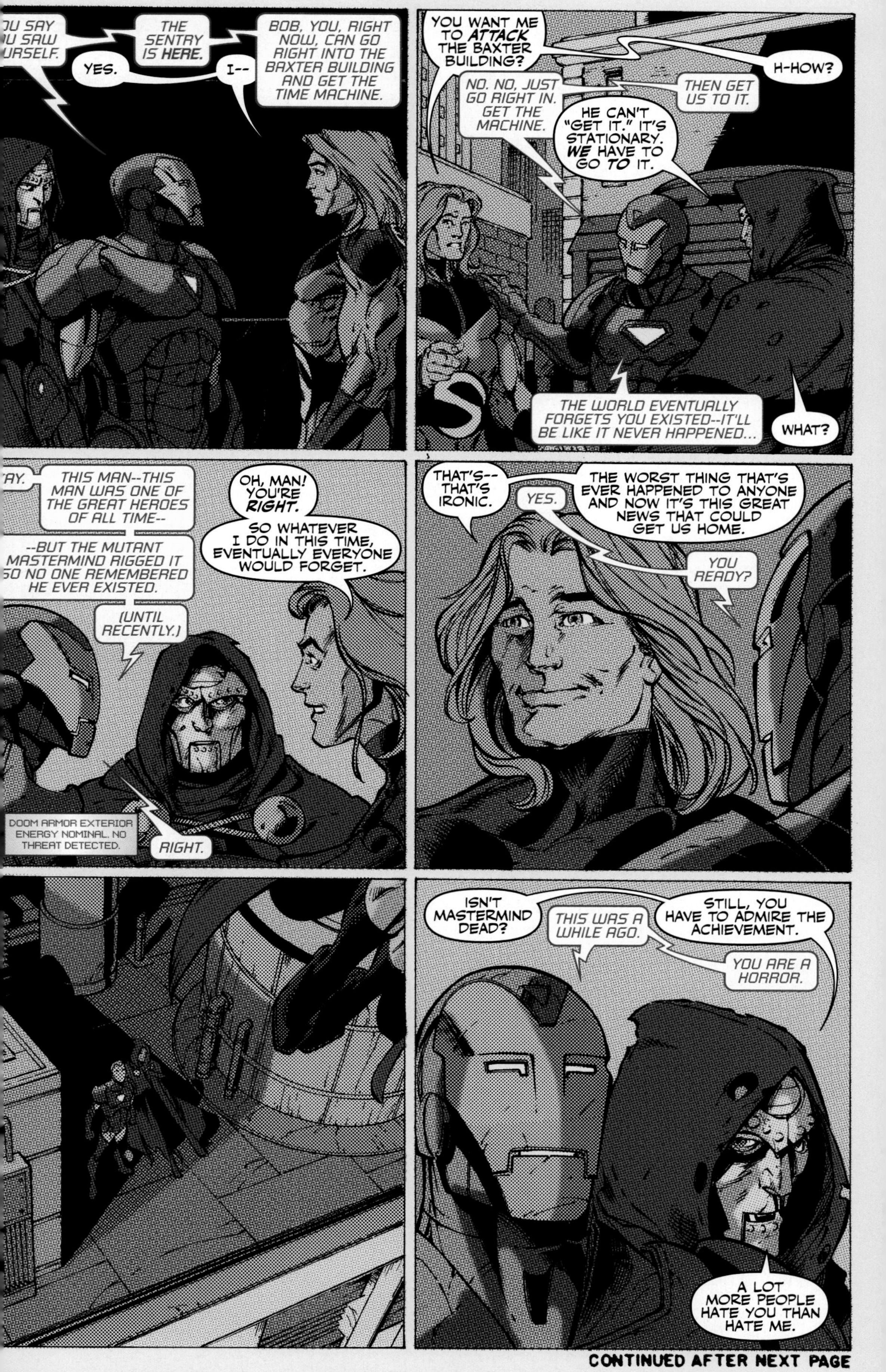

OU SAY
U SAW
URSELF.
YES.
THE SENTRY IS HERE.
I--
BOB, YOU, RIGHT NOW, CAN GO RIGHT INTO THE BAXTER BUILDING AND GET THE TIME MACHINE.
YOU WANT ME TO ATTACK THE BAXTER BUILDING?
H-HOW?
NO. NO, JUST GO RIGHT IN. GET THE MACHINE.
THEN GET US TO IT.
HE CAN'T "GET IT." IT'S STATIONARY. WE HAVE TO GO TO IT.
THE WORLD EVENTUALLY FORGETS YOU EXISTED--IT'LL BE LIKE IT NEVER HAPPENED...
WHAT?
AY.
THIS MAN--THIS MAN WAS ONE OF THE GREAT HEROES OF ALL TIME--
--BUT THE MUTANT MASTERMIND RIGGED IT SO NO ONE REMEMBERED HE EVER EXISTED.
OH, MAN! YOU'RE RIGHT.
SO WHATEVER I DO IN THIS TIME, EVENTUALLY EVERYONE WOULD FORGET.
(UNTIL RECENTLY.)
DOOM ARMOR EXTERIOR ENERGY NOMINAL. NO THREAT DETECTED.
RIGHT.
THAT'S-- THAT'S IRONIC.
THE WORST THING THAT'S EVER HAPPENED TO ANYONE AND NOW IT'S THIS GREAT NEWS THAT COULD GET US HOME.
YES.
YOU READY?
ISN'T MASTERMIND DEAD?
THIS WAS A WHILE AGO.
STILL, YOU HAVE TO ADMIRE THE ACHIEVEMENT.
YOU ARE A HORROR.
A LOT MORE PEOPLE HATE YOU THAN HATE ME.

CONTINUED AFTER NEXT PAGE

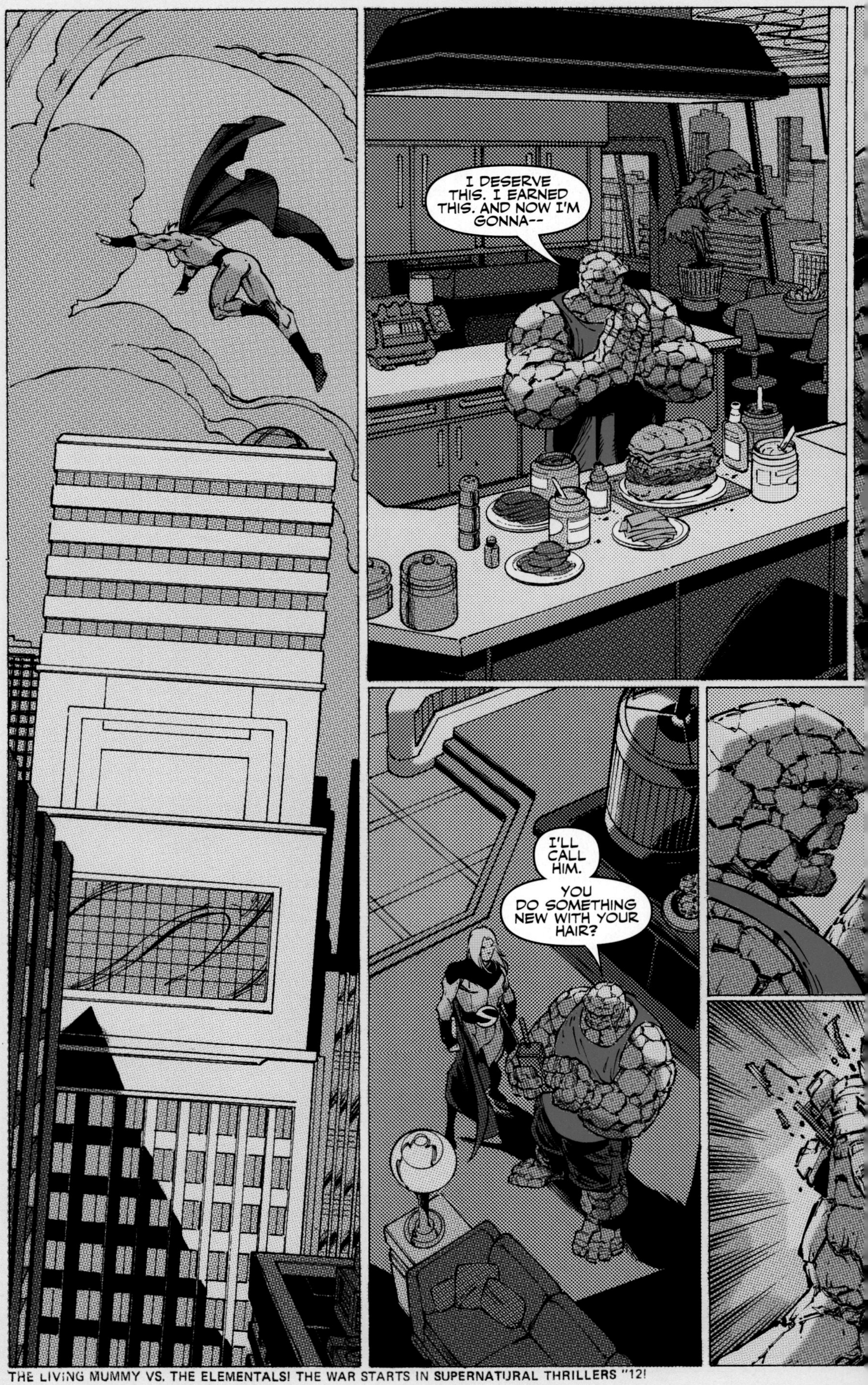
I DESERVE THIS. I EARNED THIS. AND NOW I'M GONNA--
I'LL CALL HIM.
YOU DO SOMETHING NEW WITH YOUR HAIR?

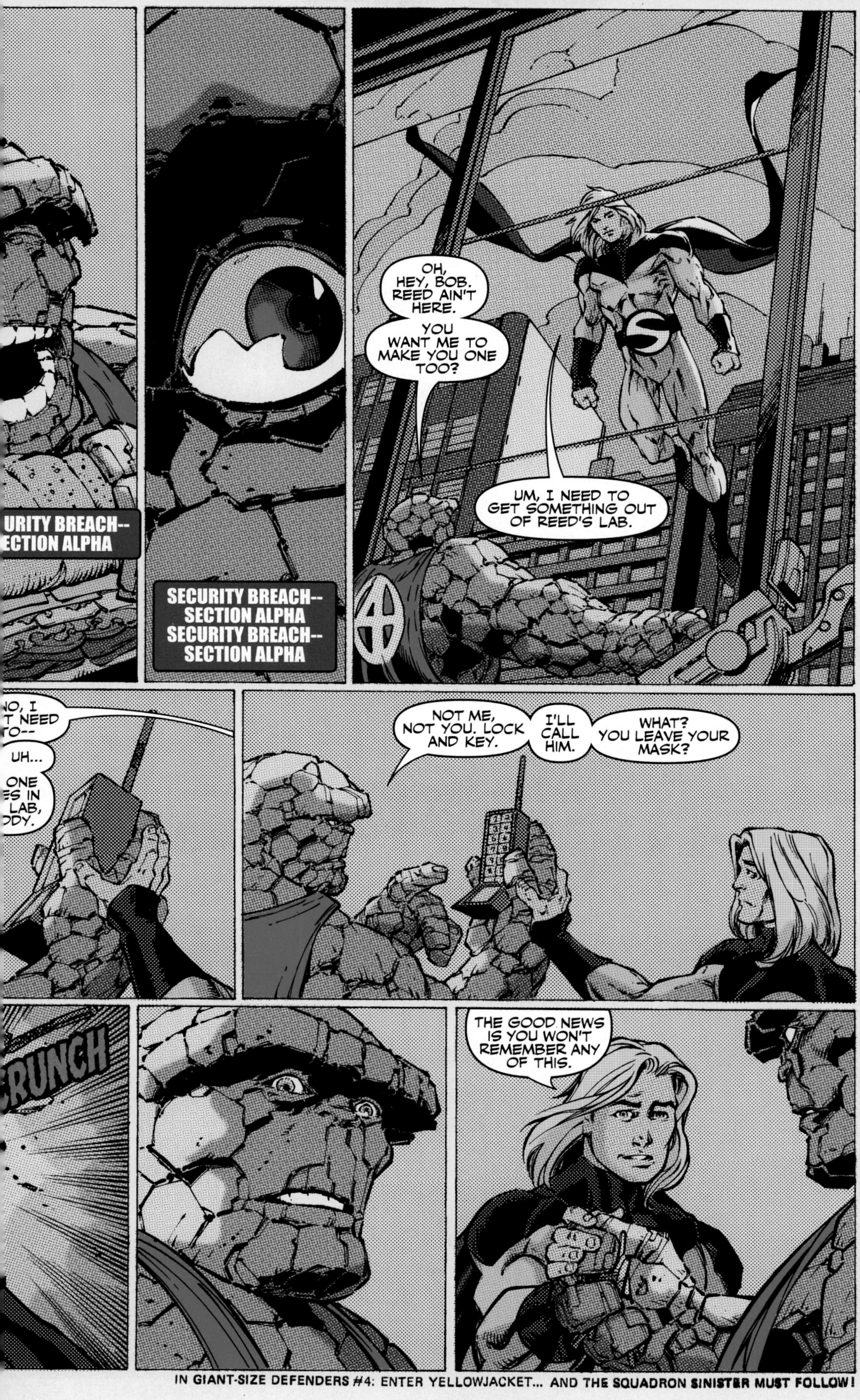

URITY BREACH--
ECTION ALPHA
SECURITY BREACH--
SECTION ALPHA
SECURITY BREACH--
SECTION ALPHA
OH, HEY, BOB. REED AIN'T HERE.
YOU WANT ME TO MAKE YOU ONE TOO?
UM, I NEED TO GET SOMETHING OUT OF REED'S LAB.
NO, I T NEED TO--
UH...
ONE ES IN LAB, DDY.
NOT ME, NOT YOU. LOCK AND KEY.
I'LL CALL HIM.
WHAT? YOU LEAVE YOUR MASK?
CRUNCH
THE GOOD NEWS IS YOU WON'T REMEMBER ANY OF THIS.

IN GIANT-SIZE DEFENDERS #4: ENTER YELLOWJACKET... AND THE SQUADRON SINISTER MUST FOLLOW!

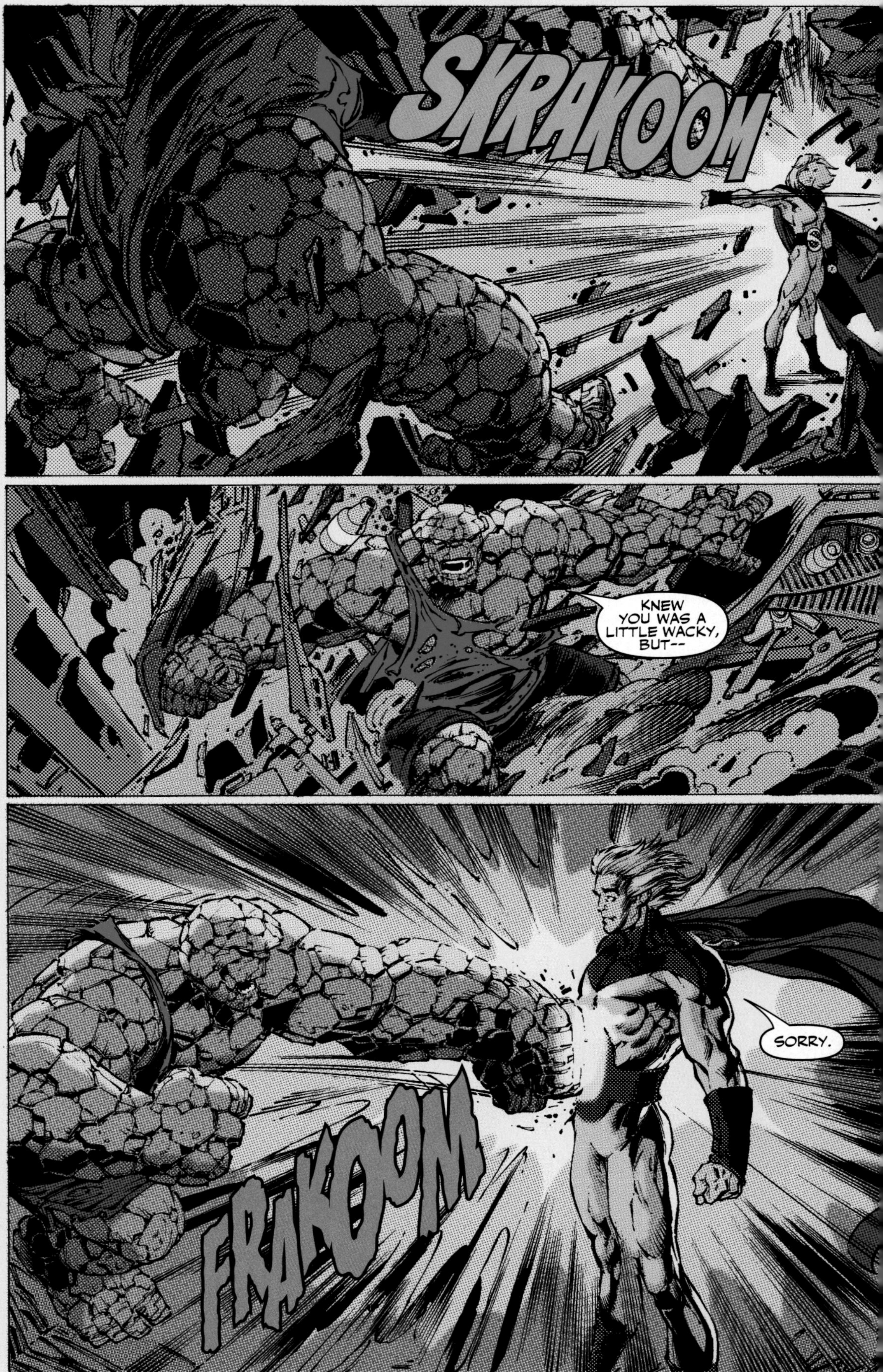
SKRAKOOM
KNEW YOU WAS A LITTLE WACKY, BUT--
SORRY.
FRAKOOM

CONTINUED AFTER NEXT

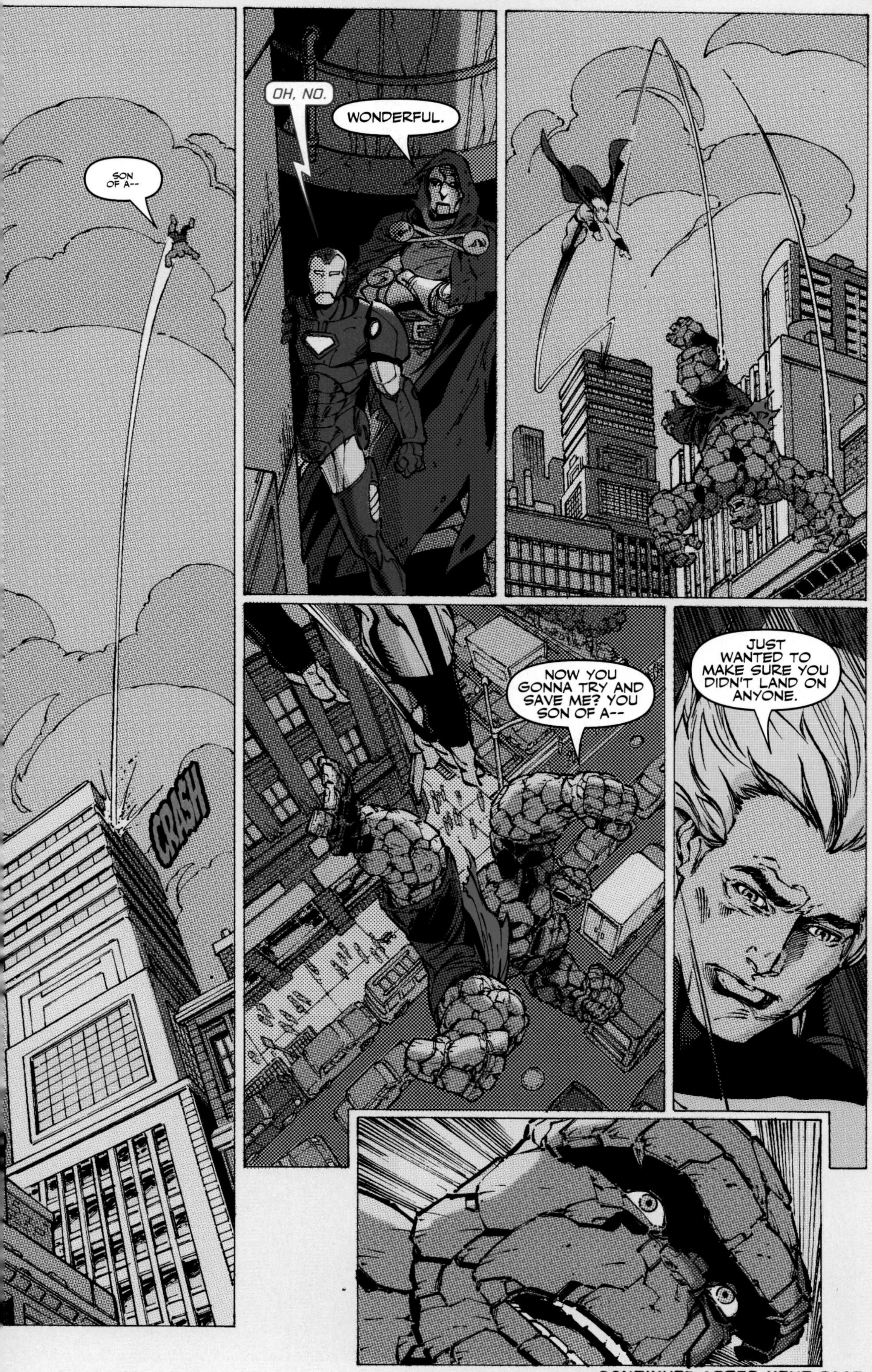
SON OF A--
OH, NO.
WONDERFUL.
NOW YOU GONNA TRY AND SAVE ME? YOU SON OF A--
JUST WANTED TO MAKE SURE YOU DIDN'T LAND ON ANYONE.
CRASH

CONTINUED AFTER NEXT PAGE

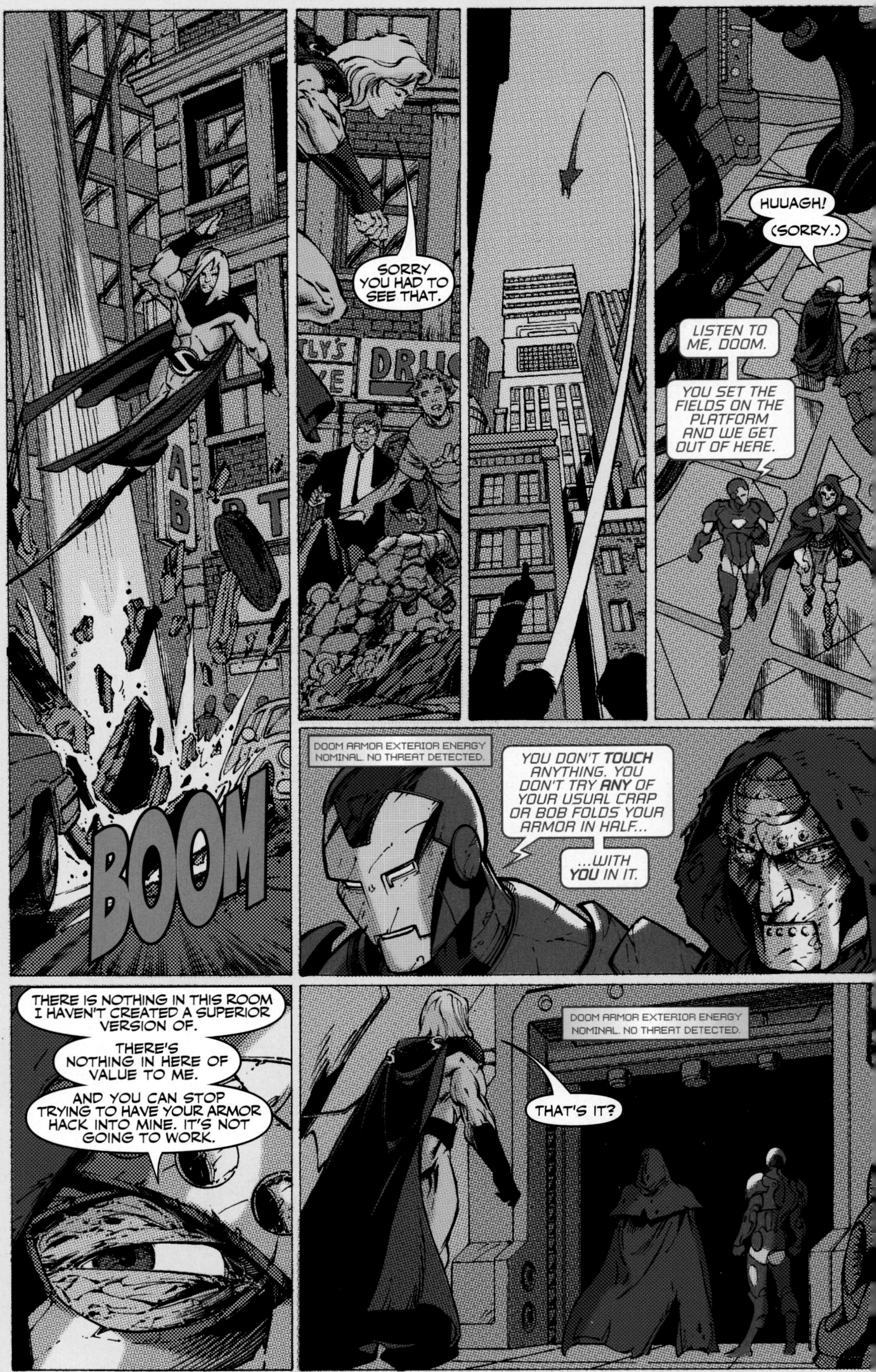
SORRY YOU HAD TO SEE THAT.
DRUG
BOOM
HUUAGH!
(SORRY.)
LISTEN TO ME, DOOM.
YOU SET THE FIELDS ON THE PLATFORM AND WE GET OUT OF HERE.
DOOM ARMOR EXTERIOR ENERGY NOMINAL. NO THREAT DETECTED.
YOU DON'T TOUCH ANYTHING. YOU DON'T TRY ANY OF YOUR USUAL CRAP OR BOB FOLDS YOUR ARMOR IN HALF...
...WITH YOU IN IT.
THERE IS NOTHING IN THIS ROOM I HAVEN'T CREATED A SUPERIOR VERSION OF.
THERE'S NOTHING IN HERE OF VALUE TO ME.
AND YOU CAN STOP TRYING TO HAVE YOUR ARMOR HACK INTO MINE. IT'S NOT GOING TO WORK.
DOOM ARMOR EXTERIOR ENERGY NOMINAL. NO THREAT DETECTED.
THAT'S IT?

THE SERPENT SQUAD STRIKES—IN CAPTAIN AMERICA #181!

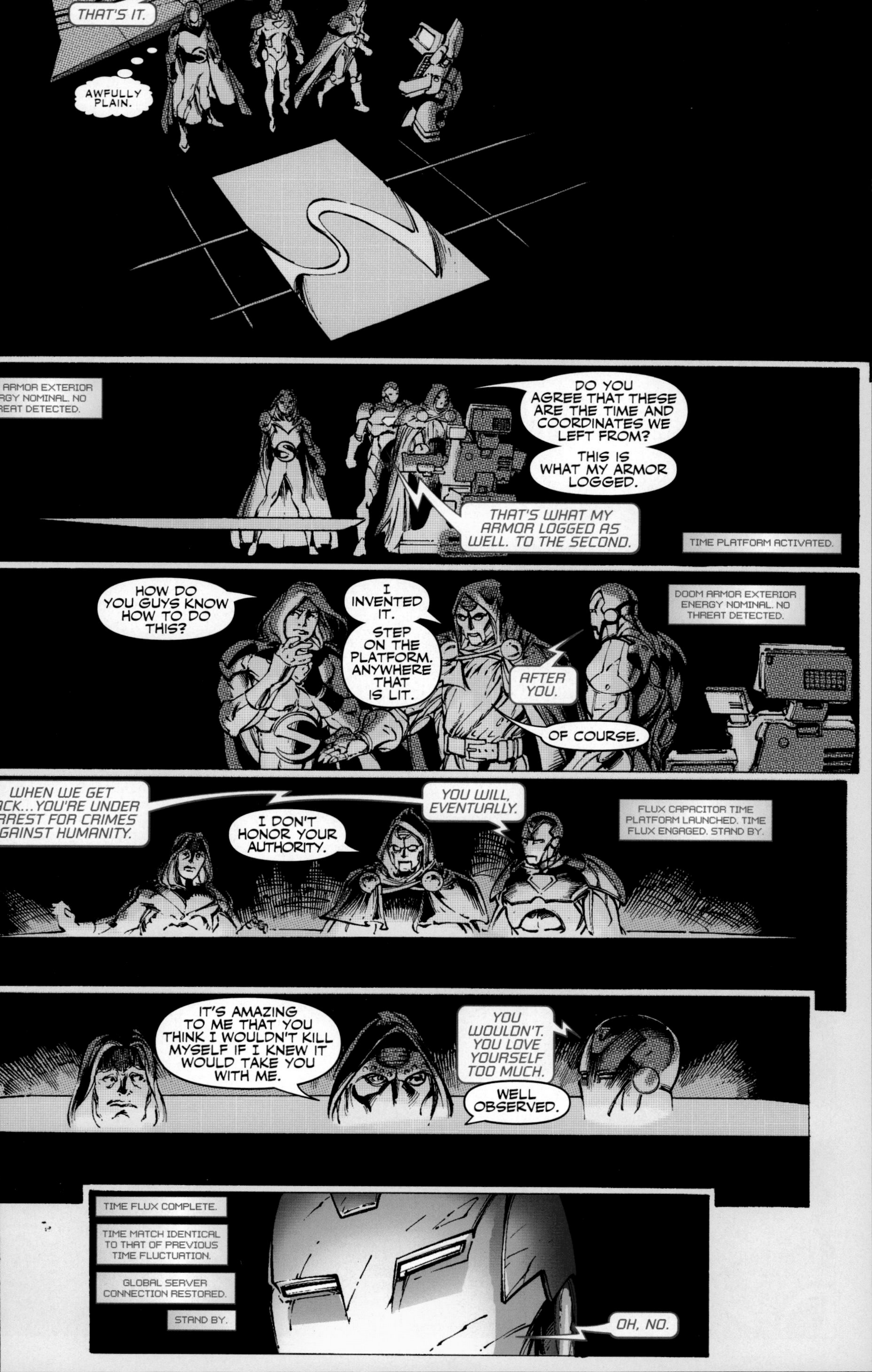
THAT'S IT.
AWFULLY PLAIN.
ARMOR EXTERIOR
ERGY NOMINAL. NO
REAT DETECTED.
DO YOU AGREE THAT THESE ARE THE TIME AND COORDINATES WE LEFT FROM?
THIS IS WHAT MY ARMOR LOGGED.
THAT'S WHAT MY ARMOR LOGGED AS WELL. TO THE SECOND.
TIME PLATFORM ACTIVATED.
HOW DO YOU GUYS KNOW HOW TO DO THIS?
I INVENTED IT.
STEP ON THE PLATFORM. ANYWHERE THAT IS LIT.
DOOM ARMOR EXTERIOR ENERGY NOMINAL. NO THREAT DETECTED.
AFTER YOU.
OF COURSE.
WHEN WE GET
ACK...YOU'RE UNDER
RREST FOR CRIMES
GAINST HUMANITY.
I DON'T HONOR YOUR AUTHORITY.
YOU WILL, EVENTUALLY.
FLUX CAPACITOR TIME PLATFORM LAUNCHED. TIME FLUX ENGAGED. STAND BY.
IT'S AMAZING TO ME THAT YOU THINK I WOULDN'T KILL MYSELF IF I KNEW IT WOULD TAKE YOU WITH ME.
YOU WOULDN'T. YOU LOVE YOURSELF TOO MUCH.
WELL OBSERVED.
TIME FLUX COMPLETE.
TIME MATCH IDENTICAL TO THAT OF PREVIOUS TIME FLUCTUATION.
GLOBAL SERVER CONNECTION RESTORED.
STAND BY.
OH, NO.

LOCATION: CASTLE DOOM, LATVERIA.

WHERE DID DOOM GO?

I DON'T KNOW.

HE-HE WAS *RIGHT HERE!*

@#%¢!

GLOBAL SATELLITE CONNECTION ENGAGED. STAND BY.

AERIAL RECON, BOB.

HE WAS RIGHT HERE!

BOB! FOCUS!

AERIAL RECON!

ARE-- ARE WE IN THE RIGHT TIME PERIOD?

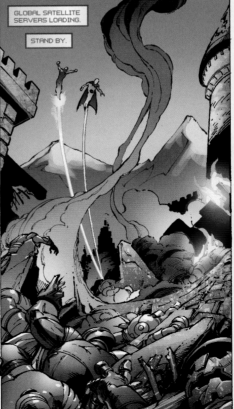

GLOBAL SATELLITE SERVERS LOADING.

STAND BY.

BOB!

WHAT IS THAT?

@#¢%!

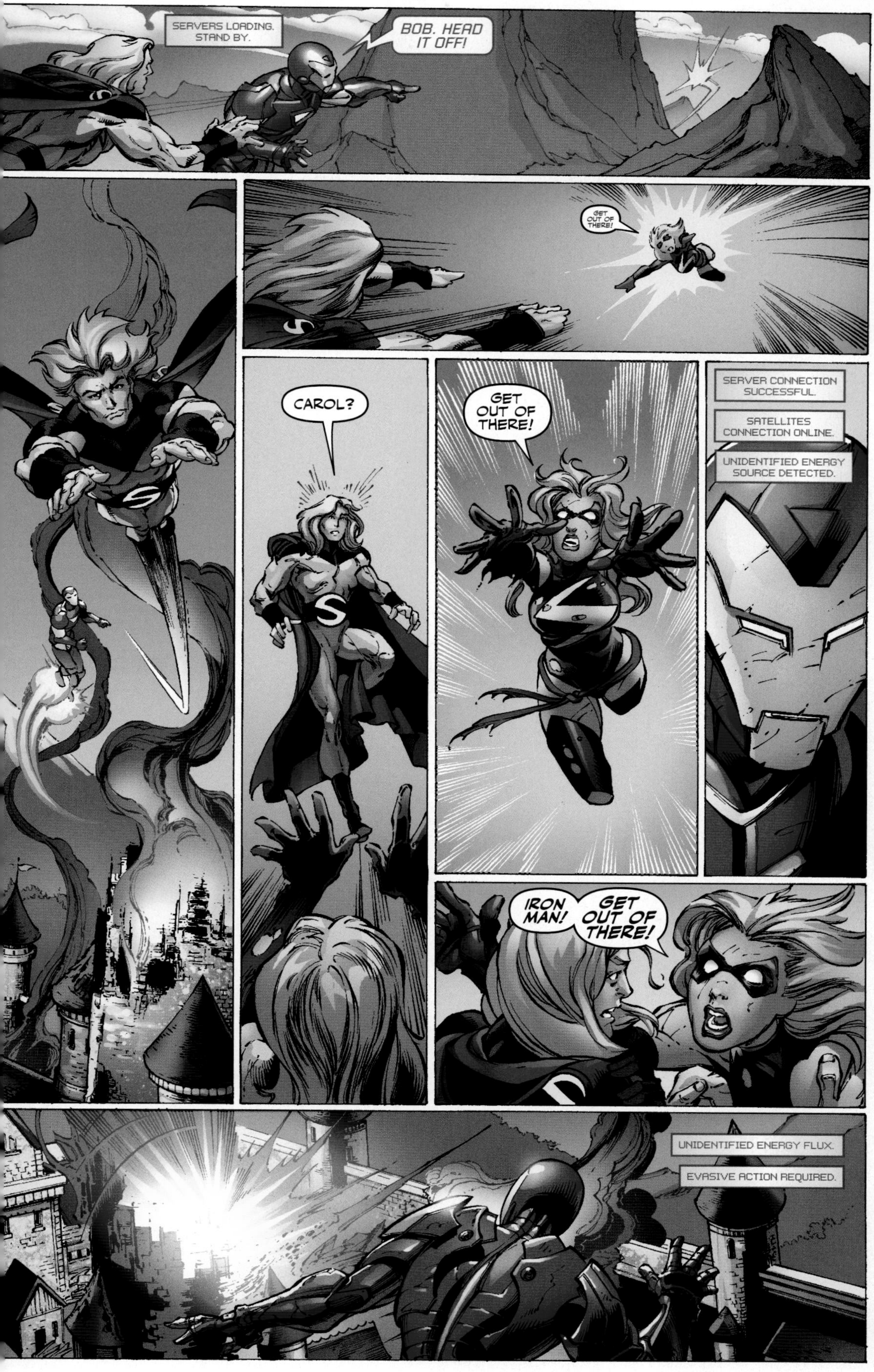
SERVERS LOADING. STAND BY.
BOB. HEAD IT OFF!
GET OUT OF THERE!
CAROL?
GET OUT OF THERE!
SERVER CONNECTION SUCCESSFUL.
SATELLITES CONNECTION ONLINE.
UNIDENTIFIED ENERGY SOURCE DETECTED.
IRON MAN!
GET OUT OF THERE!
UNIDENTIFIED ENERGY FLUX.
EVASIVE ACTION REQUIRED.

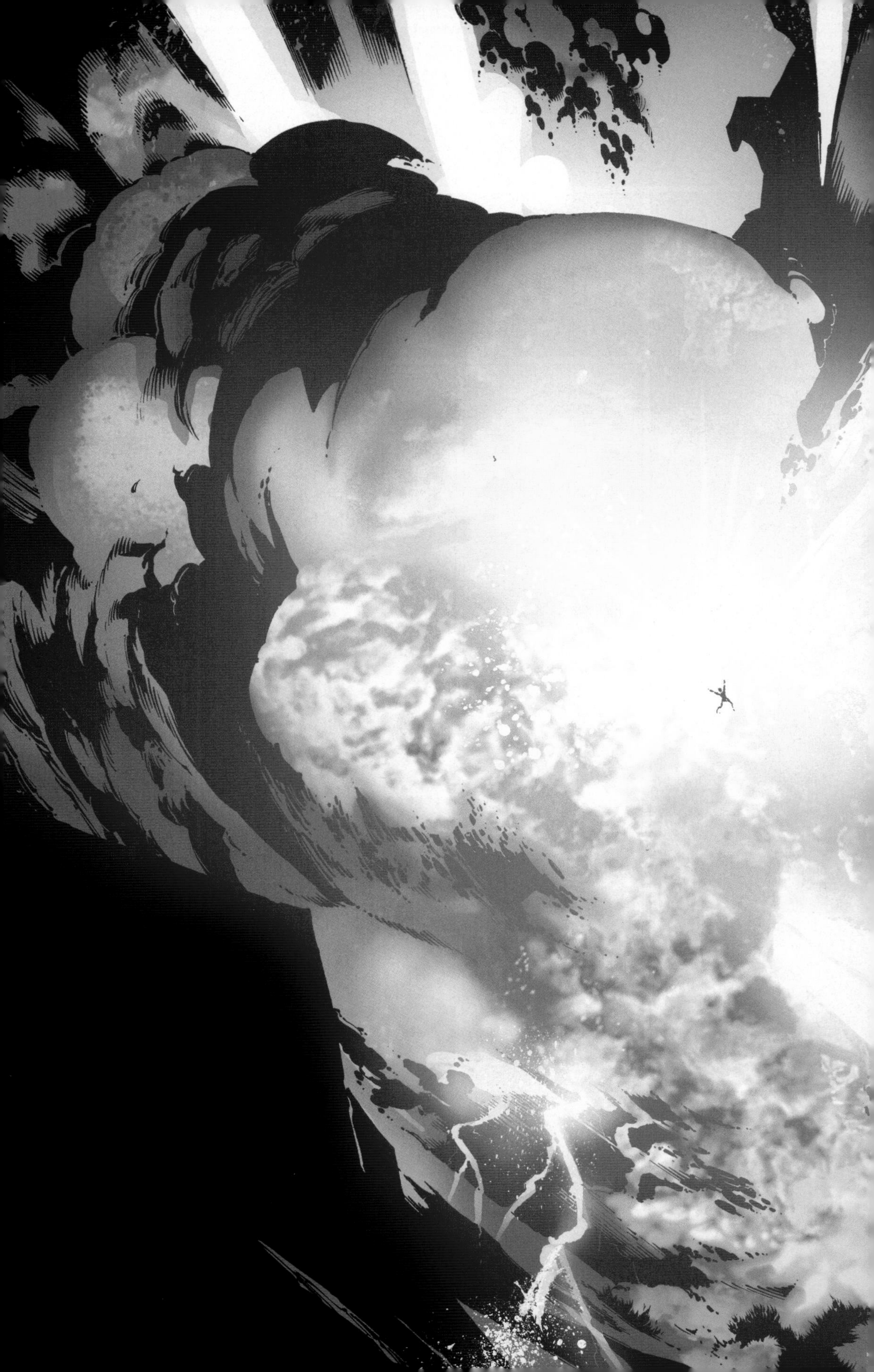

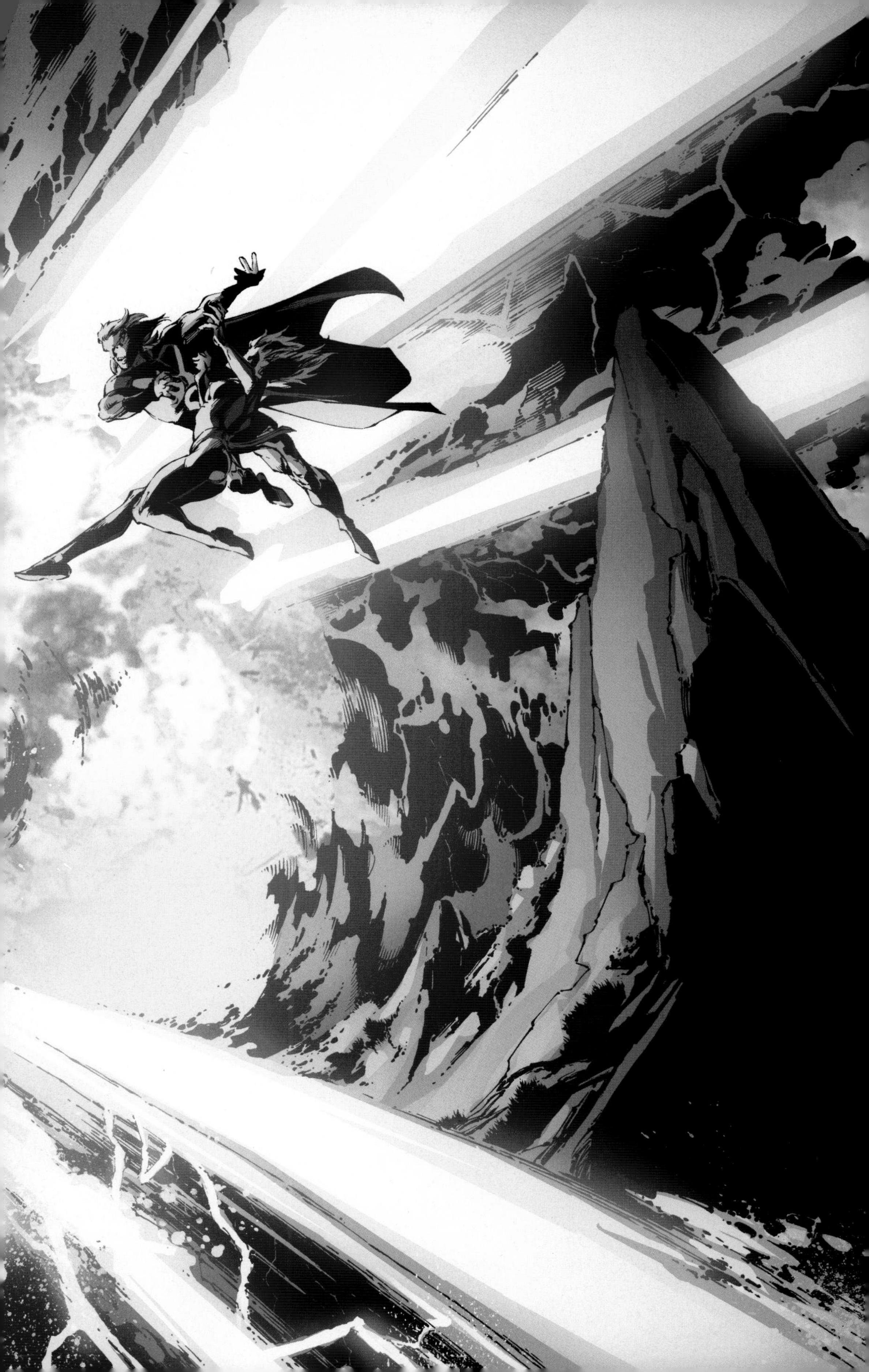

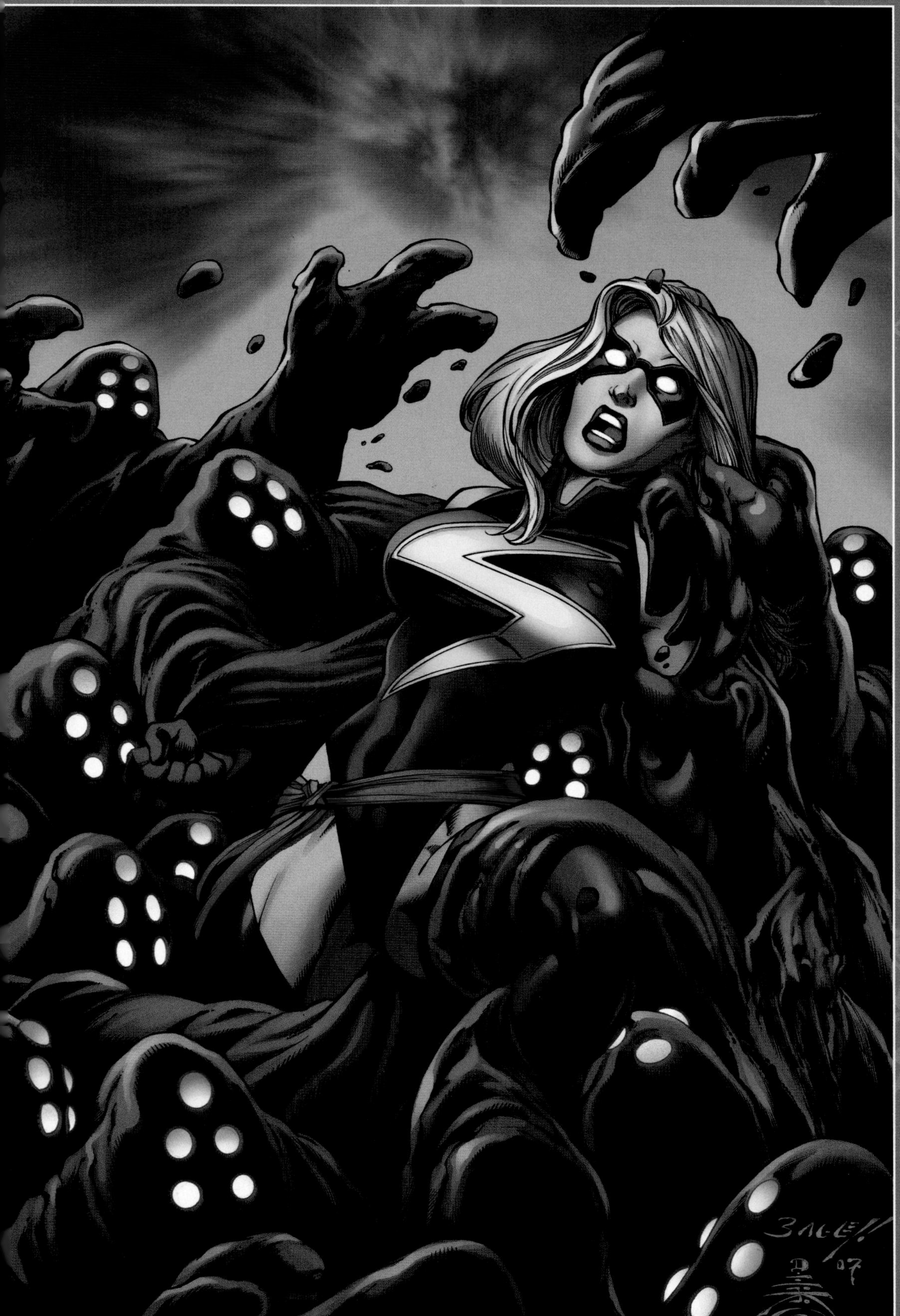

MIGHTY AVENGERS (2007) #11

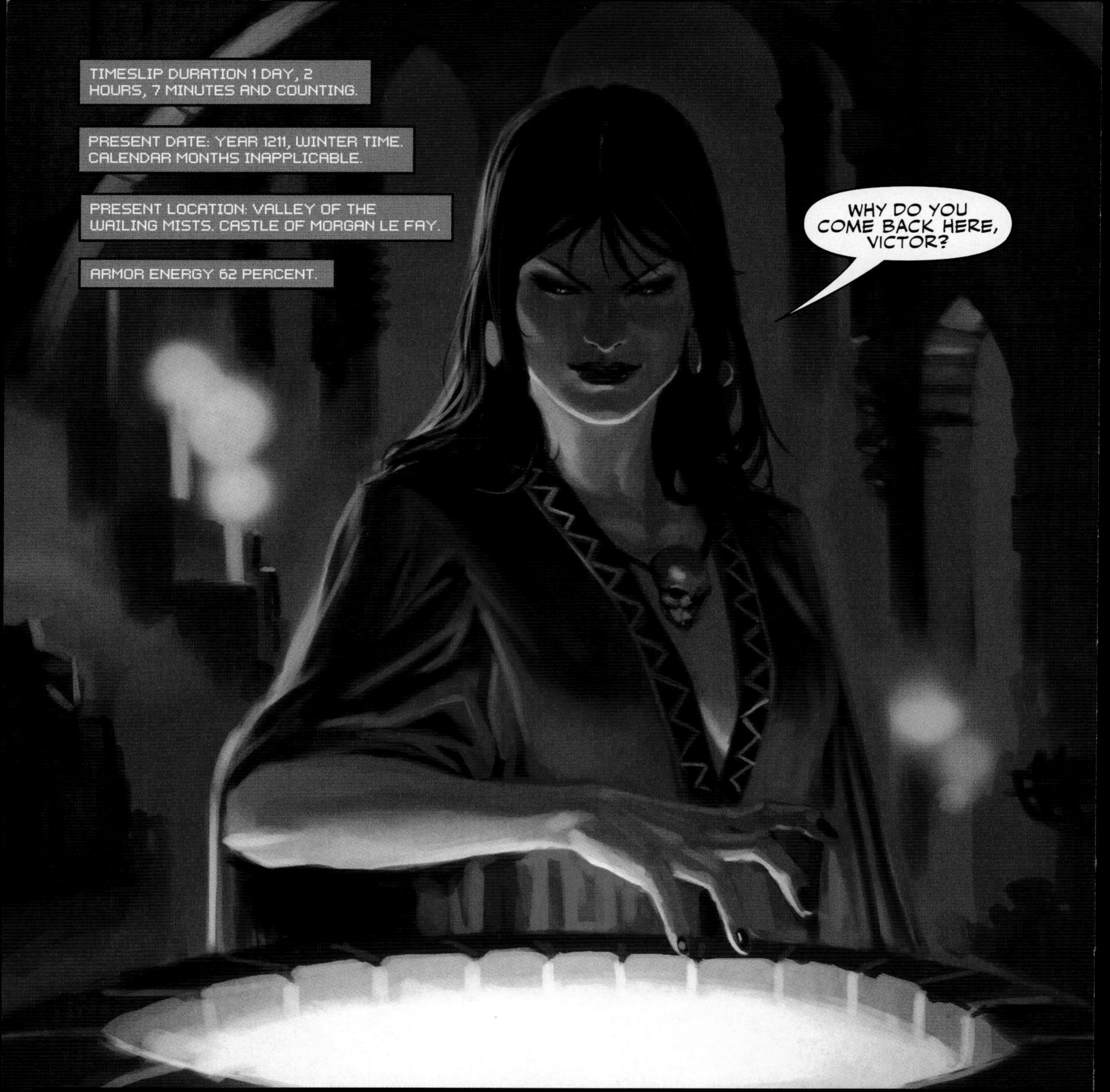
TIMESLIP DURATION 1 DAY, 2 HOURS, 7 MINUTES AND COUNTING.
PRESENT DATE: YEAR 1211, WINTER TIME. CALENDAR MONTHS INAPPLICABLE.
PRESENT LOCATION: VALLEY OF THE WAILING MISTS. CASTLE OF MORGAN LE FAY.
ARMOR ENERGY 62 PERCENT.
WHY DO YOU COME BACK HERE, VICTOR?
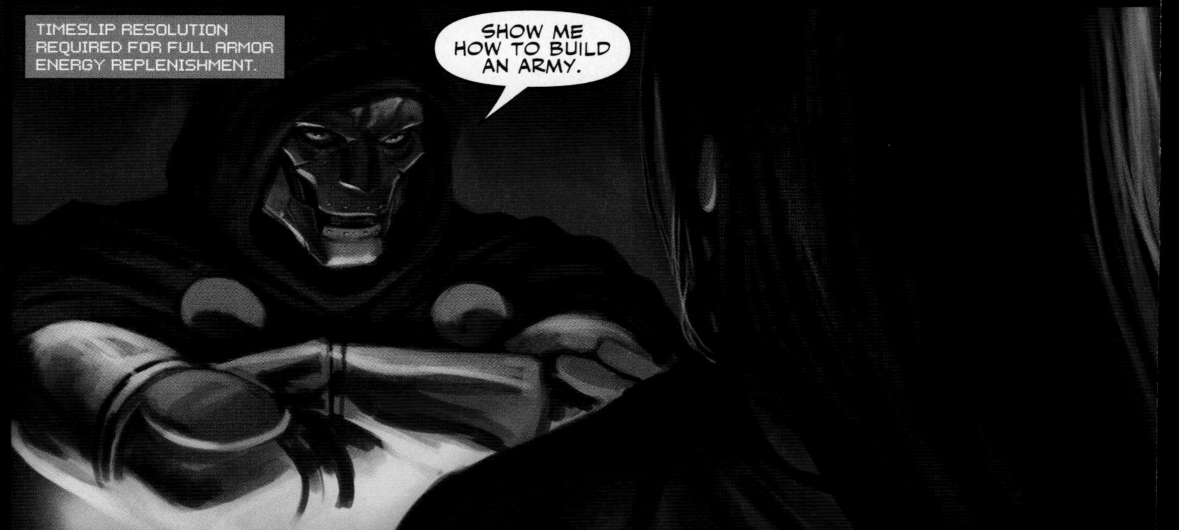
TIMESLIP RESOLUTION REQUIRED FOR FULL ARMOR ENERGY REPLENISHMENT.
SHOW ME HOW TO BUILD AN ARMY.

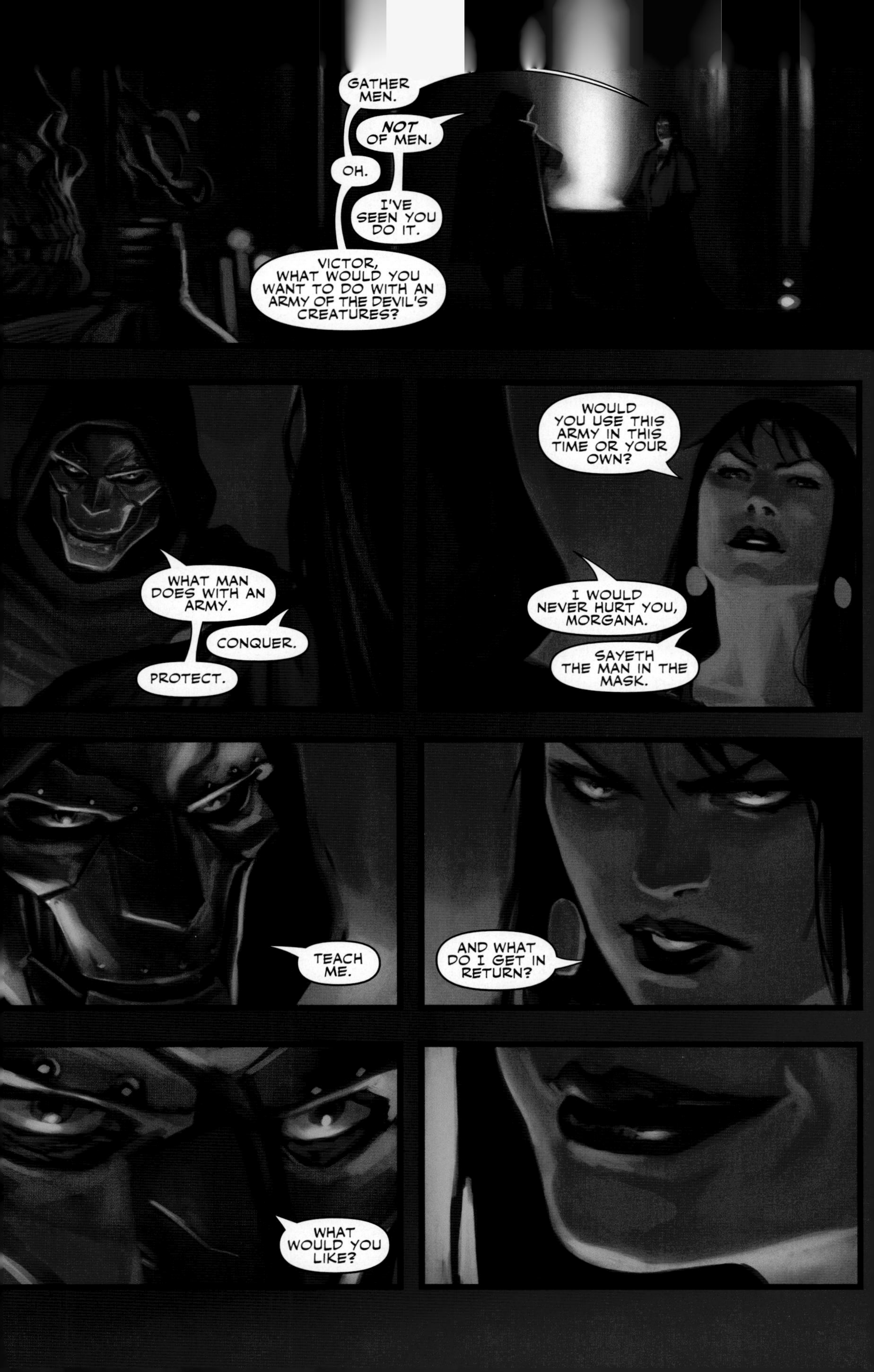
GATHER MEN.
NOT OF MEN.
OH.
I'VE SEEN YOU DO IT.
VICTOR, WHAT WOULD YOU WANT TO DO WITH AN ARMY OF THE DEVIL'S CREATURES?
WHAT MAN DOES WITH AN ARMY.
CONQUER.
PROTECT.
WOULD YOU USE THIS ARMY IN THIS TIME OR YOUR OWN?
I WOULD NEVER HURT YOU, MORGANA.
SAYETH THE MAN IN THE MASK.
TEACH ME.
AND WHAT DO I GET IN RETURN?
WHAT WOULD YOU LIKE?

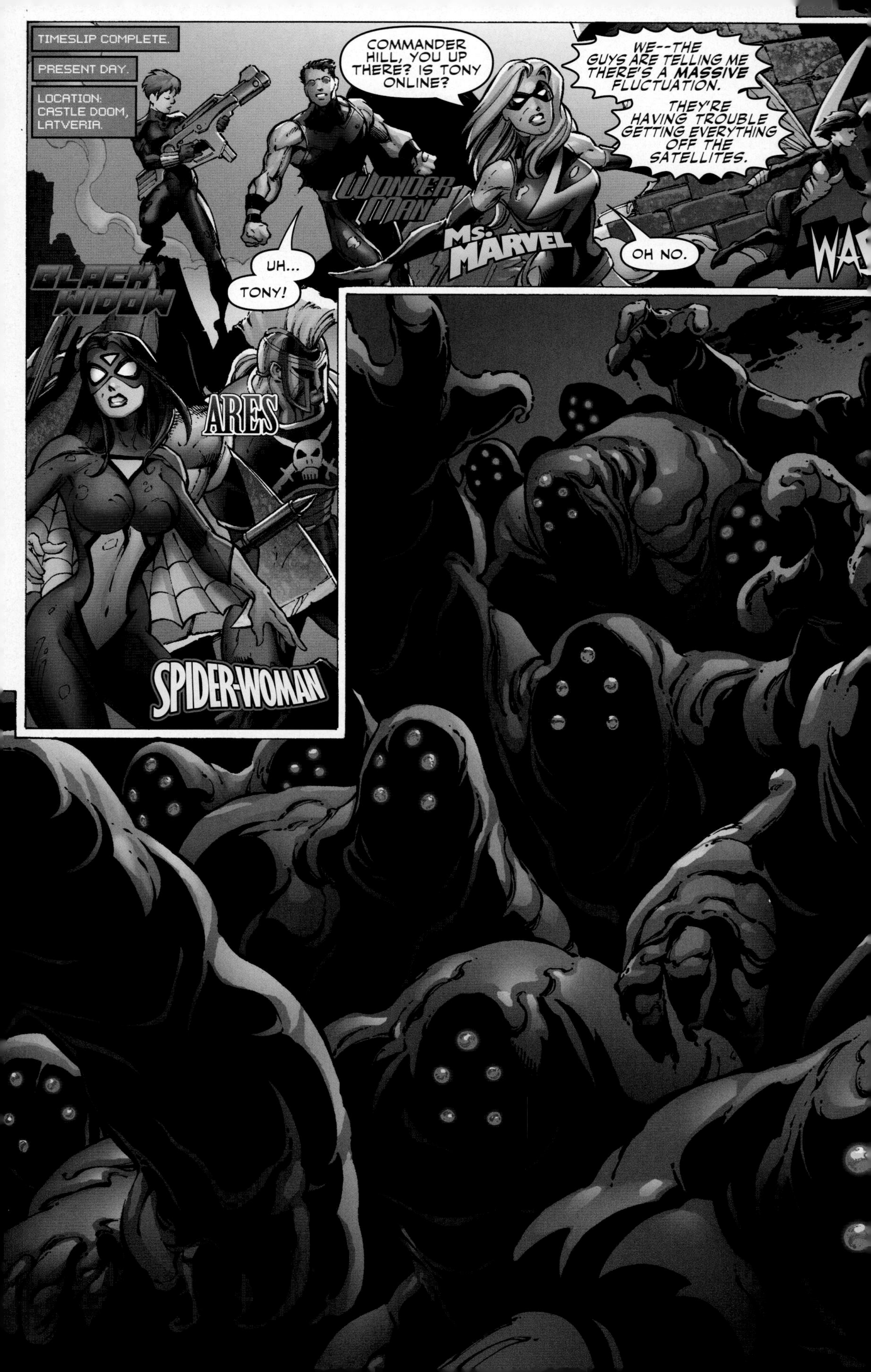
TIMESLIP COMPLETE.
PRESENT DAY.
LOCATION: CASTLE DOOM, LATVERIA.
COMMANDER HILL, YOU UP THERE? IS TONY ONLINE?
WE--THE GUYS ARE TELLING ME THERE'S A MASSIVE FLUCTUATION.
THEY'RE HAVING TROUBLE GETTING EVERYTHING OFF THE SATELLITES.
BLACK WIDOW
WONDER MAN
MS. MARVEL
UH... TONY!
OH NO.
ARES
SPIDER-WOMAN

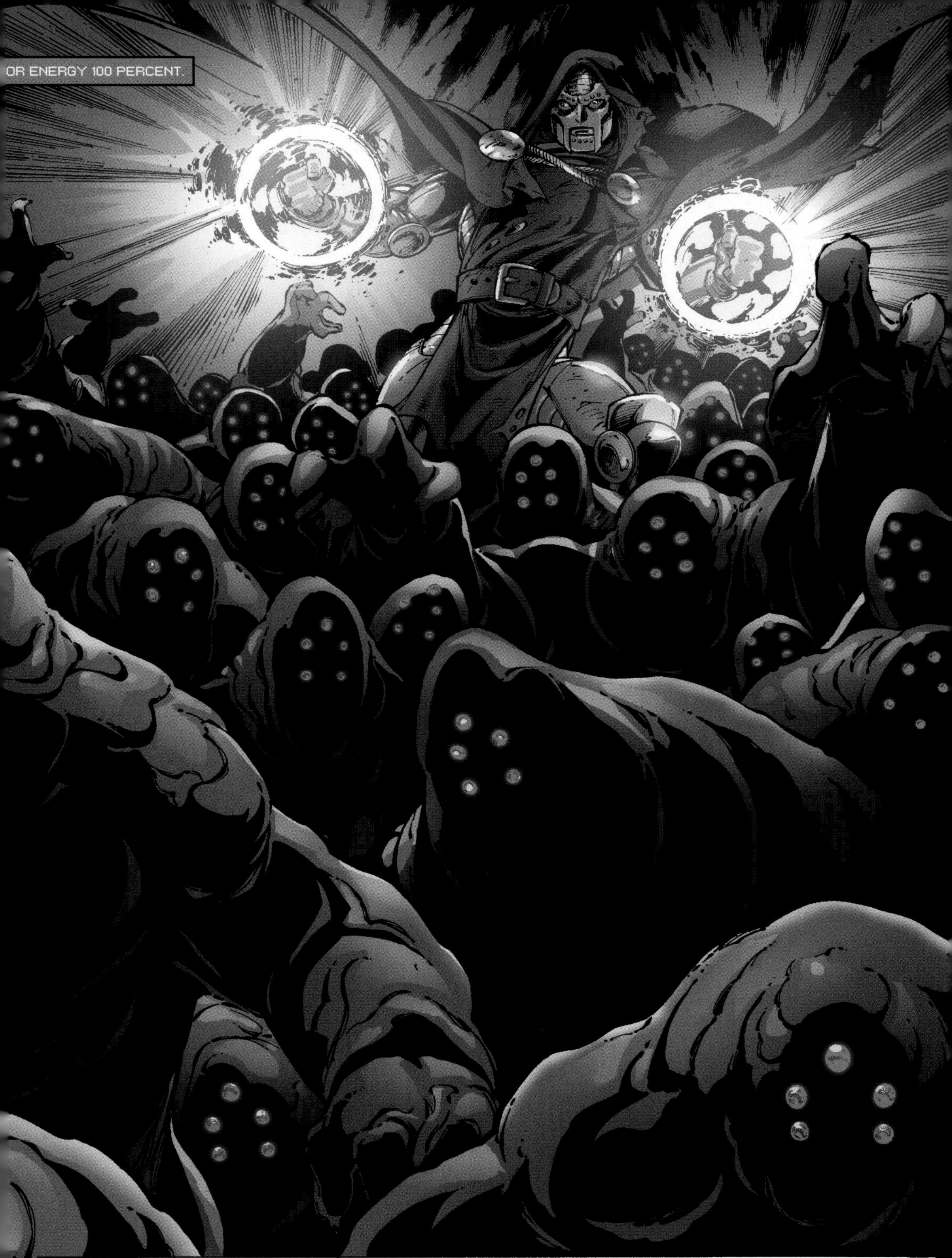
OR ENERGY 100 PERCENT.

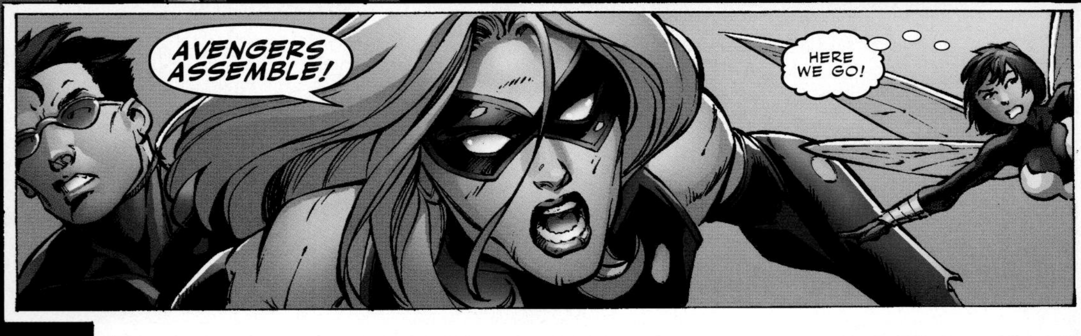
AVENGERS ASSEMBLE!
HERE WE GO!

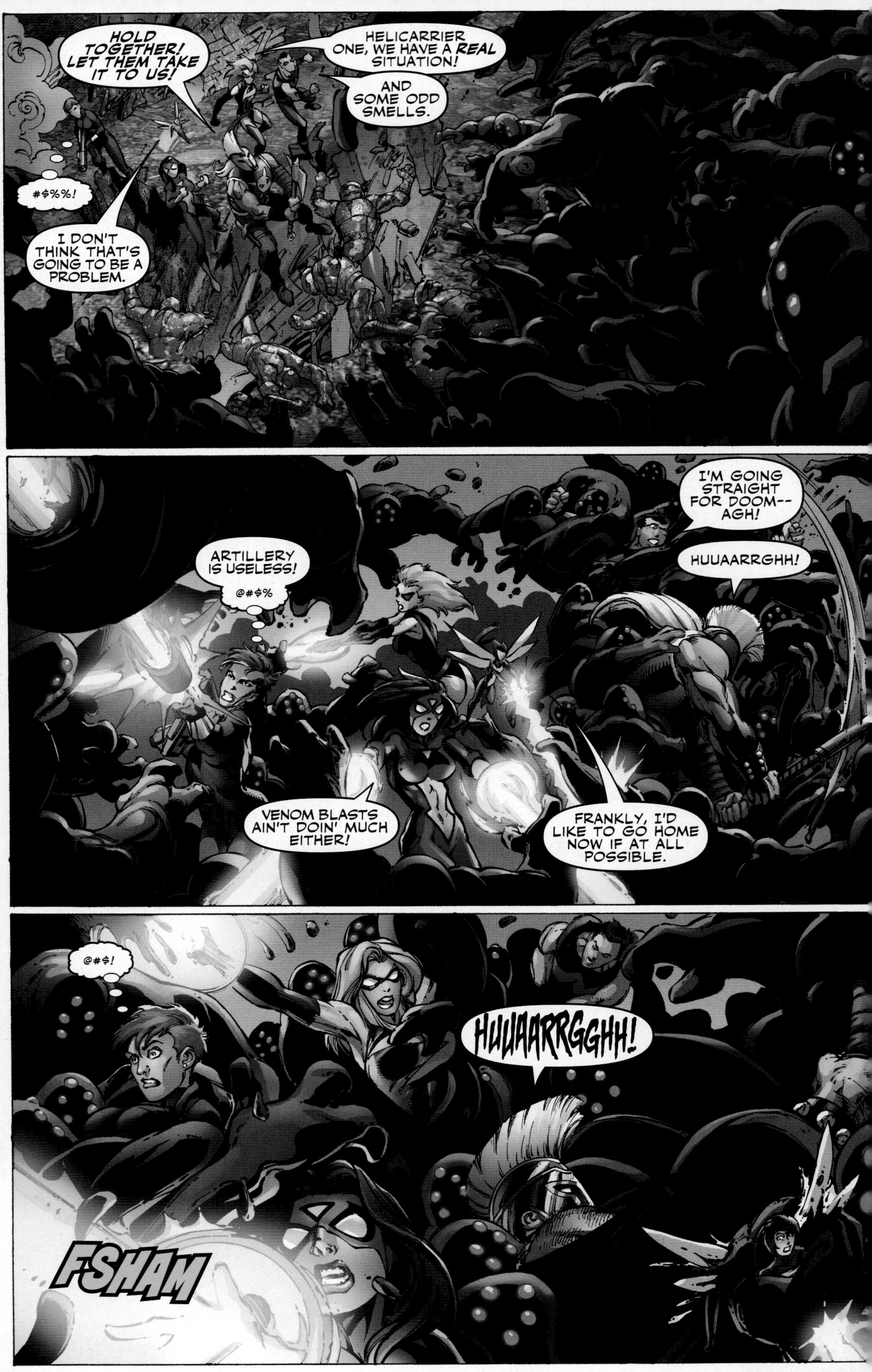
HOLD TOGETHER! LET THEM TAKE IT TO US!
HELICARRIER ONE, WE HAVE A REAL SITUATION!
AND SOME ODD SMELLS.
#$%%!
I DON'T THINK THAT'S GOING TO BE A PROBLEM.
I'M GOING STRAIGHT FOR DOOM--AGH!
HUUAARRGHH!
ARTILLERY IS USELESS!
@#$%
VENOM BLASTS AIN'T DOIN' MUCH EITHER!
FRANKLY, I'D LIKE TO GO HOME NOW IF AT ALL POSSIBLE.
@#$!
HUUAARRGGHH!
FSHAM

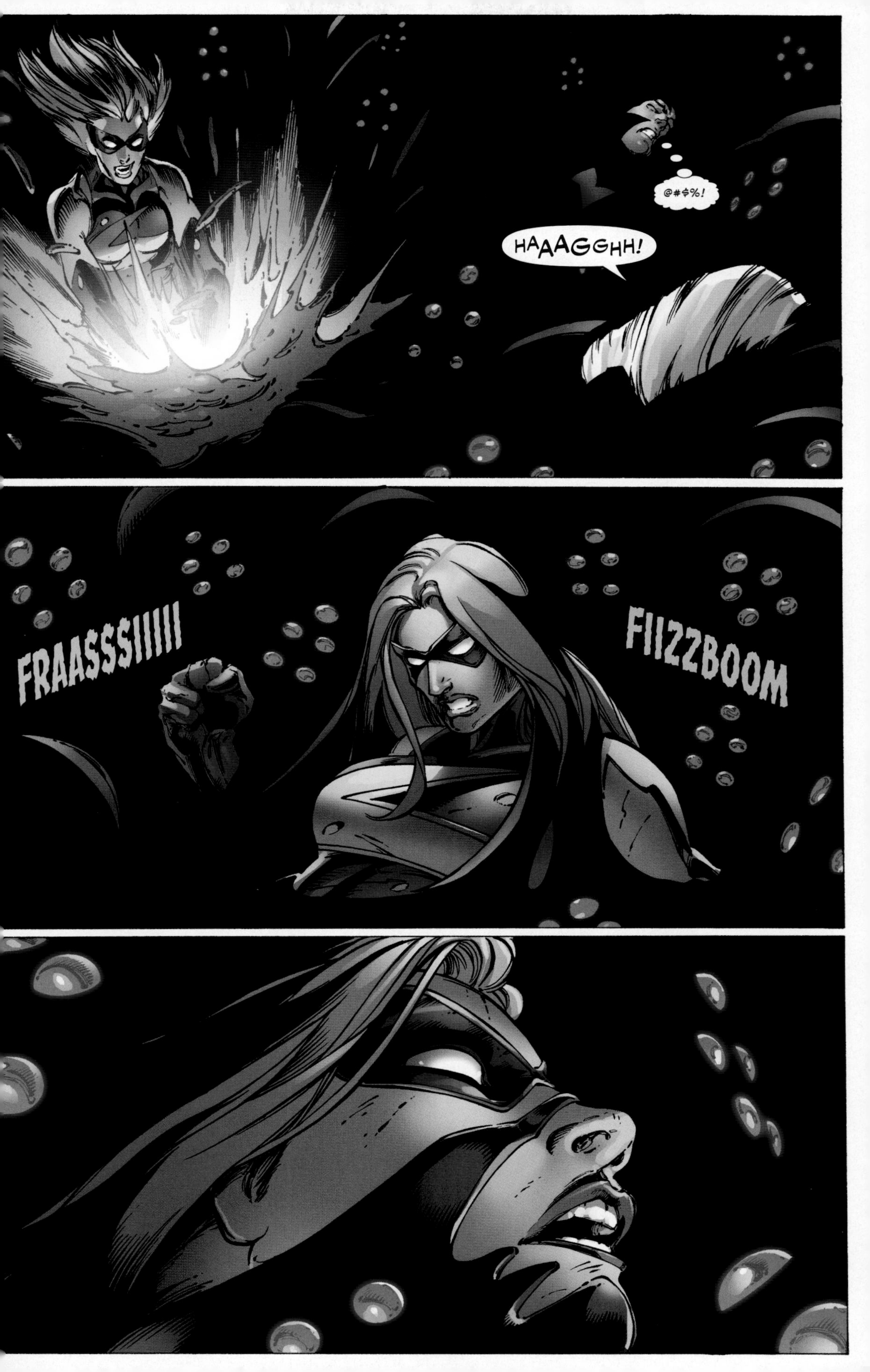
@#$%!
HAAAGGHH!
FRAASSSIIIIII
FIIZZBOOM

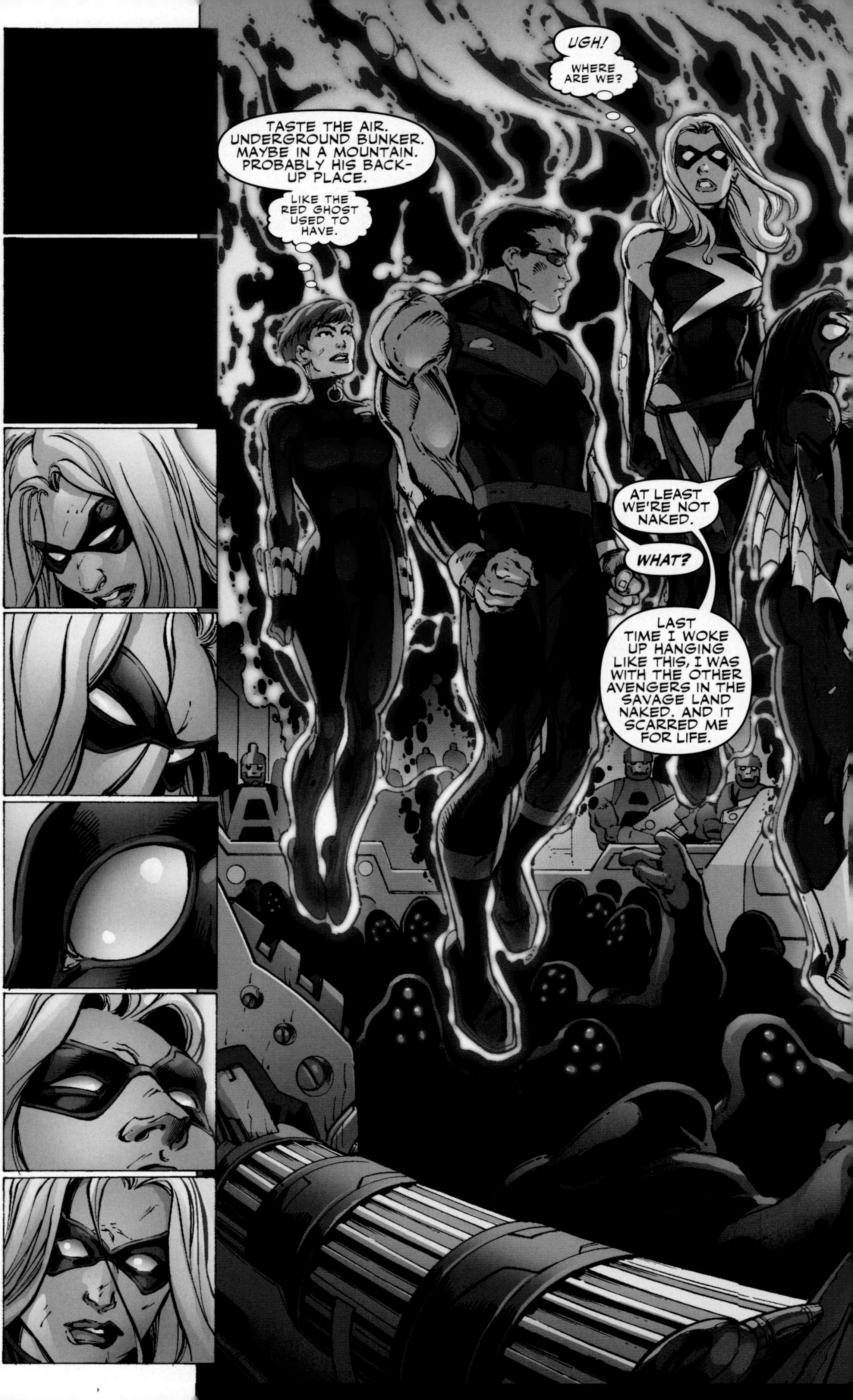
UGH!
WHERE ARE WE?
TASTE THE AIR. UNDERGROUND BUNKER. MAYBE IN A MOUNTAIN. PROBABLY HIS BACK-UP PLACE.
LIKE THE RED GHOST USED TO HAVE.
AT LEAST WE'RE NOT NAKED.
WHAT?
LAST TIME I WOKE UP HANGING LIKE THIS, I WAS WITH THE OTHER AVENGERS IN THE SAVAGE LAND NAKED. AND IT SCARRED ME FOR LIFE.

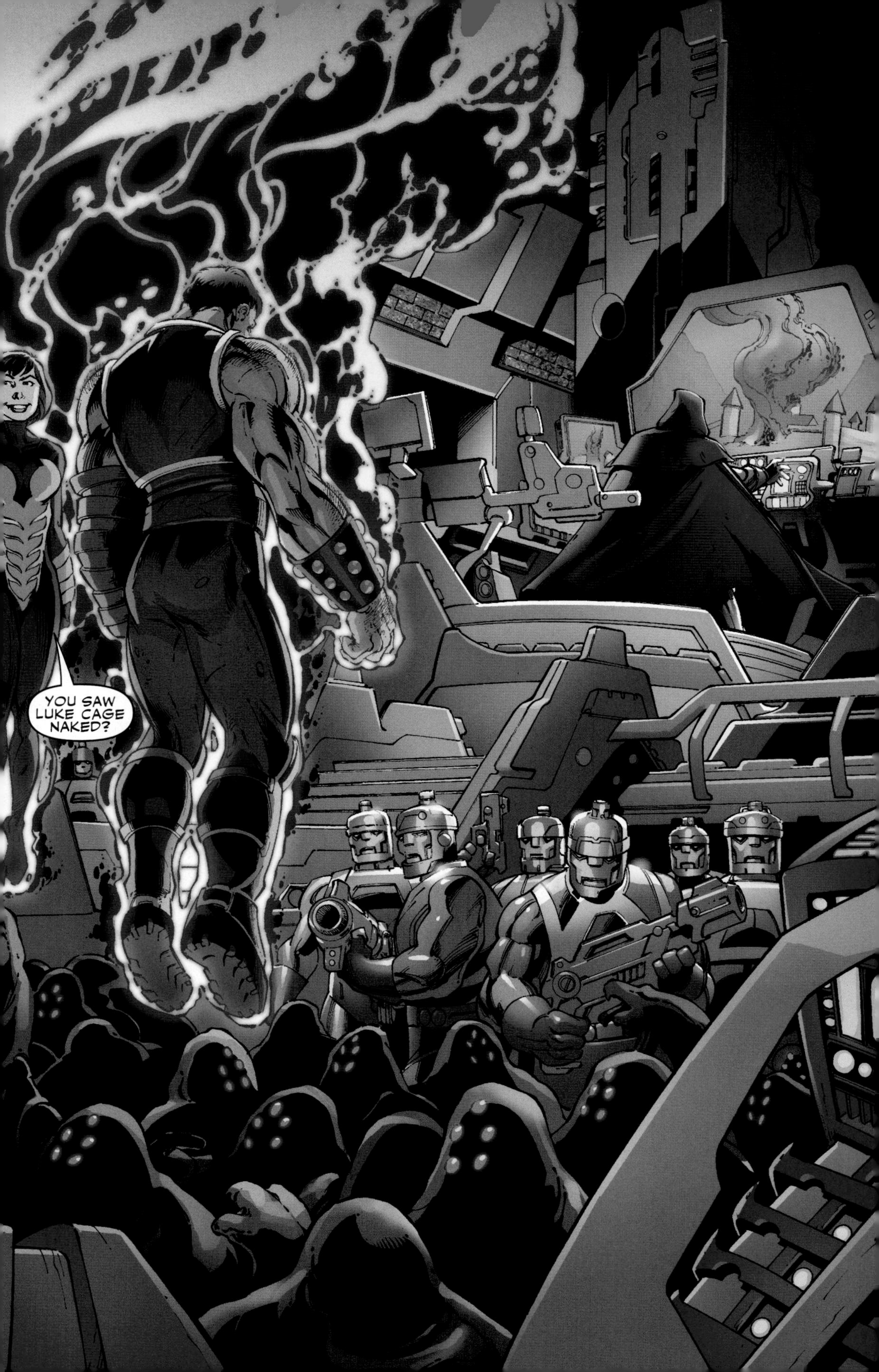
YOU SAW LUKE CAGE NAKED?

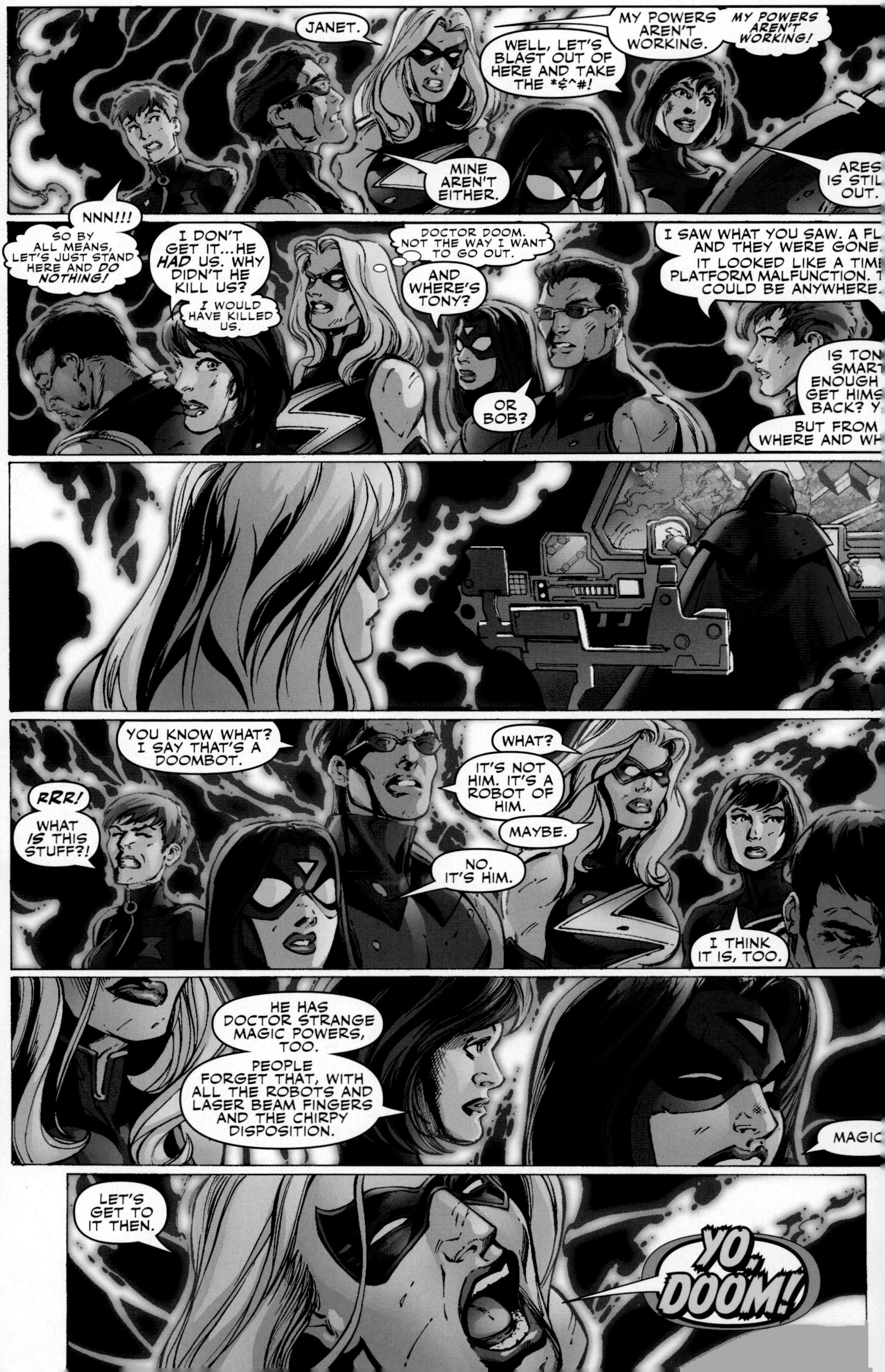

JANET.
MY POWERS AREN'T WORKING.
MY POWERS AREN'T WORKING!
WELL, LET'S BLAST OUT OF HERE AND TAKE THE *&^#!
MINE AREN'T EITHER.
ARES IS STIL OUT.
NNN!!!
SO BY ALL MEANS, LET'S JUST STAND HERE AND DO NOTHING!
I DON'T GET IT...HE HAD US. WHY DIDN'T HE KILL US?
I WOULD HAVE KILLED US.
DOCTOR DOOM. NOT THE WAY I WANT TO GO OUT.
AND WHERE'S TONY?
OR BOB?
I SAW WHAT YOU SAW. A FL AND THEY WERE GONE. IT LOOKED LIKE A TIM PLATFORM MALFUNCTION. T COULD BE ANYWHERE.
IS TON SMART ENOUGH GET HIMS BACK? Y
BUT FROM WHERE AND WH
YOU KNOW WHAT? I SAY THAT'S A DOOMBOT.
WHAT?
IT'S NOT HIM. IT'S A ROBOT OF HIM.
MAYBE.
RRR!
WHAT IS THIS STUFF?!
NO. IT'S HIM.
I THINK IT IS, TOO.
HE HAS DOCTOR STRANGE MAGIC POWERS, TOO.
PEOPLE FORGET THAT, WITH ALL THE ROBOTS AND LASER BEAM FINGERS AND THE CHIRPY DISPOSITION.
MAGIC
LET'S GET TO IT THEN.
YO, DOOM!

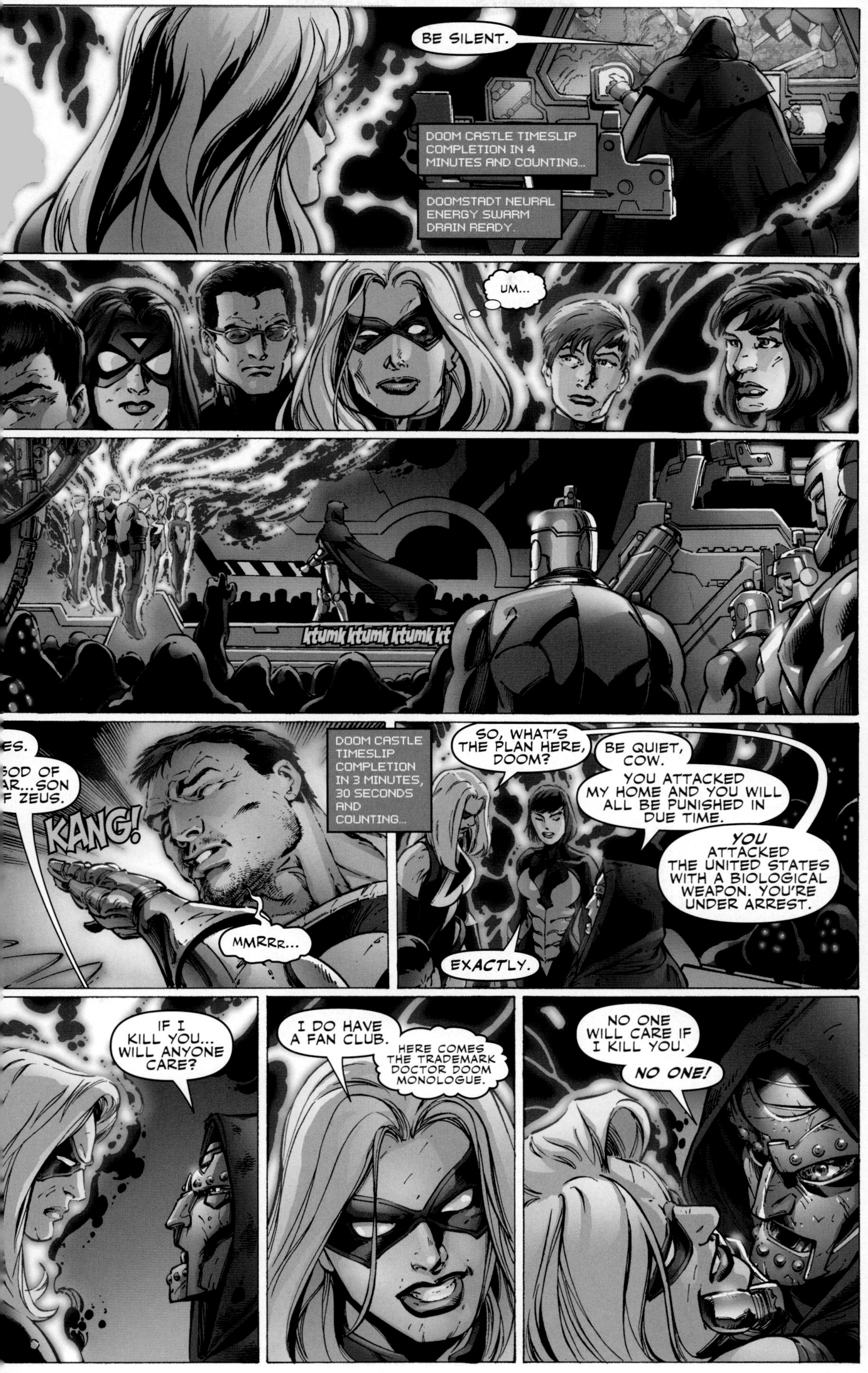
BE SILENT.
DOOM CASTLE TIMESLIP COMPLETION IN 4 MINUTES AND COUNTING...
DOOMSTADT NEURAL ENERGY SWARM DRAIN READY.
UM...
ktumk ktumk ktumk kt
ES.
GOD OF AR...SON F ZEUS.
KANG!
MMRrr...
DOOM CASTLE TIMESLIP COMPLETION IN 3 MINUTES, 30 SECONDS AND COUNTING...
SO, WHAT'S THE PLAN HERE, DOOM?
BE QUIET, COW.
YOU ATTACKED MY HOME AND YOU WILL ALL BE PUNISHED IN DUE TIME.
YOU ATTACKED THE UNITED STATES WITH A BIOLOGICAL WEAPON. YOU'RE UNDER ARREST.
EXACTLY.
IF I KILL YOU... WILL ANYONE CARE?
I DO HAVE A FAN CLUB.
HERE COMES THE TRADEMARK DOCTOR DOOM MONOLOGUE.
NO ONE WILL CARE IF I KILL YOU.
NO ONE!

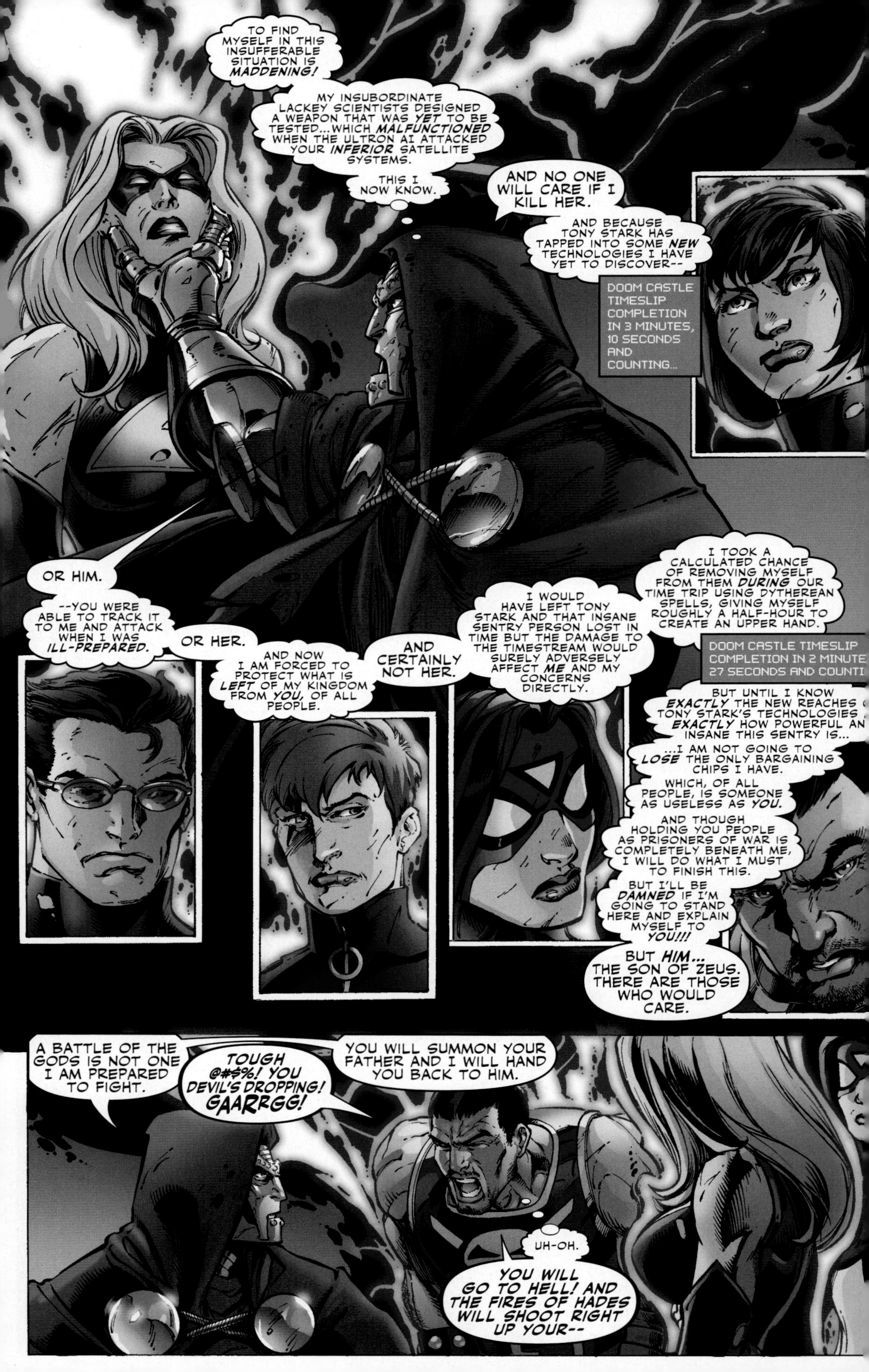
TO FIND MYSELF IN THIS INSUFFERABLE SITUATION IS MADDENING!
MY INSUBORDINATE LACKEY SCIENTISTS DESIGNED A WEAPON THAT WAS YET TO BE TESTED...WHICH MALFUNCTIONED WHEN THE ULTRON AI ATTACKED YOUR INFERIOR SATELLITE SYSTEMS.
THIS I NOW KNOW.
AND NO ONE WILL CARE IF I KILL HER.
AND BECAUSE TONY STARK HAS TAPPED INTO SOME NEW TECHNOLOGIES I HAVE YET TO DISCOVER--
DOOM CASTLE TIMESLIP COMPLETION IN 3 MINUTES, 10 SECONDS AND COUNTING...
OR HIM.
--YOU WERE ABLE TO TRACK IT TO ME AND ATTACK WHEN I WAS ILL-PREPARED.
OR HER.
AND NOW I AM FORCED TO PROTECT WHAT IS LEFT OF MY KINGDOM FROM YOU, OF ALL PEOPLE.
AND CERTAINLY NOT HER.
I WOULD HAVE LEFT TONY STARK AND THAT INSANE SENTRY PERSON LOST IN TIME BUT THE DAMAGE TO THE TIMESTREAM WOULD SURELY ADVERSELY AFFECT ME AND MY CONCERNS DIRECTLY.
I TOOK A CALCULATED CHANCE OF REMOVING MYSELF FROM THEM DURING OUR TIME TRIP USING DYTHEREAN SPELLS, GIVING MYSELF ROUGHLY A HALF-HOUR TO CREATE AN UPPER HAND.
DOOM CASTLE TIMESLIP COMPLETION IN 2 MINUTE 27 SECONDS AND COUNTI
BUT UNTIL I KNOW EXACTLY THE NEW REACHES TONY STARK'S TECHNOLOGIES EXACTLY HOW POWERFUL AN INSANE THIS SENTRY IS...
...I AM NOT GOING TO LOSE THE ONLY BARGAINING CHIPS I HAVE.
WHICH, OF ALL PEOPLE, IS SOMEONE AS USELESS AS YOU.
AND THOUGH HOLDING YOU PEOPLE AS PRISONERS OF WAR IS COMPLETELY BENEATH ME, I WILL DO WHAT I MUST TO FINISH THIS.
BUT I'LL BE DAMNED IF I'M GOING TO STAND HERE AND EXPLAIN MYSELF TO YOU!!!
BUT HIM... THE SON OF ZEUS. THERE ARE THOSE WHO WOULD CARE.
A BATTLE OF THE GODS IS NOT ONE I AM PREPARED TO FIGHT.
TOUGH @#$%! YOU DEVIL'S DROPPING! GAARRGG!
YOU WILL SUMMON YOUR FATHER AND I WILL HAND YOU BACK TO HIM.
UH-OH.
YOU WILL GO TO HELL! AND THE FIRES OF HADES WILL SHOOT RIGHT UP YOUR--

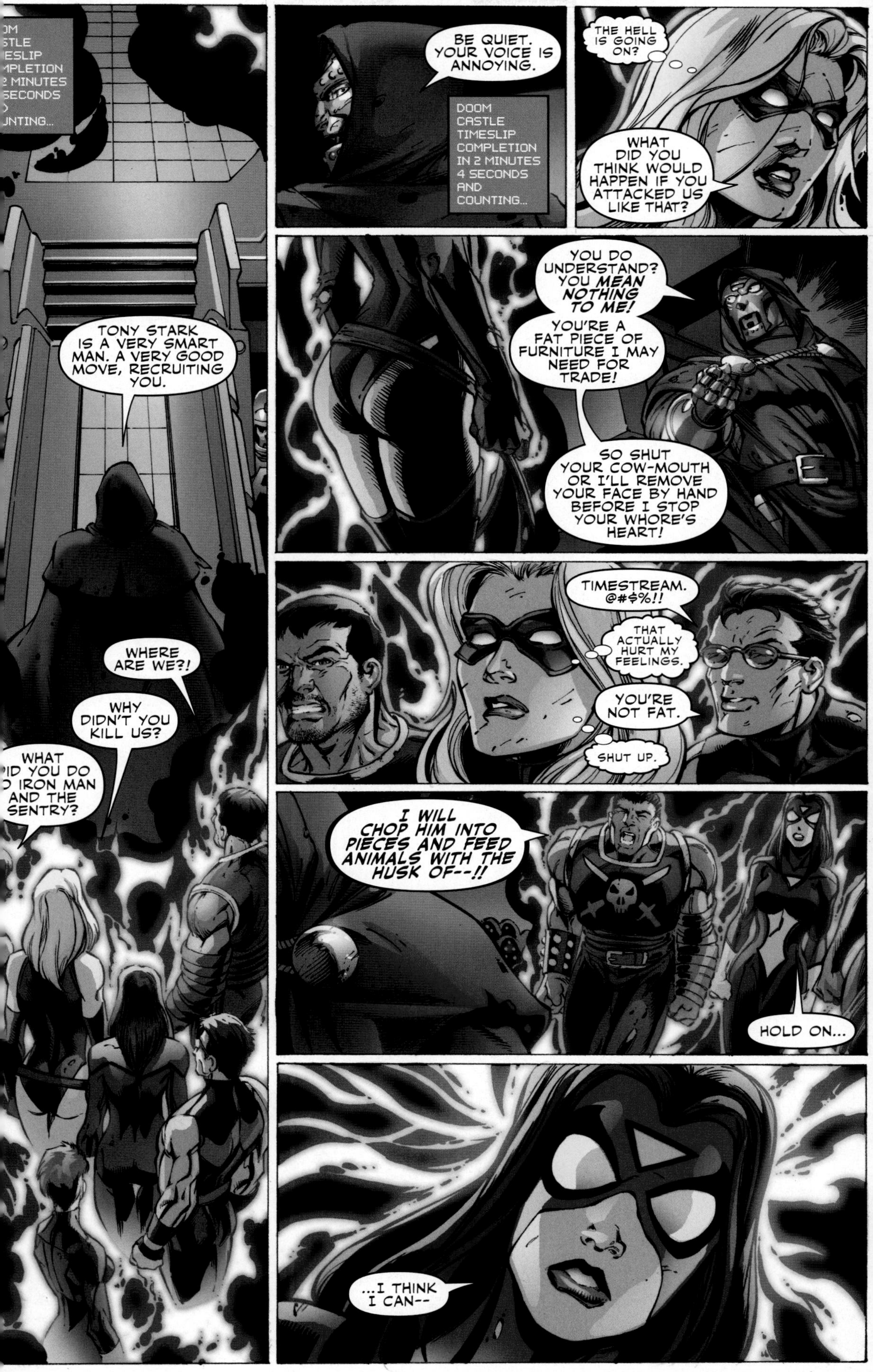

OM
STLE
ESLIP
MPLETION
2 MINUTES
SECONDS
D
UNTING...
TONY STARK IS A VERY SMART MAN. A VERY GOOD MOVE, RECRUITING YOU.
WHERE ARE WE?!
WHY DIDN'T YOU KILL US?
WHAT ID YOU DO O IRON MAN AND THE SENTRY?
BE QUIET. YOUR VOICE IS ANNOYING.
DOOM CASTLE TIMESLIP COMPLETION IN 2 MINUTES 4 SECONDS AND COUNTING...
THE HELL IS GOING ON?
WHAT DID YOU THINK WOULD HAPPEN IF YOU ATTACKED US LIKE THAT?
YOU DO UNDERSTAND? YOU MEAN NOTHING TO ME!
YOU'RE A FAT PIECE OF FURNITURE I MAY NEED FOR TRADE!
SO SHUT YOUR COW-MOUTH OR I'LL REMOVE YOUR FACE BY HAND BEFORE I STOP YOUR WHORE'S HEART!
TIMESTREAM. @#$%!!
THAT ACTUALLY HURT MY FEELINGS.
YOU'RE NOT FAT.
SHUT UP.
I WILL CHOP HIM INTO PIECES AND FEED ANIMALS WITH THE HUSK OF--!!
HOLD ON...
...I THINK I CAN--

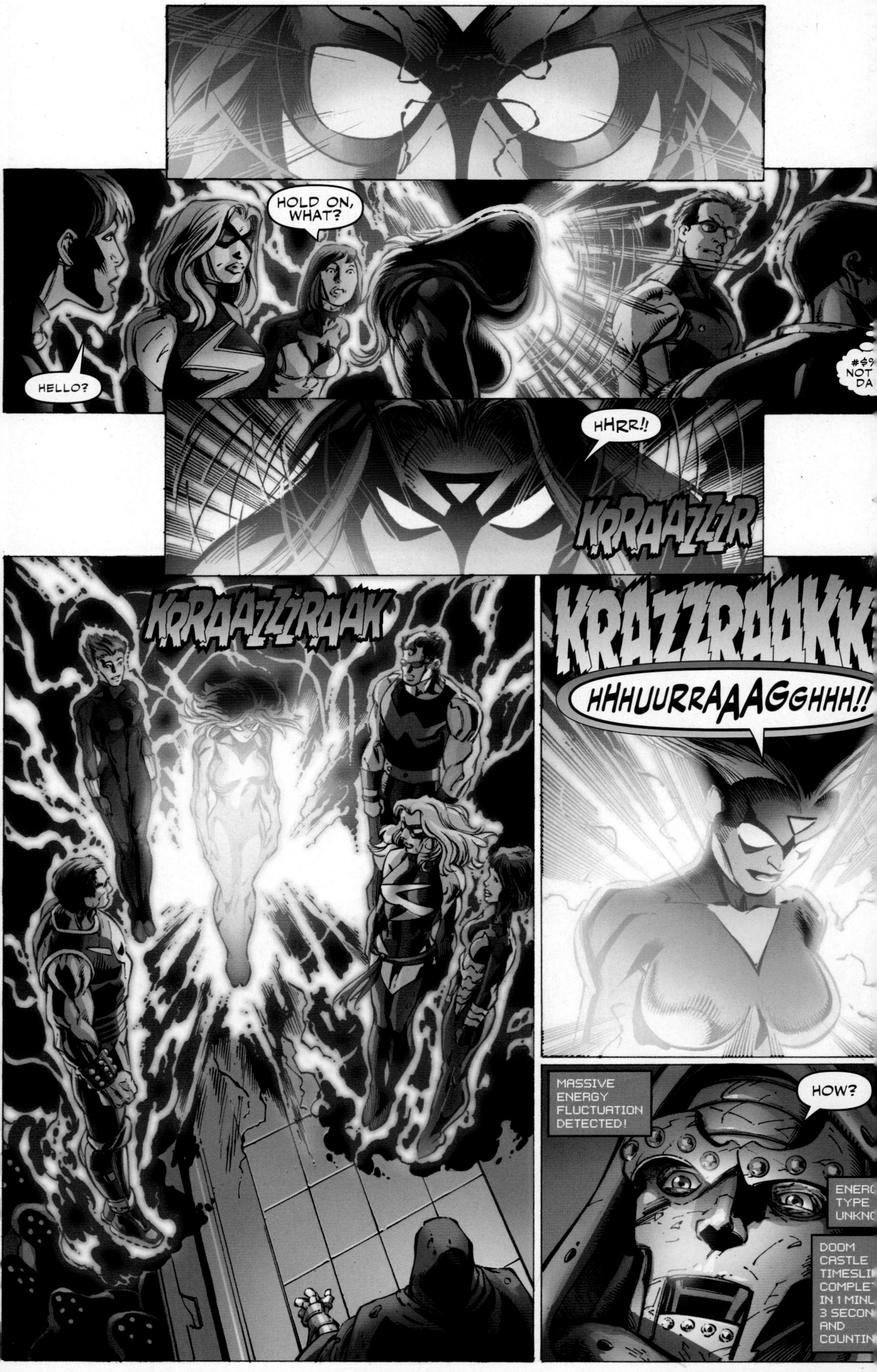
HOLD ON, WHAT?
HELLO?
HHRR!!
KRRAAZZZR
KRRAAZZZRAAK
KRAZZRAAKK
HHHUURRAAAGGHHH!!
MASSIVE ENERGY FLUCTUATION DETECTED!
HOW?

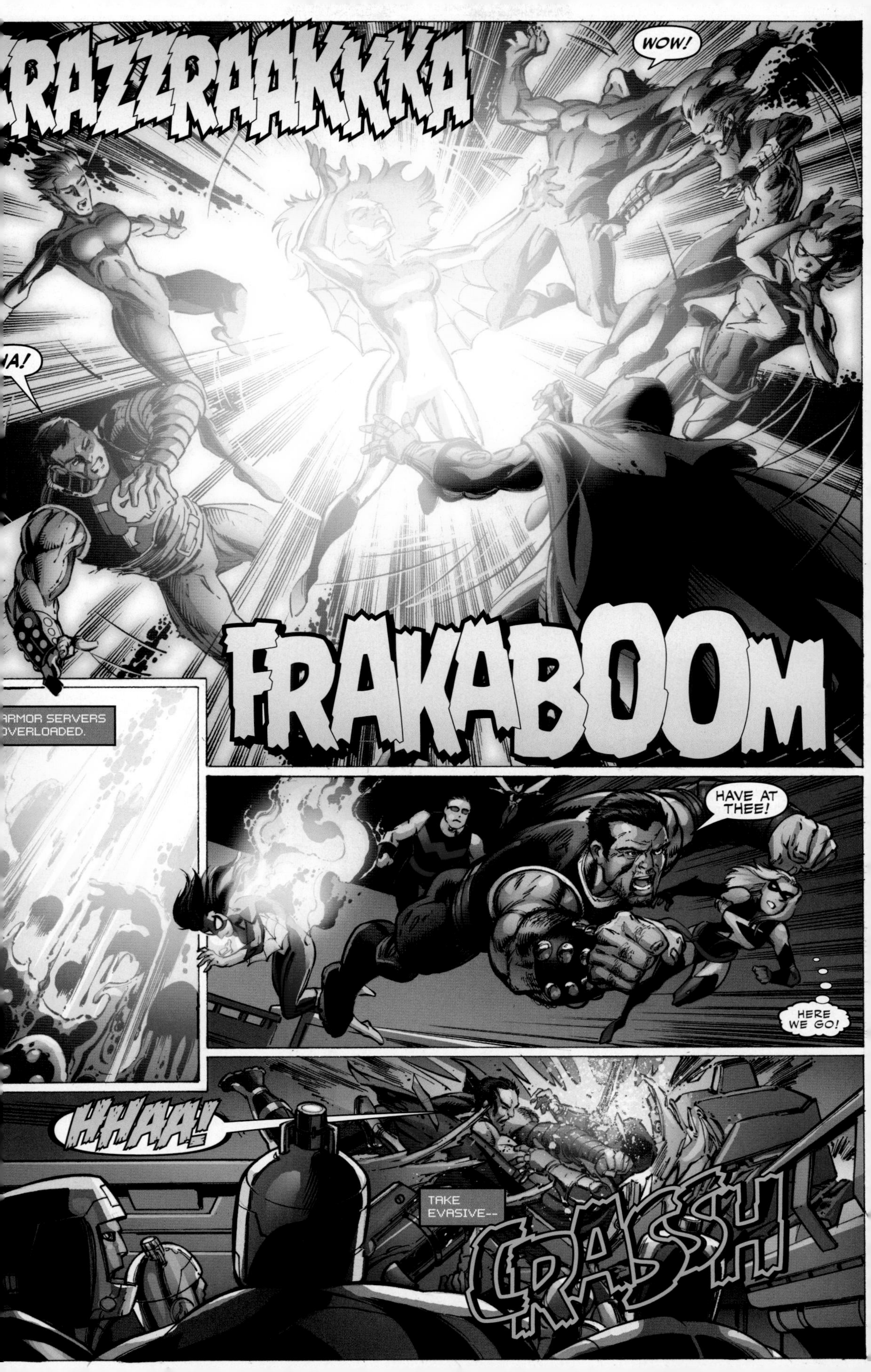
RAZZRAAKKKA
WOW!
A!
FRAKABOOM
ARMOR SERVERS OVERLOADED.
HAVE AT THEE!
HERE WE GO!
HHAA!
TAKE EVASIVE--
CRASSH

DOOM CASTLE TIMESLIP COMPLETION IN 22 SECONDS AND COUNTING...

SIMON, POUND DOOM!

WIDOW, GET THE HELICARRIER ONLINE AND FIND OUT WHERE WE ARE!

I'M GOING TO GO FIND TONY AND BOB!

THERE'S COUNTDO CLOCK

I SEE IT.

DOOM CASTLE TIMESLIP COMPLETE.

GLOBAL SATELLITE SERVERS LOADING.

SERVERS LOADING. STAND BY.

WHAT IS THAT?

BOB. HEAD IT OFF!

GET OUT OF THERE.

DOOMSTADT NEURAL ENERGY SWARM DRAIN INTERFACE ACTIVATED. LAUNCH.

DOOMSTADT NEURAL ENERGY SWARM DRAIN ACTIVATED.

OH NO!

00:00:00

CAROL?

GET OUT OF THERE!

SERVER CONNECTION SUCCE

SATELLITE CONNECTION ONL

UNIDENTIFIED ENERGY SOURCE DETECTED.

UNIDENTIFIED ENERGY F

EVASIVE ACTION REQUIR

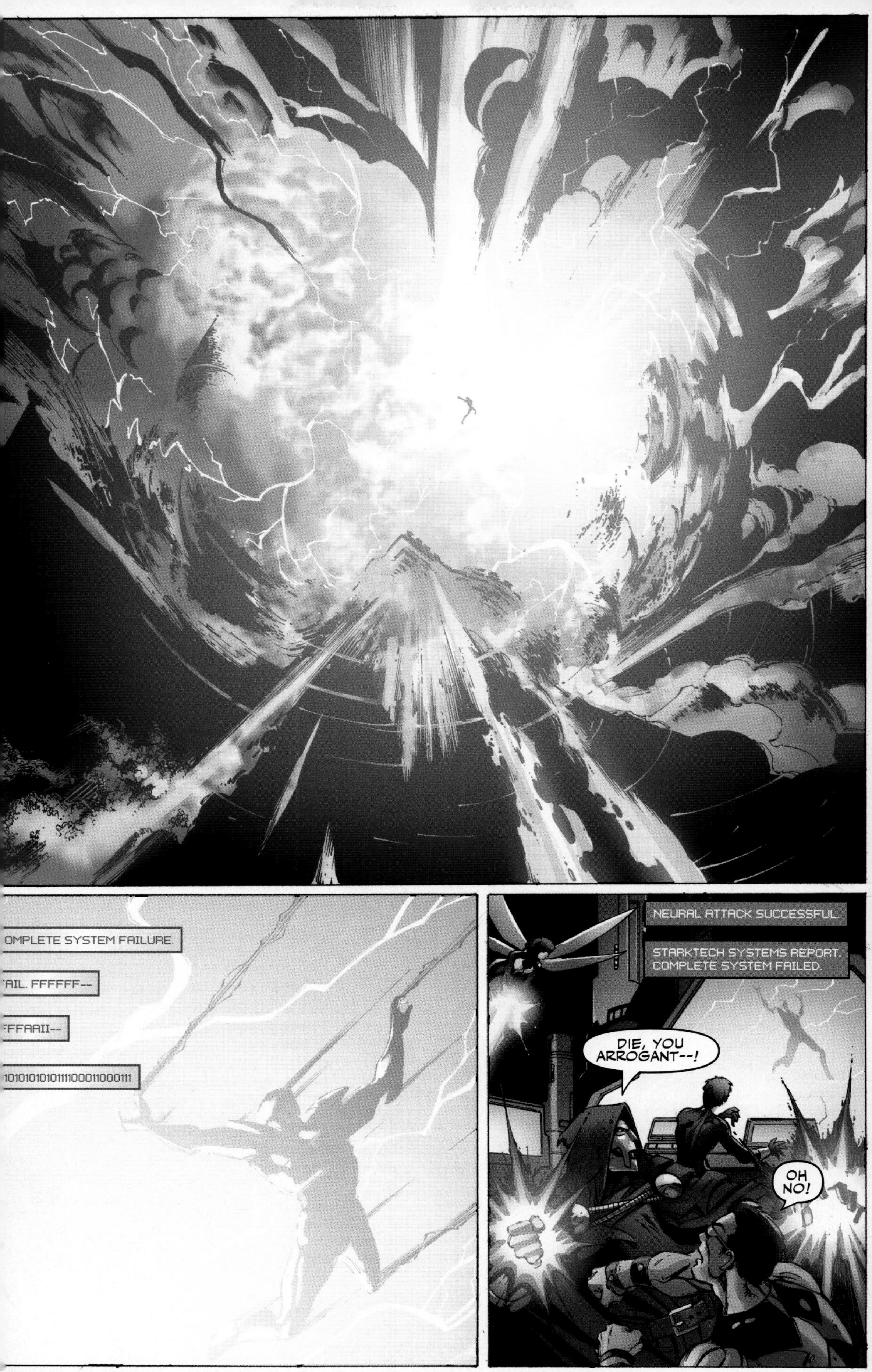
OMPLETE SYSTEM FAILURE.
AIL. FFFFFF--
FFFAAII--
1010101010111100011000111
NEURAL ATTACK SUCCESSFUL.
STARKTECH SYSTEMS REPORT. COMPLETE SYSTEM FAILED.
DIE, YOU ARROGANT--!
OH NO!

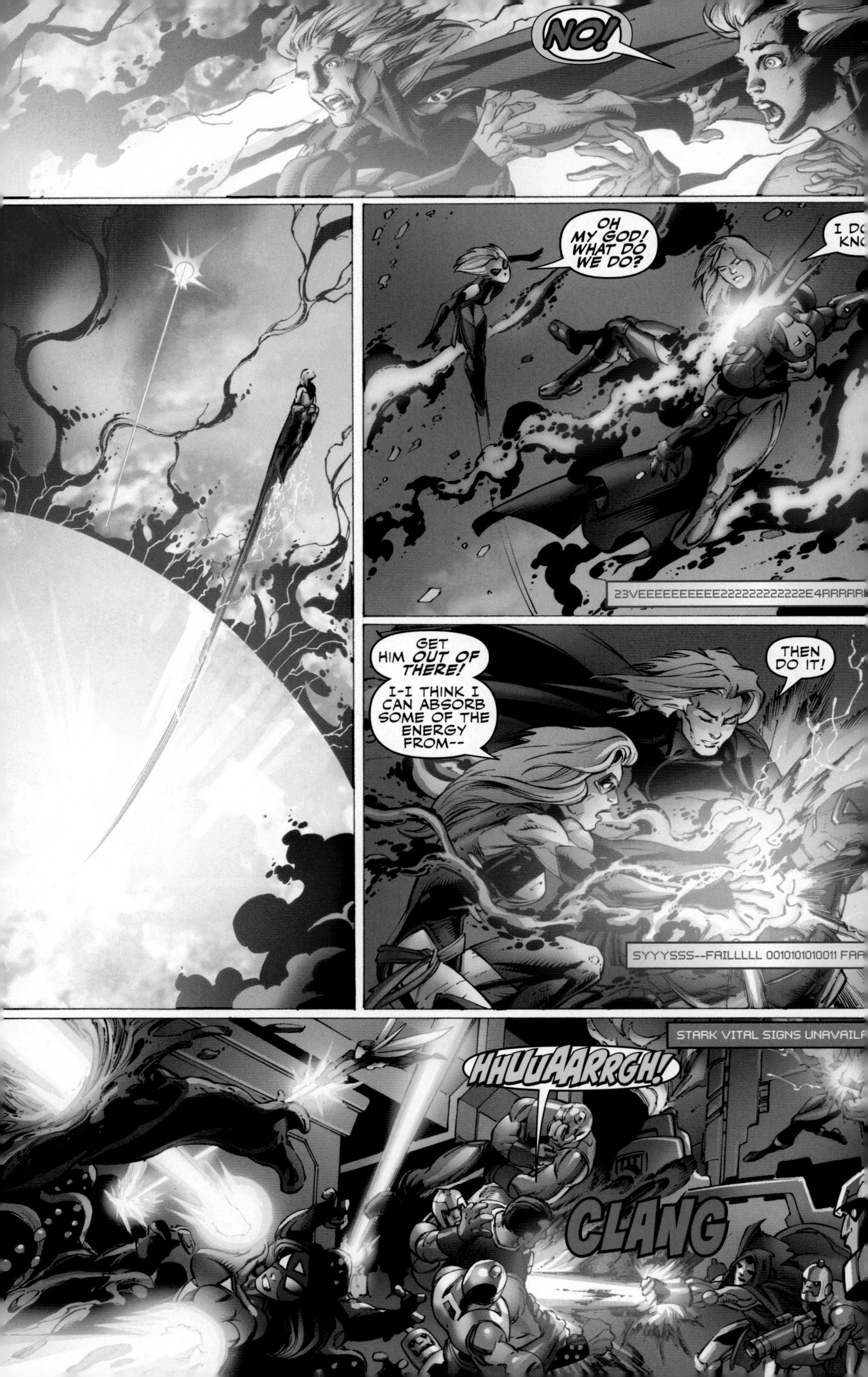
NO!
OH MY GOD! WHAT DO WE DO?
I DO KNO
23VEEEEEEEEEE2222222222222E4RRRRR
GET HIM OUT OF THERE!
I-I THINK I CAN ABSORB SOME OF THE ENERGY FROM--
THEN DO IT!
SYYYSSS--FAILLLLL 001010101010011 FAA
STARK VITAL SIGNS UNAVAILA
HHUUAARRGH!
CLANG

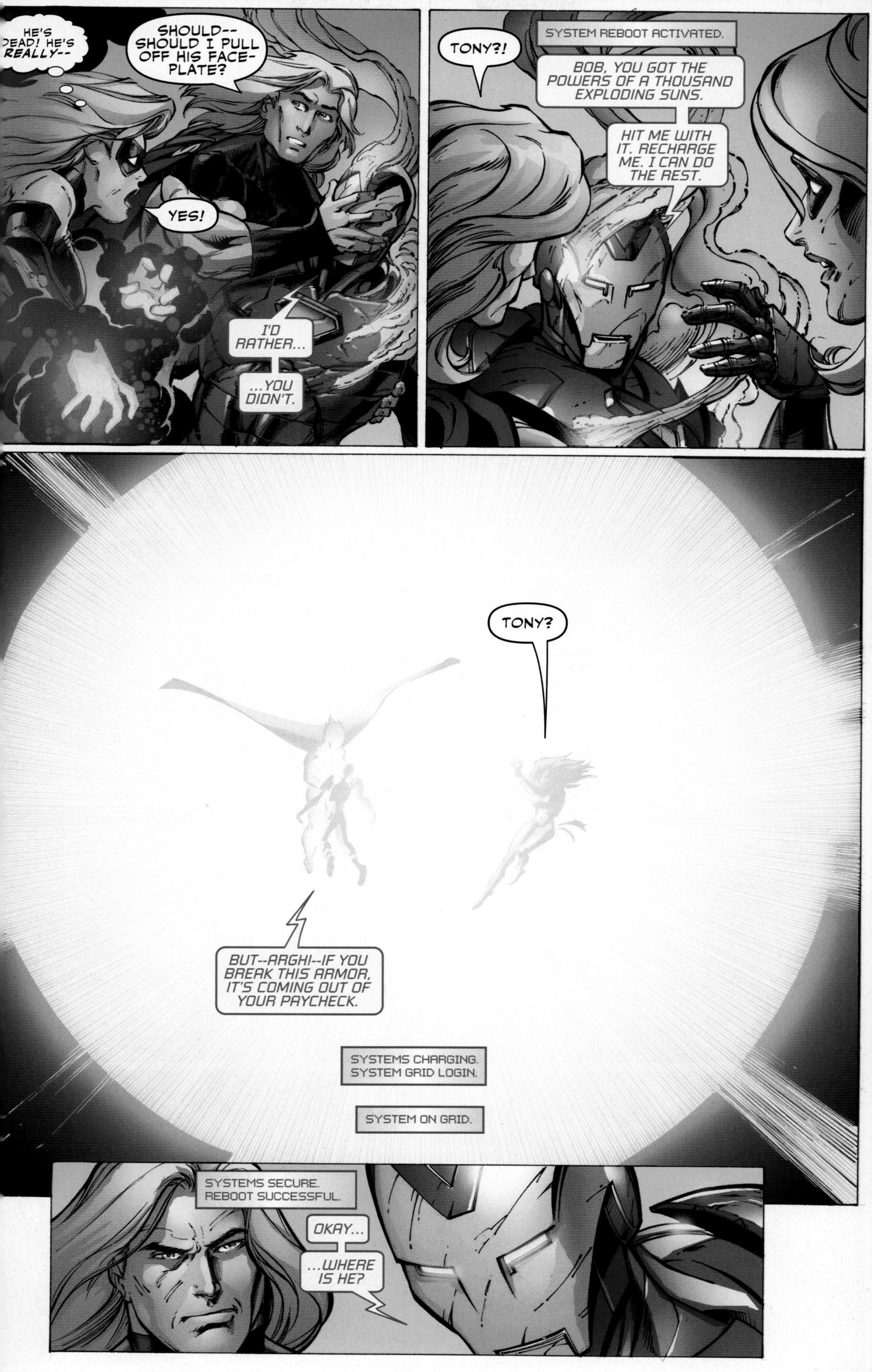
HE'S DEAD! HE'S REALLY--
SHOULD-- SHOULD I PULL OFF HIS FACE-PLATE?
YES!
I'D RATHER...
...YOU DIDN'T.
TONY?!
SYSTEM REBOOT ACTIVATED.
BOB, YOU GOT THE POWERS OF A THOUSAND EXPLODING SUNS.
HIT ME WITH IT. RECHARGE ME. I CAN DO THE REST.
TONY?
BUT--ARGH!--IF YOU BREAK THIS ARMOR, IT'S COMING OUT OF YOUR PAYCHECK.
SYSTEMS CHARGING. SYSTEM GRID LOGIN.
SYSTEM ON GRID.
SYSTEMS SECURE. REBOOT SUCCESSFUL.
OKAY...
...WHERE IS HE?

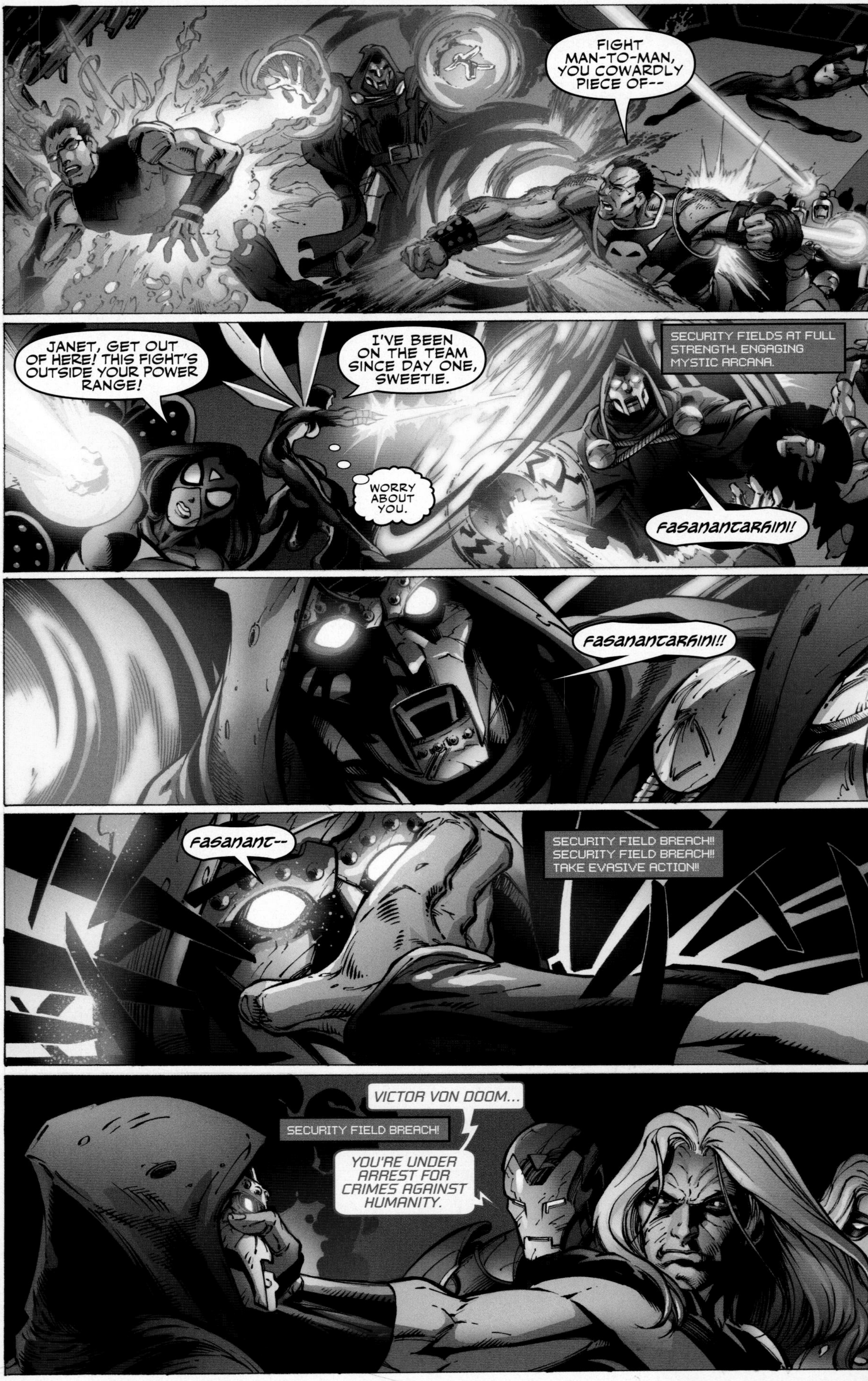
FIGHT MAN-TO-MAN, YOU COWARDLY PIECE OF--
JANET, GET OUT OF HERE! THIS FIGHT'S OUTSIDE YOUR POWER RANGE!
I'VE BEEN ON THE TEAM SINCE DAY ONE, SWEETIE.
WORRY ABOUT YOU.
SECURITY FIELDS AT FULL STRENGTH. ENGAGING MYSTIC ARCANA.
FASANANTARHINI!
FASANANTARHINI!!
FASANANT--
SECURITY FIELD BREACH!! SECURITY FIELD BREACH!! TAKE EVASIVE ACTION!!
VICTOR VON DOOM...
SECURITY FIELD BREACH!
YOU'RE UNDER ARREST FOR CRIMES AGAINST HUMANITY.

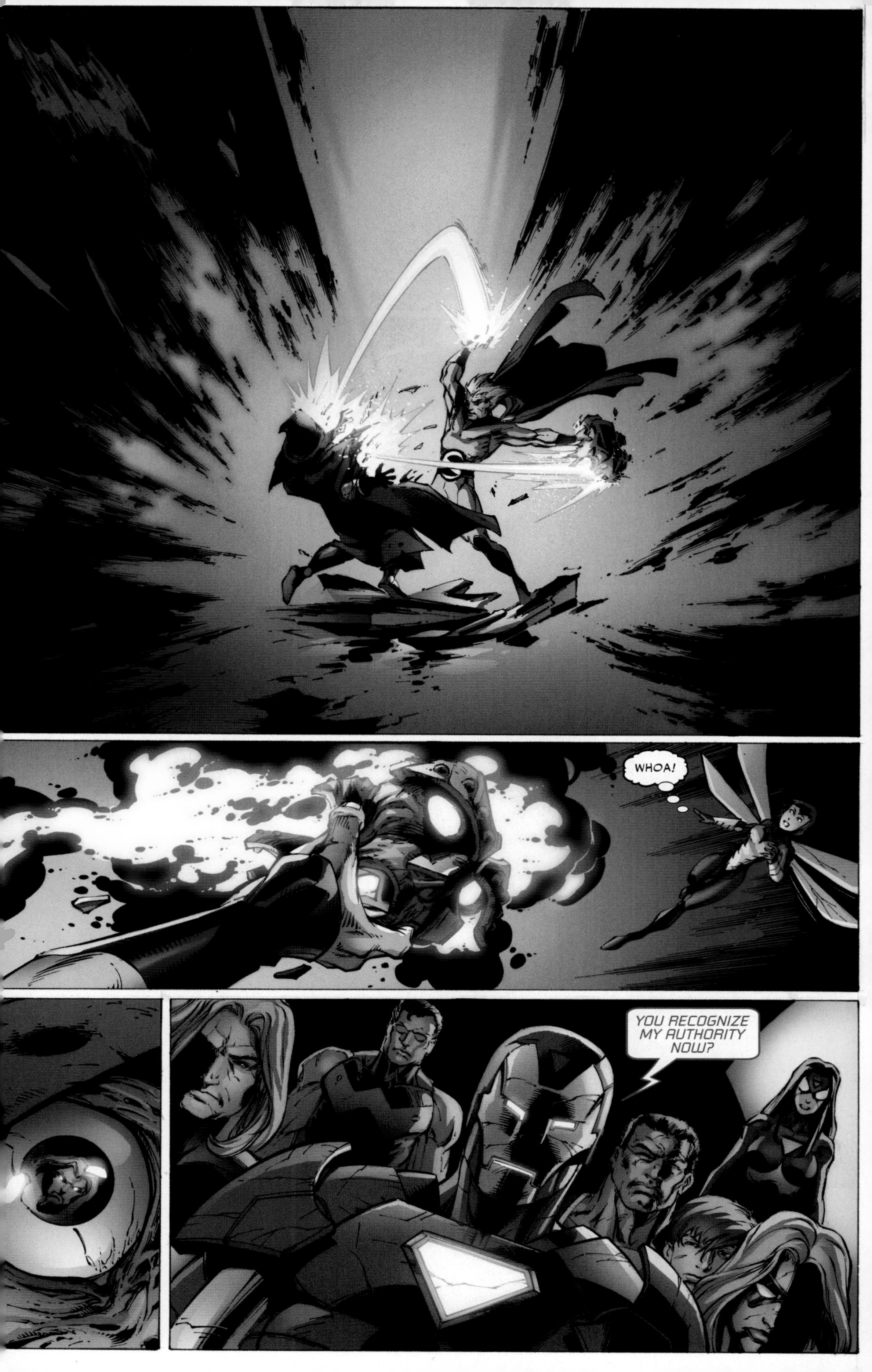
WHOA!
YOU RECOGNIZE MY AUTHORITY NOW?

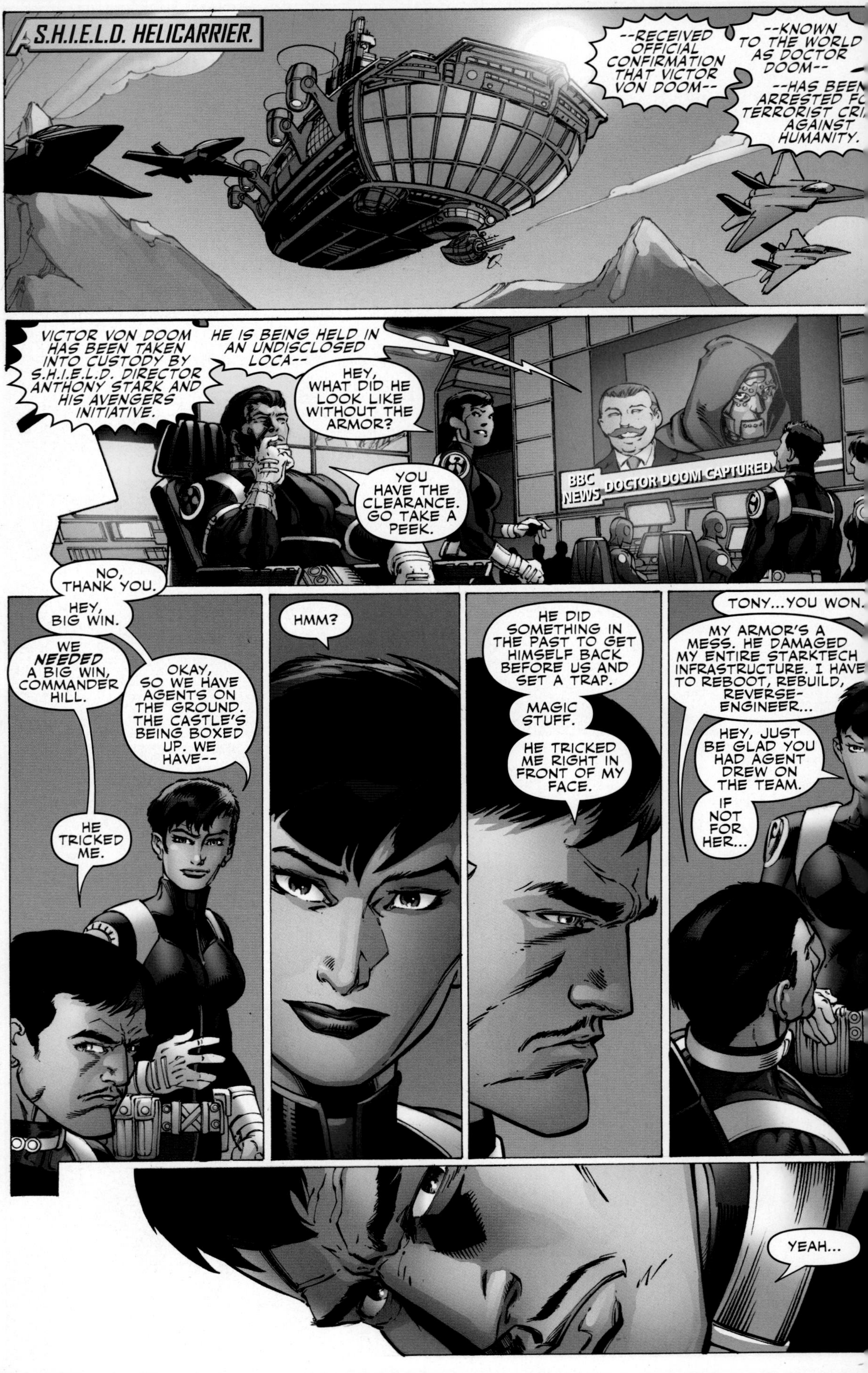
S.H.I.E.L.D. HELICARRIER.
--RECEIVED OFFICIAL CONFIRMATION THAT VICTOR VON DOOM--
--KNOWN TO THE WORLD AS DOCTOR DOOM--
--HAS BEEN ARRESTED FO TERRORIST CRI AGAINST HUMANITY.
VICTOR VON DOOM HAS BEEN TAKEN INTO CUSTODY BY S.H.I.E.L.D. DIRECTOR ANTHONY STARK AND HIS AVENGERS INITIATIVE.
HE IS BEING HELD IN AN UNDISCLOSED LOCA--
BBC NEWS DOCTOR DOOM CAPTURED
HEY, WHAT DID HE LOOK LIKE WITHOUT THE ARMOR?
YOU HAVE THE CLEARANCE. GO TAKE A PEEK.
NO, THANK YOU.
HEY, BIG WIN.
WE NEEDED A BIG WIN, COMMANDER HILL.
OKAY, SO WE HAVE AGENTS ON THE GROUND. THE CASTLE'S BEING BOXED UP. WE HAVE--
HE TRICKED ME.
HMM?
HE DID SOMETHING IN THE PAST TO GET HIMSELF BACK BEFORE US AND SET A TRAP.
MAGIC STUFF.
HE TRICKED ME RIGHT IN FRONT OF MY FACE.
TONY...YOU WON.
MY ARMOR'S A MESS. HE DAMAGED MY ENTIRE STARKTECH INFRASTRUCTURE. I HAVE TO REBOOT, REBUILD, REVERSE-ENGINEER...
HEY, JUST BE GLAD YOU HAD AGENT DREW ON THE TEAM.
IF NOT FOR HER...
YEAH...

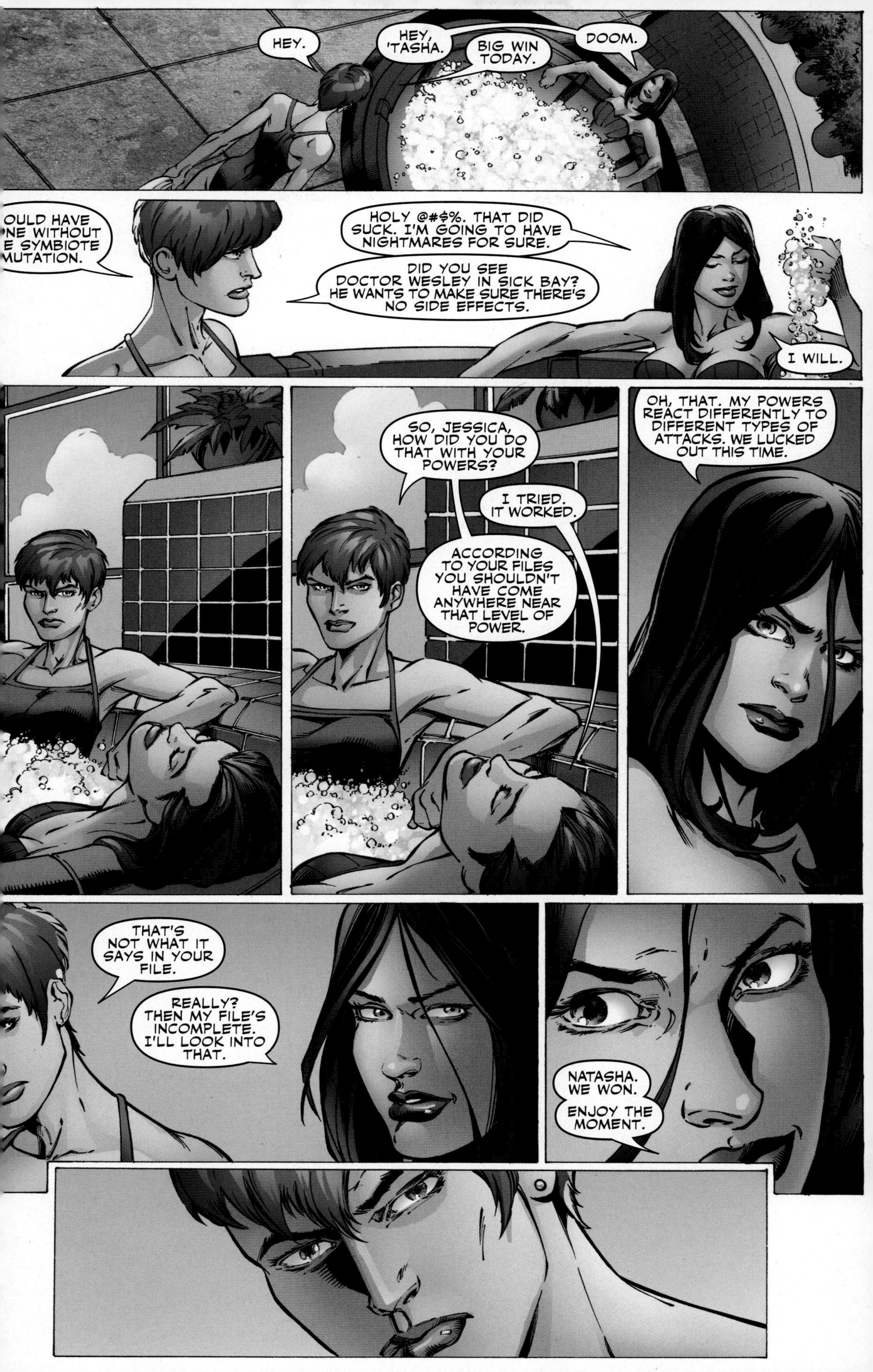
HEY.
HEY, 'TASHA.
BIG WIN TODAY.
DOOM.
OULD HAVE
NE WITHOUT
E SYMBIOTE
MUTATION.
HOLY @#$%. THAT DID SUCK. I'M GOING TO HAVE NIGHTMARES FOR SURE.
DID YOU SEE DOCTOR WESLEY IN SICK BAY? HE WANTS TO MAKE SURE THERE'S NO SIDE EFFECTS.
I WILL.
SO, JESSICA, HOW DID YOU DO THAT WITH YOUR POWERS?
I TRIED. IT WORKED.
ACCORDING TO YOUR FILES YOU SHOULDN'T HAVE COME ANYWHERE NEAR THAT LEVEL OF POWER.
OH, THAT. MY POWERS REACT DIFFERENTLY TO DIFFERENT TYPES OF ATTACKS. WE LUCKED OUT THIS TIME.
THAT'S NOT WHAT IT SAYS IN YOUR FILE.
REALLY? THEN MY FILE'S INCOMPLETE. I'LL LOOK INTO THAT.
NATASHA. WE WON.
ENJOY THE MOMENT.

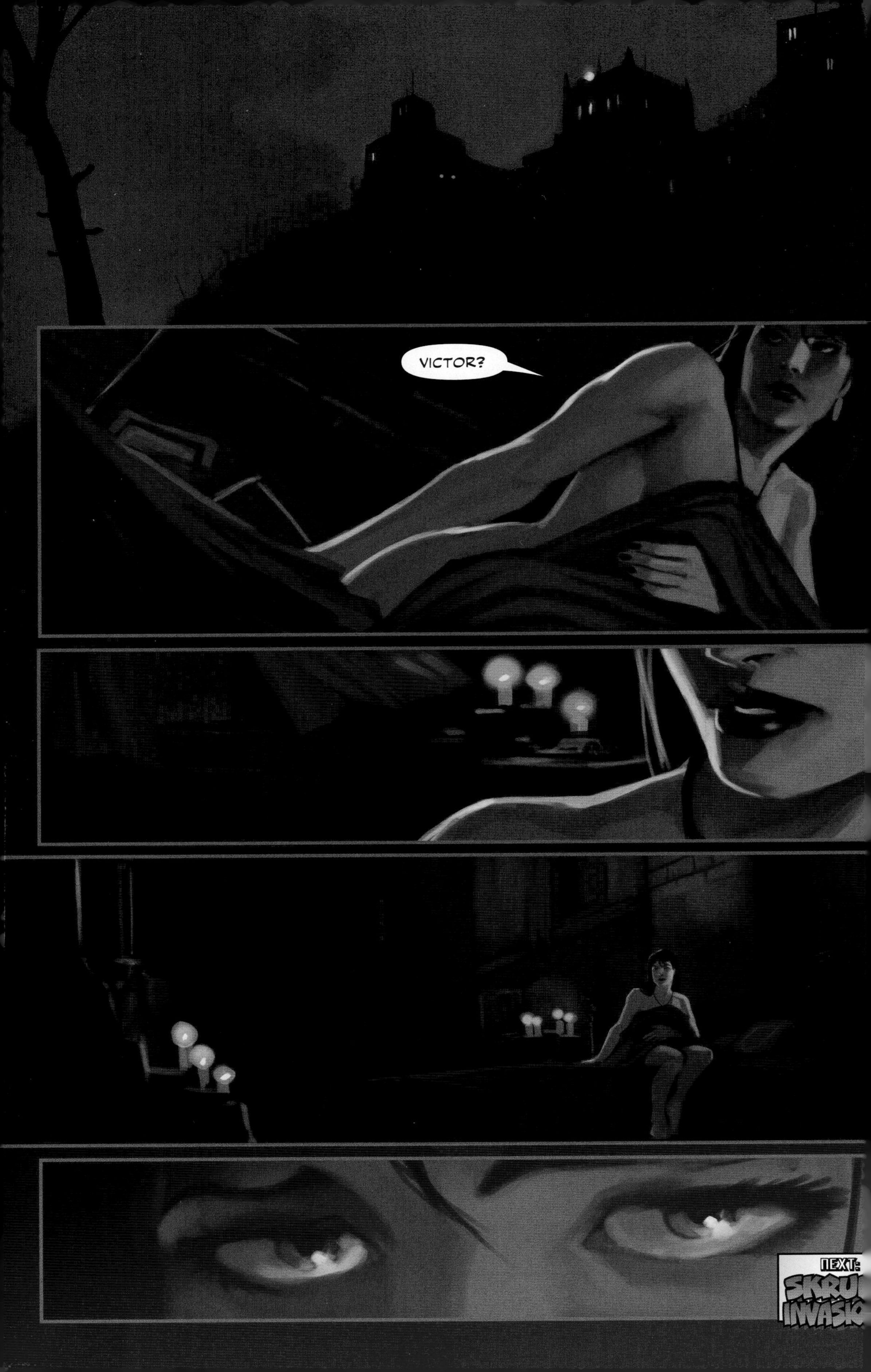
VICTOR?
NEXT:

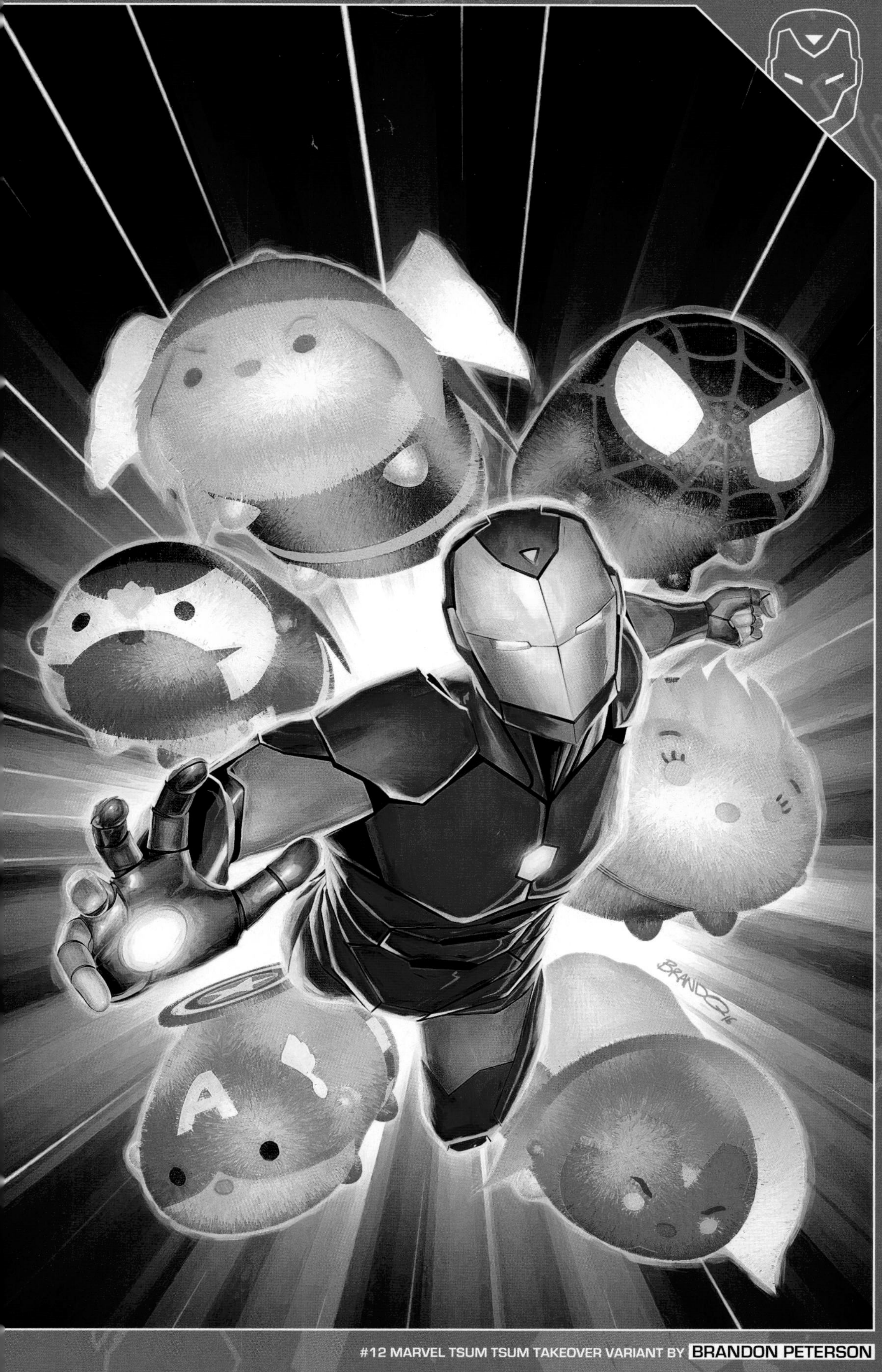
BRANDO '16

#12 MARVEL TSUM TSUM TAKEOVER VARIANT BY **BRANDON PETERSON**